YOU SHALL LOVE THE STRANGER AS YOURSELF

You Shall Love the Stranger as Yourself addresses the complex political, legal, and humanitarian challenges raised by asylum-seekers and refugees from a Biblical perspective. The book explores the themes of humanity and justice through exegesis of relevant passages in the Old and New Testaments, which are skilfully woven into accounts of contemporary refugee situations. Applying Biblical analysis to one of the most pressing humanitarian concerns of modern times, Houston creates a timely work that will be of interest to students and scholars of theology, religion, and human rights.

Fleur S. Houston is a minister of the United Reformed Church with extensive local, national, and international experience. She serves on the steering group of the Churches Refugee Network, a UK-based ecumenical body concerned with refugees and those who seek asylum.

BIBLICAL CHALLENGES IN THE CONTEMPORARY WORLD

Series Editors: J.W. Rogerson, University of Sheffield, and Mark Harris, University of Edinburgh

ACCORDING TO THE SCRIPTURES?
J.W. Rogerson

JUSTICE: THE BIBLICAL CHALLENGE
Walter J. Houston

THE BIBLE AND THE ENVIRONMENT
David G. Horrell

THE CITY IN BIBLICAL PERSPECTIVE
J.W. Rogerson and John Vincent

THE NATURE OF CREATION
Mark Harris

YOU SHALL LOVE THE STRANGER AS YOURSELF
Fleur S. Houston

YOU SHALL LOVE THE STRANGER AS YOURSELF

The Bible, Refugees, and Asylum

Fleur S. Houston

Routledge
Taylor & Francis Group
LONDON AND NEW YORK

First published 2015
by Routledge
711 Third Avenue, New York, NY 10017

and by Routledge
2 Park Square, Milton Park, Abingdon, Oxon, OX14 4RN

Routledge is an imprint of the Taylor & Francis Group, an informa business

British Library Cataloguing in Publication Data
A catalogue record for this book is available from the British Library

Library of Congress Cataloging in Publication Data
Houston, Fleur S.
You shall love the stranger as yourself : the Bible, refugees and asylum /
Fleur S. Houston. -- 1
[edition].
pages cm. -- (Biblical challenges in the contemporary world)
Includes bibliographical references and index.
1. Emigration and immigration in the Bible. 2. Refugees. 3. Asylum, Right of--Religious aspects--Christianity. 4. Emigration and immigration--Religious aspects--Christianity. 5. Church work with immigrants.
6. Church work with refugees. I. Title.
BS680.E38H68 2015
261.8'328--dc23
2014039884

ISBN: 978-1-138-85930-2 (hbk)
ISBN: 978-1-138-85931-9 (pbk)
ISBN: 978-1-315-71738-8 (ebk)

Typeset in Sabon
by Taylor & Francis Books

Printed and bound in the United States of America by
Edwards Brothers Malloy on sustainably sourced paper

IN MEMORY OF MY MOTHER AND FATHER, CHRISTINE AND ARCHIE WHITELEY, WHO FIRST TAUGHT ME TO LOVE THE STRANGER

CONTENTS

ABBREVIATIONS

AC	Appeal Cases
ALR	American Law Reports
ANET	Ancient Near Eastern Texts (James B. Pritchard, ed., Princeton: Princeton University Press, 1955).
AV	Authorized Version of the Bible (1611)
BCE	Before the Common Era (= BC)
CA	Court of Appeal
CE	Common Era (= AD)
CG	Country Guidance (applied to Tribunal cases)
CLR	Commonwealth Law Reports
DACA	Deferred Action for Childhood Arrivals
DFT	Detained Fast Track
EEA	European Economic Area
ECHR	European Court of Human Rights reports
EHRR	European Human Rights Reports
EWCA	England and Wales Court of Appeal
EWHC	England and Wales High Court (Administrative Court)
FGM	female genital mutilation
FRLANT	Forshungen zur Religion und Literatur des Alten und Neuen Testaments
HC	High Court
IAC	Independent Asylum Commission
ICE	Immigration and Customs Enforcement
IDP	Internally Displaced Person
JCWI	Joint Council for the Welfare of Immigrants
JSOT Sup	Journal for the Study of the Old Testament Supplement Series
NCADC	National Coalition of Anti-Deportation Campaigns
NGO	Non-governmental organization
NRSV	New Revised Standard Version
NZLR	New Zealand Law Reports
NZSC	Supreme Court of New Zealand

PLO	Palestine Liberation Organization
PTSD	Post-Traumatic Stress Disorder
R	*regina* (= "the queen") or *rex* (= "the king"); i.e. the Crown, that is, the state as prosecuting authority in the UK
RICE	Refugee Integration Capacity and Evaluation
RSV	Revised Standard Version
SBL	Society of Biblical Literature
SCR	Supreme Court Reports
SIAC	Special Immigration Appeals Commission
SIEV	Suspected Illegal Entry Vessel
SSHD	Secretary of State for the Home Department
SSSS	Secretary of State for Social Security
UKAIT	United Kingdom Asylum and Immigration Tribunal (precursor of UKUT)
UKBA	United Kingdom Border Agency
UKIAT	United Kingdom Immigration Appeal Tribunal (precursor of UKAIT)
UKLGIG	United Kingdom Lesbian and Gay Immigration Group
UKUT	United Kingdom Upper Tribunal
UNHCR	United Nations High Commission(er) for Refugees
UNRWA	United Nations Relief and Works Agency
WLR	Weekly Law Reports

PREFACE

The invitation to write this book, the sixth in the Biblical Challenges in the Contemporary World series, came from the Bible and Society Group, and I would like to record my thanks to the group for entrusting me with this project.

I am grateful for this opportunity to reflect on issues with which I have been increasingly preoccupied since September 2003, when a visitor from Iran was brought by his landlady to the Church of the Holy Family, Blackbird Leys, where I was serving as a minister of the United Reformed Church. He soon became fully involved in the life of the Church, and on 11 April 2004 he was baptized. Although my colleagues and I were fully persuaded of the profound sincerity of his Christian conviction, his claim for asylum in the UK was refused on the grounds that it was not credible. The evidence of expert witnesses was disregarded. The chief basis for assessment by the Tribunal was a series of questions, more or less ludicrous, which betrayed scant knowledge of the Bible, the Church or the Christian faith. With a sense of justice outraged, I collaborated with Nicholas Coulton, canon of Christ Church, Oxford, in assembling a dossier of similar Tribunal evidence from churches of many traditions and from all over the UK. Under the auspices of the then Churches Main Committee, we met with a succession of government ministers to discuss appropriate guidelines for tribunals. On joining the steering group of the Churches Refugee Network, I became increasingly aware of the rapidly worsening plight of many refugees and asylum-seekers; the catastrophic effects of government legislation, policies, and practices; the courage shown by people in often desperate circumstances; and the commitment of individuals and organizations that seek, despite draconian financial restrictions, to bring some humanity to bear on their situation. And I also became increasingly aware of the urgent ethical and moral questions regarding asylum-seekers which are currently being raised.

While this book is an attempt to reflect critically on the significance of the Bible for Christian life and action in this field, I hope that it will also be accessible to non-Christians. Except for instances where the Hebrew or Greek text indicates a need for greater precision, Biblical references and quotations are from the New Revised Standard Version (NRSV). In chapters four to six,

I have used the Tetragrammaton, the personal name for God revealed to Moses (Exod. 3.14), which represents the four Hebrew letters that are commonly transliterated in Roman script as YHWH.

In thanking my colleagues in the Churches Refugee Network for their ongoing interest and encouragement, I would like to express particular appreciation to Louise Zanre, who generously read the second chapter of the book and sharpened my thinking, and to James Davies, who set aside precious time to critique chapter three. I am also grateful to Jerome Phelps, who clarified the finer points of detention practice, to Puck de Raadt, who kept me up to date on asylum cases, and to Zrinka Bralo, who introduced me to Remzije Sherifi, who keeps hope alive in Maryhill. Thanks are also due to Iona Hine and Susie Snyder, who shared some of their work with me at an early stage, and to Amy Hole, who in the midst of a busy life cast an eagle eye over my legal references and saved me from *bêtises*. From its gestation, this book has known three publishers. Tristan Palmer steered it supportively through the transition stages from Equinox to Acumen Press, and Eve Mayer of Routledge, who inherited the project fully fledged, has been helpful and encouraging. My copy-editor, Michael Helfield, has been most assiduous. I am grateful as well to the anonymous reviewers of my original proposal and of the final manuscript, who encouraged me to think that this project is worthwhile, and to Mark Harris, who, as co-editor of the series, read through the manuscript in successive drafts and made helpful comments. Above all, I would like to thank my husband, Walter, who read through all the chapters in draft, in some cases more than once, for his acute and perceptive critique, his constant encouragement when progress seemed hard, and his patience with a wife who became more and more absorbed with the Bible and refugees as time went on.

1

INTRODUCTION

As the number of desperate people forced to leave their homes in 2013 exceeded fifty million for the first time since the Second World War, the political, legal, and humanitarian challenges raised by the situation of refugees and asylum-seekers are amongst the most significant and complex in our world today. Refugee camps are overflowing, the Mediterranean has become a huge cemetery, and, from the US to Ukraine, walls and borders are being reinforced not to protect, but to exclude.

This book tries to do justice to the complexity of the issues, many of which are contested, but it offers no easy solutions. It does seek, however, to move the reader to a deeper awareness that throws into perspective the posturing of politicians and the ideological arguments that are so often a feature of national discourse. And it does this by an examination of Biblical texts which enable us to discern the broad thrust of Biblical teaching. As it does so, it explores how this Biblical perspective may shape the lives of the faithful today and provide a basis upon which the institutions, structures, and policies of our societies may be challenged.

A definition of terms

Although I try as much as possible for present purposes to differentiate the category of refugees from the general category of migrants, and the category of asylum-seekers from the category of other immigrants, a hard and fast distinction is not always possible. With this in mind, some sort of working definition of terms may be helpful.

The word "refugee" is used in three ways: first, in the most general sense of a person who has been forced to leave his or her home on a temporary or permanent basis chiefly because of war or persecution; second, in terms of the United Nations Refugee Convention of 1951, which defines a refugee more narrowly as a person who is judged to have "a well-founded fear of being persecuted for reasons of race, religion, nationality, membership of a particular social group or political opinion" and who "is outside the country of his nationality, and is unable … or … unwilling to avail himself of the protection of that country" (Article 1A(2)); and third, the term is used of a person who has been granted asylum. The term is used in this book in all three of these senses, and I hope that the meaning in each case will be clear from the context.

The term *asylum-seeker* is used in a technical sense to refer to a person who has arrived at an international border claiming to be a refugee, but who has not yet been given official recognition as such. It is also used more generally to mean a person whose asylum claim has been refused, yet who continues to live in the country without leave to remain.

Those who cross international borders to settle in another country, for a short or long period of time, are described as *immigrants*. The move may be for a variety of reasons – economic, political, or personal – and these may or may not be refugees. These persons are frequently described as *illegal* if they lack appropriate documentation. But they are not criminals, and so I prefer to use the term *undocumented*.

How can the Bible inform the debate?

In the first volume of the series *Biblical Challenges in the Contemporary World*, John Rogerson has this to say: "Any responsible use of the Bible must acknowledge that it comes from a culture completely different from that of modern western society ... Further, it must be acknowledged that the Bible says nothing about many modern problems ... This does not mean that the Bible cannot be used to address modern issues. It does mean that ... against all the odds, the Bible can bring light and hope into a world still darkened by so much ignorance and inhumanity" (2007: 105). But how may this best be achieved? The question is hermeneutical: the Scriptural text is one link in a chain of communication between the original speaker, the situation of their hearers, and those who read the text in a different time and place, whose experiences shape the act of interpretation. For those who maintain that Biblical study and theological reflection have a significant role to play, it is not an option just to read off from the text to the issues of today. But for the life of faith, it cannot be right either simply to treat the Biblical literature as ancient texts, of purely archaeological interest, with no particular relevance to today's world.

A middle way between the two alternatives is posited by Paul Ricoeur, the distinguished French philosopher and theologian, who steers a careful path between a "literalist" approach to the Bible and a "critical" approach (Stiver 2001: 77–79), and this is the method I adopt in this book. There are, he suggests, three stages in finding meaning, what he calls a "hermeneutical arc". First, we read the passage carefully and allow it to "speak" to us as it stands. Then we make a careful critical examination of the text, allowing for form and redaction criticism and reflecting on the narrative in its historical context. And finally, we go back to the passage, now rich with meaning and giving us new understandings and insights (Ricoeur 1981, 1984: 77–81; Mudge 2001: 114). The text now seems different from the way it did on the first reading. It projects a world which may or may not coincide with the intentions of the author or editor, a "world in front of the text" (Stiver 2001: 92), and the reader experiences a new way of living, of feeling, and of seeing. Ricoeur describes this process as *mimesis*, a dynamic link between life and the text (1982). But the process doesn't rest there. It invites the reader to make a creative response using "ethical imagination" (Thomasset 2005: 525–541). This highlights a tension between the world as it is and the world as it ought to be, and it calls inhumanity and injustice into question.

This ethical imagination comes into play in two main respects. First, it stirs solicitude and compassion, as it invites the reader to stand in another person's shoes (Ricoeur 1986). Second, imagination keeps human relations personal. It combats the anonymity of relationships in bureaucratic societies. It feeds into a sense of justice. With this exercise of creative imagination, the Biblical texts educate our moral and affective sensibilities and inspire our ethical vision, as well as our relations to our neighbours and to our social institutions.

The Biblical texts in chapters three to eight have been chosen because they are relevant. While not exhaustive, they cover a broad range of experiences. Different perspectives avoid foreclosing debate and embracing easy conclusions. I explore the texts in some detail, bringing them as appropriate into conversation with archaeology, sociology, refugee and diaspora studies, and disaster and trauma studies. Although these have to be brought into contact carefully – comparisons of this type between ancient and modern societies involve critical reflection as to whether such insights are comparable – they can enable us to gain a more realistic estimation of human experience and ethical responsibility both in the world of the Bible and in the world of today. Some contemporary narrative sources are legal. Tribunal judges work with a logic of uncertainty and qualitative probability (Stiver 2007: 152). This can involve arguments, evidence, and conclusions that are probable but that are not proofs. Knowing the technicalities of the law is not enough to guide the difficult decisions they have to make; rather, the capacity to imagine and feel how a "reasonable person" in a very different situation might respond is critical. This capacity for empathetic imagination varies from judge to judge.

References are made chiefly to the policies and practices of three countries: the US, traditionally the largest provider of refugee protection, Australia, with a particular emphasis on "unauthorized" asylum-seekers who try to reach the country by sea, and the UK, where the humanitarian process of refugee resettlement is being turned into a politically motivated form of refugee deterrence. But the issues raised are not, by any means, exclusive to these three countries.

After looking in some detail at the situation of refugees and asylum-seekers in today's world in chapters two and three, we turn to the Biblical texts that concern the sojourner in chapter four, with particular reference to the Torah and narratives. We then examine the ambiguities of the Exodus narrative and the trauma associated with the Babylonian Exile in chapter five before moving on to explore the challenges of "return" in chapter six. The evangelists highlight the way in which Jesus' life and teaching exemplifies and develops the Torah in chapter seven, and in chapter eight we further explore the relevance of this for the life of the early church and the church of today. Texts that illustrate hospitality to the stranger, fundamental to both Testaments, are examined in chapter eight. Chapter nine then draws some conclusions.

2

A WORLD OF REFUGEES

This chapter examines the protection that is available for refugees under international law and the relationship between this and the need for humanitarian protection. It considers the bearing of international refugee law on inter-state relationships and the rights and duties of states towards refugees before going to explore a series of questions that arise.

The need for protection

> When families in Mustafa's neighbourhood were brutally killed, including his sister, and her husband and children, he took his family and left Syria. Hungry and sick, he eventually reached Jordan – but as winter storms sweep the country, refugee families like Mustafa's are at risk.

This story illustrates the appeal for aid in 2014 by the international Non-Governmental Organization (NGO), Islamic Aid. Mustafa's story is that of millions of people in our world today. Men, women, and children are forced to leave their homes in fear for their lives. Immediate humanitarian needs are imperative, but so is political protection. The two provisions are distinct but interlinked, and this is reflected in international law. The general principle of the right to seek and enjoy asylum is part of international customary law, as it is part of the 1948 United Nations Universal Declaration of Human Rights. But it was not until 1951 with the United Nations Convention Relating to the Status of Refugees that the international obligations of states towards refugees, based on broad humanitarian principles, were set out in international law. A legal definition of "refugee" was internationally agreed upon, and a controversial label was thereby created (Zetter 1999: 46; see p. 1).

The Refugee Convention was designed to address the plight of Holocaust survivors and refugees from the Second World War, and, with the advent of the Cold War, new refugees from central and eastern Europe. In this respect, it was timely. However, its Eurocentric focus meant that it was not then applied to the huge population displacements that took place outside Europe. As fresh refugee-producing situations emerged worldwide, the 1967 Protocol was added to remove time restrictions and geographical limitations. Other legal instruments on refugees apply regionally in Africa, Latin America, and the European Union (EU), but the Refugee Convention remains the only global legal instrument dealing with the status and rights of refugees. Amongst the first to accede to the Convention in 1954 were Australia and the UK, the latter having been amongst the first signatory nations. While the US did not at the time ratify the Refugee Convention, it did ratify the New York Protocol in 1968, thereby binding itself derivatively to it. And the governing statute in the US, namely, the Refugee Act of 1980, generally follows the Convention's definition of "refugee". While each individual state has discretion to decide whether a person on its threshold qualifies for refugee status, the Convention obliges the host state to protect those who have reached its borders from forced return to the country from which they have fled; this is the principle of *non-refoulement* (Article 33).

State protection

Forcibly displaced over the border

International law until recently dealt primarily with inter-state relationships and with the rights and duties of states. The role of the state in protection has been stretched to the limit by the increasingly huge numbers of people who have had to take refuge across the border in "countries of overspill". The majority of refugees flee, like Mustafa and his family, over the borders of their own country to take refuge in a neighbouring territory. Studies suggest that "local populations in receiving countries have shown remarkable signs of tolerance and solidarity with fleeing victims of colonial oppression in earlier decades and of ethnopolitical violence in the most recent ones" (Westin 1999: 29). A possible explanation may lie in the fact that "refugees from one country will generally be treated kindly by ethnic or tribal compatriots on the other side of the border". The different host countries in Africa show "incredible generosity and openness" (Türk 2012b), but the huge numbers of displaced people stretch their resources, already scarce, to the limit. There is an urgent need for an international humanitarian response. With the agreement of the host country, this is supplied by the United Nations High Commission for Refugees (UNHCR) in close partnership with NGOs who deliver and operate the relief programme. Fundraising is imperative. The bulk of the UNHCR's activities are entirely funded by voluntary contributions: "UNHCR's funding arrangements put a political and diplomatic price on the lives of refugees depending on the effectiveness of its appeals and the claim an emergency makes on the world's humanitarian conscience" (Zetter 1999: 58). But does the perception that the UNHCR is "the servant to the world's humanitarian conscience" allow individual states to abdicate responsibility? In the International Covenant on Social, Economic and Cultural Rights (1966), Articles 2(1) and 11 are usually interpreted as implying an obligation to contribute to international aid for the benefit of refugees in poor countries, though "under present interpretations of international human rights law, the failure of a government to provide foreign aid ... is probably not legally actionable" (Hathaway 2005: 495).

Unlike the industrialized nations of the West, these "countries of overspill" have usually no domestic asylum procedures and institutions; where possible, registration, documentation, and refugee status determination are carried out by the UNHCR. This can take very many years – the primary focus of the organization has to be on ensuring that basic survival needs for food, shelter, and hygiene are met. Desperate to escape the misery of war, thousands of these men, women, and children make their homes in refugee camps. Some, like the camps for refugees from Syria or South Sudan, may have been set up relatively recently; others, like the Somalian or Palestinian refugee camps, may be of longer standing, reflecting the intractability of the conflicts that brought them into being.

Somalia presents one of the world's worst refugee crises. The conflict situation was exacerbated by the worst drought to hit the Horn of Africa in sixty years. Around half the population live in forced displacement from their own homes, some across borders and around half a million of them in the Dadaab camp in Kenya. Many had trekked for thousands of miles; when they reached the border town of Liboi, some were too weak to walk any more – the onward journey to Dadaab could take up to four days. In 2012, hundreds of thousands of refugees in Dadaab were facing a humanitarian emergency. In a sobering report, *Médecins sans Frontières* states:

> The refugees in Dadaab – and others on their way – need the continuous support of the UNHCR, the Kenyan government and humanitarian organisations to be able to survive. It is the responsibility of the decision makers to find solutions to reverse the current trends where refugees are paying the price for a conflict they are trying to escape and are at risk of becoming victims of the system that should assist them. The priority should remain the provision of assistance and protection to the thousands of refugees.
>
> (MSF 2012)

As fighting escalated in Syria in August 2012, the flow of refugees into neighbouring countries increased dramatically, giving rise to a serious humanitarian emergency. In Jordan, the Za'atar camp found its resources stretched to the utmost with hundreds of refugees arriving daily, mainly women and children travelling in fear under the cover of darkness; many of the children were severely traumatized. Humanitarian organizations and the United Nations (UN) agencies worked around the clock to accommodate the new arrivals (the *Guardian*, 4 September 2012). Meanwhile, authorities in Turkey struggled to cope with a huge influx of refugees from Syria. Many of these tried desperately to put the Turkish camps and the misery of war behind them and find refuge in Europe through Greece. But Greece, where anti-immigrant popular sentiment fed upon a spiralling economic recession, was under pressure to seal off its borders with Turkey. With border controls tightening between Turkey and Greece, asylum-seekers increasingly tried to enter Europe through Bulgaria. Mahmoud and his wife Fadwa were among them. An eyewitness reporter for the *Guardian* had this to say:

> As Damascus collapsed around them, they packed up their four children and left. The family has spent six months at an open camp in Pastrogor, an isolated border village in Bulgaria. Farouk is living at the same camp. "We don't know what to do. We cannot go back because there is a problem with our country. We cannot continue, because we have no money. We are like slum dogs. Before we came here we heard that Europe is a country [sic] of humanity. But after all these experiences, we see the opposite."
>
> (*Guardian*, 8 December 2012)

Resettlement

Those who have the most pressing humanitarian needs are usually unable to return to their country of origin or to integrate locally. Around one per cent of these are resettled in a third country by orderly programmes coordinated chiefly through the UNHCR and the International Red Cross. The status of the refugees is established prior to entry. The scheme offers "legal and physical protection, including access to civil, political, economic and cultural rights similar to those enjoyed by nationals. It should allow for refugees to become naturalized citizens" (UNHCR 2014). Although a relatively small number of states participate in the scheme, quotas are agreed as one way of fulfilling their humanitarian responsibility. The US, with a reputation for having one of the most open and generous immigration policies in the world (Smith 1995), has taken in large numbers of displaced persons annually since 1990, more than any other Western country; in 2010, the number was 54,077. But the numbers do not necessarily reflect an ideological commitment set in bronze to welcome the hungry and tired masses "yearning to breathe free". Different factors come into play. Over the years, US policy has been at times "inconsistent, racist and surprisingly un-American" (Smith 1995). Abraham Lincoln's wry statement that should the nativists have their way, the Declaration of Independence would be rewritten to say "All men are created equal, except Negroes, foreigners and Catholics" might be exemplified by the National Origins Act of 1924, the chief aim of which appeared to have been to protect a dominant core of White, Protestant, Anglo-Saxons from dilution. Not until the Immigration and Nationality Act of 1965, in the context of the Civil Rights movement of the 1960s, was the quota system based on national origin abolished. Advocates for displaced persons appealed to an alternative account of US obligation "for the simple reason that all of them are the descendants of displaced persons – everybody in this country" (Truman 1963), and the Executive, with a greater responsibility for foreign affairs, was often proactive in its attempts to initiate enabling asylum legislation. But it cannot be said that this was exclusively for humanitarian reasons. Even after the end of the Cold War, concern for displaced persons was linked with the foreign policy interests of the US: displaced persons from the former Soviet Union and eastern Europe were welcomed in huge numbers in the belief that to do so would contribute to the ultimate defeat of Communism. Political dissidents from the Middle East were also welcome. But since the 1990s, the number of refugees resettled annually in the US has continued to decline. This may be related to a steady increase in refugees from Africa (Gibney 2004). The rise of terrorism and the increasing numbers of paramilitary organizations throughout the world – but especially in Africa – has led to enhanced security checks being implemented (most of them after 9/11) to ensure that terrorists do not gain access to US territory. Those individuals in the camps who hope to benefit from resettlement are normally subject to lengthy delays in getting travel documents to the US and other countries.

In 2002, the British government announced a resettlement scheme called "Gateway," which, with the help of voluntary groups and NGOs, catered annually for 500 refugees. Ten years on, the annual quota has been raised to a conservative 750 people. Even so, given the high rate of unemployment in the UK and the strains on the national economy, refugee resettlement is increasingly experienced as a burden (Westin 1999: 37). Sheffield, the first city to welcome a quota of Liberian refugees under the scheme in 2004, told the government in May 2014 that despite the City Council's willingness to accept Syrian refugees, it could not do so without adequate funding support. Other local authorities followed suit (Merrill & Dugan 2014).

Since 2009, Australia has also received a generous quota of Convention refugees, although this includes family members who might not themselves be refugees. Farida Fozdar makes the point that, to be serious about offering sanctuary to refugees, a state must have as a goal the re-establishment of security among these communities. This does not, she suggests, mean merely doing the minimum necessary to foster material security, but treating people as those "whose interests must be considered as legitimate as one's own" (Fozdar 2012: 50). Although such refugees are provided with government-funded services and assistance, this is experienced as a "limited and contingent humanitarian response that expects gratitude and assimilation" (2012: 60). Many feel that their culture is at best marginalized and that they are not allowed to be different. They feel insecure (Aidani 2010: 62–63).

Burden-sharing

Yet the resettlement programme deals with only a fraction of the numbers of people in the refugee camps. Sweden and Germany have notably taken significant steps to ease the refugee burden on Syria's neighbours by taking in a significant quota of Syrian refugees. Sweden grants asylum-seekers from Syria permanent residence so that they can immediately start integration. But on a global scale, the countries of the North have made a significantly smaller contribution towards refugee protection than the poorer nations of the South, who, with far fewer material resources, carry the burden of the bulk of the world's refugees. Equitable burden-sharing criteria would ensure that proposals be developed with each country's capacities in mind. But a major problem with most proposals for burden-sharing is the continued insistence that the largest share of the world's refugees be confined to the poorer countries of the South. Given the increasing inability of such countries to cope, even with UN help, this insistence is immoral. Satvinder Singh Juss argues that proposals based on the provision of temporary protection and the voluntary repatriation of refugees are "unworkable on moral and practical grounds". In practice, there is often little distinction between "voluntary" and "forced". Under certain circumstances, Western governments may apply pressure on people to induce them to leave. There are cultural factors: "most Northern countries are more likely to repatriate refugees from the poorer South who are ethnically and culturally different from their populations" (Juss 2006: 235). A distinction may be drawn according to the way refugees arrive in a host country: spontaneous arrivals are often harshly treated and induced to leave, while those who have been resettled tend to be regarded in a more favourable light. There are also variable regimes associated with public opinion or the involvement of the host government in a specific conflict, as was the case with the temporary protection measures afforded to the Kosovans who came to the UK in the mid-1990s. These proposals, Juss suggests, are advocated "on instrumentalist, rather than moral grounds … (they rest) on the conviction that the dominant states of the North will not honour the new system unless they believe that it serves their long-term interests" (2006: 221). Such proposals will not protect human dignity. They "do not reject the role of nativism and racism in shaping state refugee policy" (2006: 221). One is faced with the stark question: "is nation-centred 'burden-sharing' replacing the historical tradition of asylum, which has provided 'freedom from seizure' to refugees since the time of antiquity" (2006: 219)?

Can humanitarian need be reconciled with sovereign state control?

Questions arise, which were not envisaged in 1951, about the role of the state in refugee law. Of what relevance is the failure of the state to protect its citizens? The question is not a matter of purely academic importance, for whether or not a person's claim for asylum succeeds will often depend on the way decision-makers answer it. Broadly speaking, in asylum jurisprudence there are two main approaches: a "state-centred accountability" approach and a "protection" approach (Kneebone 2003). But can humanitarian need be reconciled with sovereign state control?

Where the focus is on state-centred accountability, it is only when the state cannot or will not carry out its duty to defend the interests of its citizens that international law comes into play – the Refugee Convention offers surrogate national protection until the role of protector is assumed by the receiving state. This is consistent with an authoritarian model of the state. It diverts attention away from the individual asylum-seeker, according less weight to his or her personal circumstances and context, and according more weight to external factors with bearing on the general risk of harm. Where there are reasons for persecution, these are seen as arising mainly from a person's civil or political status (Kneebone 2003). This may be illustrated by three key cases in the UK (Adan 1999; Islam & Shah 1999; Horvath 2000) which diverge significantly from the traditional understanding of protection theory. In these, a "protection" approach to non-state persecution is based on a conception of state culpability.

It may be argued, however, that the basis of protection under the Refugee Convention is a matter not so much of internal state accountability as of external or diplomatic protection (Kneebone 2003: 283–284). For those who adopt this line of reasoning, the basis for protection in international law is a person's presence in a territory, not his or her citizenship. The notion of citizenship may even be irrelevant (Adler & Rubinstein 2000). This "protection approach" emphasizes the link between persecution and protection rather than the link between persecution and the state, and has a primary focus on the reasonableness of a well-founded fear of persecution. Some would argue that the Convention is focused on the state to such an extent that it is "not sufficiently sympathetic of the human imperatives driving people away from their homes" (Juss 2006: 191). As Susan Kneebone observes, it is important to recognize the tension between the state approach and the protection approach, and to attempt to ensure that the emphasis on protection is not overshadowed (Kneebone 2003: 283–284).

Is a broader definition of "refugee" required, one that reflects contemporary historical circumstances? As early as 1985, Andrew Shacknove was arguing that the Refugee Convention was too focused on the state. As he saw it, too narrow a conception of refugeehood could mean the denial of international protection to people in desperate need, whereas too broad a conception could financially exhaust refugee relief programmes (1985: 276) and have an adverse impact on domestic stability (Juss 2006: 207). Shacknove makes two important observations. First, "persecution is but one manifestation of a broader phenomenon, the absence of state protection of the citizen's basic needs. It is this absence of state protection which constitutes the full and complete negation of society and the basis of refugeehood" (1985: 277). Second, refugees need not necessarily cross an international border to qualify for international protection. They may be defined as "persons whose basic needs are unprotected by their country of origin, who have no remaining recourse other than to seek international restitution of their needs, and who are so situated that international assistance is possible" (Shacknove 1985: 277). The 1951 definition, however, is more flexible than it would seem at first sight. First, the record of the UNHCR shows a broad interpretation of the Refugee Convention with clear linkage between Internally Displaced Persons (IDPs) and refugees, and attentiveness to the humanitarian needs of IDPs within a sovereign state. Second, the explosion of refugee populations in Africa and Latin America led to the adoption of regional instruments which are based on the Refugee Convention, but which more closely reflect the historical and political experiences of the two continents. And third, "the model of the Convention as the central but essentially reactive tool to tackle the phenomenon of refugees is being refocused on the role of the international community to mitigate the onset of humanitarian disasters and to define the form of response when this is enacted" (Zetter 1999: 54). No longer is the role of the international community conceived of primarily in terms of burden-sharing or responding in appropriate ways to the humanitarian needs of exiled refugees. Aid is now being seen as conditional on the attempt to address root causes of refugee flows such as human rights abuse (Zetter 1999: 76). Should we then give up on protecting individuals from the gross humanitarian abuses that lead them to flee for their lives? Surely not. And until the humanitarianism that lies behind the creation of the Refugee Convention becomes a widespread reality, that Convention is indispensable.

Stateless

What happens when a person "is not considered as a national by any State under operation of its law"? This is how the 1954 Convention Relating to the Status of Stateless Persons defines a stateless person (Article 1(1)). The problem may arise when state boundaries shift, when particular ethnic groups are stripped of nationality, or when new countries are created. By having no national authorities to protect their rights, these are especially vulnerable groups – their children are commonly stateless too, which makes the problem worse. In the case of refugees, the absence of proof of birth, origins, or legal identity can increase the risk of statelessness. This may be instanced by a case where a man claiming asylum in the UK in 2007 alleged that he was a member of a particular ethnic group, the Bedoon, which is uncontestably at risk of persecution in Kuwait. His claim and subsequent appeal failed on the basis that the only documentary evidence he had to show he was Bedoon was an identity card which was found to be fake. He was refused asylum, and the appeals court found him to be Kuwaiti. However, because he had no documents to show he was Kuwaiti, the Kuwaiti authorities would not allow him to enter their state. He could neither enter the UK nor return to Kuwait. This is the Catch-22 situation of many refugees who are unable to establish a right to reside in one state, but who have no other state to return to. Such people are forced to live out a liminal existence "stranded in legally ambiguous situations, unable to conduct a normal life in one state, but unable to leave to enter a different state" (AS 2011).

The 1954 Convention and the 1961 Convention on the Reduction of Statelessness are key legal instruments in the protection of stateless people around the world. Completed by regional treaty standards and human rights law, these are the "most comprehensive codification of the rights of stateless persons yet attained at the international level" (Statelessness Convention 1954). The state is required to facilitate the assimilation and naturalization of stateless persons. This does not, however, entail an unconditional right to refugee status. As in the Refugee Convention, those grounds exclude from refugee status persons who have committed a crime against peace, a war crime, a crime against humanity, or a serious non-political crime and persons who have been guilty of acts contrary to the purposes and principles of the UN.

Since it was established in 1951, the UNHCR is mandated, through a series of General Assembly resolutions, to take the lead in assisting "stateless persons as a distinct population of persons of concern". But what happens when an international humanitarian organization is implicated in the political situation that has led to these persons being stateless? What happens when the UN acts in a quasi-state capacity? This question is posed by the enduring plight of the Palestinian refugees.

Palestinian refugees

This is a long-term situation. It predates both the Refugee Convention and the Statelessness Convention. Since 1947, when Britain, involved in a three-way struggle with Arabs and Jews over Palestine's future, abandoned its Mandate under the League of Nations, the UN inherited a grim struggle over living space that has since grown progressively more intractable. In the convulsions that followed the abortive partition in 1948, a Jewish state emerged a quarter larger in territory than had been assigned to it and over 600,000 Arabs became refugees. In his comprehensive report to the General Assembly, Count Folke Bernadotte, the UN Mediator, made it clear that this particular refugee problem entailed UN responsibility (Buehrig 1971: 11). The Palestinians were without citizenship in their countries of refuge. As residents of a former mandated territory "for which the international community has a continuing responsibility until a final settlement is achieved", the refugees, he said, "understandably look to the United Nations for assistance". He maintained that it would be "an offence against the principles of elemental justice if these innocent victims of the conflict were denied the right to return to their homes while Jewish immigrants flow into Palestine, and ... offer the threat of permanent replacement of the Arab refugees who have been rooted in the land for centuries"

(Bernadotte 1948: 14). On the next day, Bernadotte was assassinated, and from then on, as the conflicting interests of Israelis and Palestinian Arabs remain opposed in an unequal and increasingly bloody power relationship, the refugee issue remains unresolved.

Bernadotte pointed to one feature which makes the Palestinian refugees distinctive from all others. Whereas in most situations that are handled by the UNHCR, the refugees are seeking refuge elsewhere – they cannot countenance being sent back to the countries from which they have fled – the Arab refugees cannot accept rehabilitation or resettlement in another territory as a viable option. They want to "go home". The huge size of the exodus from Palestine, the circumstances of their flight, and the apparent refusal of Arab governments, except that of Jordan, to allow them to be integrated into their respective host communities have combined to defeat any attempts at resettlement elsewhere. Buehrig (1971: 8) observes that "though group identity among the refugees was at first amorphous, the simple longing to return to homes left in sudden flight, in itself, constituted a psychological obstacle to resettlement in the countries of refuge". Yet as the "right of return" was denied the refugees, a sentimental attachment to the homeland gradually evolved into organized political expression, and after the profound shock of the 1967 War, the Palestine Liberation Organization (PLO) became an increasingly significant factor. As long as the refugees had no organization of their own, they lived under the authority of their host states, and within that, the United Nations Relief and Works Agency for Palestinian Refugees (UNRWA) had overall responsibility for their humanitarian needs while being itself exempt from territorial authority. The PLO, however, has helped them become a self-conscious community.

Buehrig (1971: 64) points to the irony of the situation in which UNRWA found itself. Established in 1949 as a welfare agency to bring humanitarian help to displaced Palestinians in Jordan, Lebanon, Syria, the West Bank, and the Gaza Strip, the UNRWA was overtaken by the political character of the problem. Its programmes were carried out within the territorial jurisdiction of states, and in its constant encounter with territorial authority it had to have political reinforcement. In the area of health, the UNRWA's relations with governments have been quite straightforward; but in other areas, such as economic rehabilitation, education, and welfare, the agency has encountered difficulties. At any rate, these remedies in themselves would not have solved the refugee problem.

The mode of operation of the UNRWA has been quite distinct from that of the UNHCR. Unlike any situation with which the UNHCR has been involved, the UN has been engaged in Palestine as a third party along with Jews and Arabs since the end of the British Mandate. It performs functions that are normally assigned to states. It is against this background that we see an international organization assume responsibility for the welfare of the Arab refugees in a manner that would be inappropriate in any other context (Buehrig 1971: 60). Its services continue in principle to be available to Palestinians.

But what happens when Palestinians who have been assisted by the UNRWA are forced to flee the camps where they had settled and seek refuge in Europe?

From stateless person to refugee

A Council Directive of the EU sets out "minimum standards for the qualification and status of third country nationals or stateless persons as refugees or as persons who otherwise need international protection and the content of the protection granted" (2004/83/EC). Referring to the Refugee Convention, the Directive states that persons who are currently receiving protection or assistance from UN organs or agencies other than the UNHCR, such as the UNRWA, are excluded from being refugees. However, where such protection or assistance has ceased for any reason, without the position of such persons being definitely settled, it provides that those persons are entitled to protection.

This was tested out when a number of stateless persons of Palestinian origin were forced to leave the UNRWA refugee camps in Lebanon either as a result of the destruction of their homes during clashes between armed groups or as a result of receiving death threats. They fled to Hungary, where they applied for refugee status. Although the authorities rejected their applications for asylum, they permitted the applicants to remain in Hungary.

The Palestinian applicants for refugee status brought proceedings before the Fővárosi Bíróság (Municipal Court of Budapest) which asked the Court of Justice of the European Union whether, under these circumstances, the applicants should automatically be recognized as refugees in the EU. In its judgement on 19 December 2012, the Court reminded the Fővárosi Bíróság that persons who are at present receiving assistance from the UNRWA cannot qualify as refugees (El Karem & El Kott 2012). But if a Palestinian applicant is able to show that their personal safety is seriously at risk and that it is impossible for the UNRWA to guarantee their continuing protection, then they are entitled to the protection conferred by the Council Directive so long as they are not caught by any of the grounds for exclusion. That interpretation is in keeping with the objective of ensuring that Palestinian refugees continue to receive effective protection.

By the end of the year, there were further attacks on established refugee settlements, which drew the attention of the world to the plight of Palestinian refugees. On 16 December 2012, Syrian government forces bombed Yarmouk refugee camp, a sprawling settlement in south-west Damascus. With around 180,000 inhabitants, this is the largest concentration of Palestinians in Syria, an established township where Palestinians have enjoyed Syrian protection since 1957 and where they have lived at peace with their Syrian neighbours ever since. But as the civil war that raged around them became more brutal and indiscriminate, thousands of Palestinians, many of them refugees for a second time, were forced to flee Damascus for camps in Lebanon and Jordan. Amongst them was Souha. She was spotted by a journalist, who described her as

> a distraught-looking woman sitting alone, tightly holding two babies, at one corner of the vast parking lot of the central Damascus bus station known as Al-Soumariyeh. One thought was about a character out of a Charles Dickens novel and the other was "waif, frail, malnourished, frightened", so the lady, holding the babies, appeared. She managed a polite but weak smile as I passed and she said "hello". Long story made short, the lady and I chatted and it turned out that Souha was fleeing the al-Hajar al-Aswad neighborhood on the southern edge of Yarmouk Palestinian refugee camp.
>
> Souha, who is studying English literature, had lost her husband and was trying to travel to Ein el Helwe refugee camp in Saida, Lebanon. She had the name of a distant relative she thought was still living in Ein el Helwe, but she was unsure how to find her but knew that she desperately needed to get out of Syria.
>
> (Almanar News 2012: http://www.almanar.com.lb/english/)

That morning, according to an estimate by the UNRWA, ninety per cent of the Yarmouk camp residents had fled.

Displaced within a state

At the other end of the spectrum of international involvement, there are the thousands of people who flee their homes and who are displaced within their own country. The rapidly growing number of IDPs (IDMC 2012) may be defined as "persons or groups who have been forced or obliged to flee or leave their homes or habitual residence, in particular as a result of or in order to avoid the effects of armed conflict, situations of generalized violence, violations of human rights or natural or human-made disasters, and who have not crossed an internationally recognized state border" (Deng 1998). These IDPs may find it hard to get assistance. They could be said to have similar protection needs to those of refugees, and they too are forced to flee their homes. They need international protection. But they have not crossed an internationally recognized state border to find sanctuary; they have remained inside their home country. According to international law, they are in theory under the protection of their own government – even though that government might be the cause of their flight. The figures are huge, and they continue to grow. In Côte d'Ivoire, violence following the November 2010 presidential elections forced an estimated half a million people to flee their homes. In Somalia, the worst drought in decades aggravated the country's chronic instability and led to one of the worst humanitarian emergencies of 2011. In Mali, in 2012, the number of IDPs reached almost 150,000, and according to the Syrian Red Crescent, there were 400,000 to 500,000 IDPs in Syria (Türk 2012b).

The UNHCR's mandate does not specifically cover IDPs, and the agency faces a dilemma in this regard (Goodwin-Gill 1999; Gonzaga 2003). In theory, according to traditional understandings of sovereignty, IDPs should be under the state's protection. The UNHCR is not supposed to provide a substitute for this, but because of its expertise in displacement, it has the lead role in overseeing their protection and shelter needs as far as practicable, as well as the coordination and management of camps (UNHCR 2012a). However, the US Refugee Act of 1980 *does* make provision for IDPs. Unlike the UN instruments, it offers an opportunity of resettlement to those who might qualify as refugees according to the definition of the Refugee Convention were it not for the fact that they are still in their country of origin.

Where the state is ineffective: flight from civil war

There is a further category of people who are in obvious need of international protection, but who do not qualify on a narrow interpretation of the Refugee Convention: those who fear persecution by non-state agents or rebel groups.

According to a rigorist interpretation of the Refugee Convention, an individual who is caught up in generalized violence or civil war may not be judged to be entitled to protection under international law, however great his or her fear of persecution may be. Kneebone illustrates this approach by citing Ibrahim 2000 (Kneebone 2003: 299–305). Mr Ibrahim was born in Somalia in 1960 and was a member of the Rahanwein clan. Until 1991, Somalia was ruled by a dictator of the rival Darod clan who was overthrown in that year. In the ensuing civil warfare involving rival clans, thousands were killed. In 1991, Mr Ibrahim's house was destroyed, he was captured, his wife was raped, and he was forced to labour in the fields. He escaped in 1992 and left Somalia in 1995. Two years later, he made his way to Australia via Thailand. His claim for asylum was rejected in the first instance because his fear of persecution arose from a situation of "instability and anarchy". After an unsuccessful application for judicial review followed by an appeal which held that the Tribunal had erred in law, the Australian High Court decided by a narrow majority of four to three to restore the initial decision of the Federal Court and reject the claim. The majority reasoning represented by Gummow J was of the opinion that the Convention does not apply where there is no effective state: "The protection spoken of in the Convention definition is not that of a 'country' in an abstracted sense, divorced from the notion of a government with administrative organs" (Ibrahim 2000 para [153]). This judgement reflects the ways in which an overemphasis on the state may actually hinder the recognition of new categories of refugees as persons requiring protection against persecution.

The degree to which protection is afforded by the 1951 Convention to victims of oppression by non-state actors has been much debated in law, and there have been widely differing interpretations in different jurisdictions. If we compare the judgement in the case of Mr Ibrahim to analogous cases in the UK, we will see the different ways in which local domestic legislation does, in this respect, enact the Refugee Convention (Wilsher 2003). The matter is complex. There is no entirely satisfactory interpretation of "protection" in the Convention. Goodwin-Gill & McAdam point out that "neither the 1951 Convention nor the *travaux préparatoires* say much about the source of the persecution feared by the refugee, and no necessary linkage between persecution and government authority is formally required" (2007: 98).

Non-refoulement

The emphasis on protection is enshrined in the provision against *refoulement*. A state may not send a person back to the country from which he or she has fled because of a well-founded fear of persecution. Article 33 of the Refugee Convention provides that "[n]o Contracting State shall expel or return (*refouler*) a refugee in any manner whatsoever to the frontiers of territories where his life or freedom would be threatened on account of his race, religion, nationality, membership of a particular social group or political opinion". This core principle, solidly rooted in international human rights law and refugee law, is also generally considered to be a rule of customary international law, binding on all states, whether or not they are signatories of the Refugee Convention or Protocol. *Non-refoulement* does not convey a right to asylum, but it does place strict limits on what a state may lawfully do. As Goodwin-Gill makes clear, "it applies independently of any formal recognition of refugee status or entitlement to other forms of protection, and it applies to the actions of States, wherever undertaken, whether at the land border, or in maritime zones, including the high seas" (Goodwin-Gill 2011).

Non-refoulement *and "boat people"*

In such "maritime zones, including the high seas", the principle of *non-refoulement* has been severely put to the test. "Boat people" first came to international attention following the fall of Saigon in 1975, when desperate men, women, and children fled Vietnam in boats which were not suitable for navigating open waters. On 10 June 1977, an Israeli cargo ship en route to Japan crossed paths with a boat full of sixty-six people from Vietnam. They were out of food and water, they were lost, and their boat was leaking. The captain and crew decided to bring the passengers on board and transported them to Israel. There, Prime Minister Menachem Begin authorized their Israeli citizenship, comparing their situation to the plight of Jewish refugees seeking a haven during the Holocaust. As Begin explained to US President Jimmy Carter, "we never have forgotten the boat with nine hundred Jews, the *St Louis*, having left Germany in the last weeks before the Second World War ... traveling from harbor to harbor, from country to country, crying out for refuge. They were refused ... Therefore it was natural ... to give those people a haven in the land of Israel". The Government of Israel offered a ceremonial welcome, and the Minister of Absorption David Levy exhorted other governments to "do as we have. May they lend a hand to save women and children who are in the heart of the sea without a homeland, and lead them to safe shores" (Bryen 2012). Over the next two years, large numbers were picked up by British merchant ships in the South China Sea and taken to camps in Hong Kong, still at the time a British colony. By July 1979, there were more than 60,000. On the eve of the UN conference convened to find a solution to this problem, the British government reluctantly agreed to take in 10,000 of these refugees spread out over three years. The US admitted 430,000 refugees from Vietnam. By 1981 around 50,000 Indo-Chinese had been allowed to enter Australia as refugees, and the government committed itself to accepting a further 15,000 a year.

But attitudes were hardening towards the boat people. The spontaneous arrivals tended to provoke an immediate political reaction in a way that did not happen with orderly resettlement programmes. In the US, this may be illustrated by the waves of boat people from Cuba and Haiti. The facts of the Mariel Boatlift are well known. In April 1980, Fidel Castro declared the port of Mariel open for any Cubans who so desired to depart for the US. Over the next six months, in hundreds of lobster boats and shrimpers, around 125,000 *Marielitos* set out for Florida. An immediate political backlash in the US was fuelled by concern that asylum was becoming a vehicle for the entry of criminals and those who were mentally unstable. The dominant narrative shifted from one in which thousands of Cubans were fleeing Communism to one where, in the words of a *New York Times* columnist, Fidel Castro was "exporting his failures". In the face of popular anger, exacerbated by the aborted attempt to save the American hostages held in the US embassy in Tehran, President Carter lost his bid for re-election. The sense that Americans were under siege was exacerbated by the simultaneous arrival of an armada of tiny, fragile boats from Haiti carrying people who were desperate to flee the venal regime of Jean-Claude Duvalier. Around 40,000 of these claimed asylum. Haitian refugees had been excluded before, but this could happen again only if the US administration was now prepared to violate the law. The Refugee Act of 1980 carried the obligation not to *refoule* any one at or within US borders who had a legitimate claim to refugee status. Could the administration continue to accept Cubans for asylum for reasons of foreign policy, while denying entry to Haitians in obvious need? Under the new Reagan regime, Haitians were subjected to harsh treatment (Reagan 1982). Those who managed to avoid being intercepted at sea and returned to Haiti were detained for lengthy periods of time in the US before their asylum claim was rejected. Summary and discriminatory treatment was also meted out to those who were fleeing in large numbers to the US from right-wing dictatorships in Guatemala and El Salvador. Refugee advocates, human rights groups, churches, and the judiciary mobilized in opposition to these actions. The matter was not yet over. In 1994, as the US was once more coming to grips with the arrival of boatloads of desperate people from Haiti, Castro increased the pressure on the US by allowing the departure of *balseros* (rafters) from Cuba. The US administration responded to domestic lobbies and signalled that spontaneous arrivals would not be tolerated. Harsh measures were introduced. The Cuban Adjustment Act of 1966 had enabled Cuban natives or citizens with accompanying spouses or children to obtain permanent resident status in the US provided that they had resided in the country for at least one year. This was applicable regardless of whether or not they had entered the US at a "designated port of entry". The Act was now suspended, US captains were to be prosecuted if they picked up Cuban emigrants, and the Coast Guard was to send all those who were picked up at sea to a new camp in Guantanamo Bay on the island of Cuba. Meanwhile, the deepening human rights crisis in Haiti after Jean-Bertrand Aristide was overthrown meant that President Clinton was faced with the choice of either admitting Haitian boat people or intervening to restore Aristide to power. Afraid of an electoral backlash, he chose the latter option, citing a desire to "protect the integrity of US borders". The decision was challenged, but the US Supreme Court ruled that it was not a violation of US or international law to intercept boats from Haiti before they reached US territorial waters and return their occupants to Haiti before they could make an asylum claim (Sale 1993). As Andrew Pizor demonstrates (Pizor 1993), this was an erroneous decision based on a legally dubious interpretation of *non-refoulement*, which "should be rejected by other nations facing similar refugee situations". The judiciary had given its imprimatur to a double standard of growing significance: refugees within US territory would enjoy the rights and privileges of the state – whereas those outside its territorial waters could be treated summarily.

The need for humanitarian protection is clear, but who has the juridical obligation to protect the boat people? In what sense could it be said that states are liable to protect them? Under whose territorial jurisdiction do they come? Because they are at sea, it could be argued that they are outside the literal provisions of the Convention. It is possible, however, to affirm the core principles of the Convention and maintain the possibility that existing rights may be given a wider interpretation. A good example of a "living instrument" interpretation may be seen in a landmark judgement of the Grand Chamber of the European Court of Human Rights on 23 February 2012:

> The Court considers that the Italian government must take steps to obtain assurances from the Libyan government that the applicants will not be subjected to treatment incompatible with the Convention, including indirect *refoulement*. This is not enough. The Italian government also has a positive obligation to provide the applicant with practical and effective access to an asylum procedure in Italy. The words of Justice Blackman are so inspiring that they should not be forgotten. Refugees attempting to escape Africa do not claim a right of admission to Europe. They demand only that Europe, the cradle of human rights idealism and the birthplace of the rule of law, cease closing its doors to people in despair who have fled from arbitrariness and brutality.

> That is a very modest plea, vindicated by the European Convention on Human Rights. We shall not close our ears to it.
>
> (Hirsi Jamaa 2012)

The facts are these: a group of about two hundred refugees from Somalia and Eritrea left Libya in 2009 on board three boats bound for Italy. On 6 May 2009, when the boats were thirty-five miles south of Lampedusa, an island belonging to Italy, they were intercepted by Italian Customs and Coast Guard vessels. The passengers were transferred to the Italian military vessels and taken to Tripoli. The Italian authorities did not tell them where they were being taken, or check their identity. Who were they? Where had they come from? Why were they on the move? It appears that nobody asked, although one might reasonably infer that some, if not all, were in need of international protection. Once in Tripoli, after a ten-hour voyage, they were handed over to the Libyan authorities in accordance with bilateral agreements concluded by Italy with Libya. It was alleged that this policy discouraged criminal gangs involved in people smuggling and trafficking, helped save lives at sea, and substantially reduced landings of clandestine migrants along the Italian coast. On 26 February 2011, the Italian Defence Minister declared that the bilateral agreements with Libya were suspended following political developments in Libya.

The legal and diplomatic issues are complex. The moral issues, however, are transparently clear. *Hirsi* effectively imposed a special duty of care on a state and translated the obligation not to harm into a positive duty to protect: responsibility in law has to go hand in hand with moral responsibility. As if there were need to illustrate this, in 2011 a particularly shocking incident was beamed to the world. An inflatable dinghy set off from Tripoli with seventy-two refugees on board. They had been told they would reach Lampedusa within eighteen hours. Two days later, the island was still out of sight. The boat suffered fuel loss and engine failure, and drifted at sea for a further two weeks. During this time, a military helicopter hovered overhead and dropped food and water, indicating that it would return; but it never did. Two fishing vessels refused to help. NATO ships close by failed to respond to distress calls. Around the tenth day, when half of those on board were already dead, a large naval vessel allegedly came alongside the ship, but despite obvious distress signals, sailed away. When the ship was finally washed back up on to Libyan shores, all but nine of those on board had died from thirst and starvation or in storms, including two babies. A damning Council of Europe report, published on 29 March 2012, identifies the "human, institutional and legal" failure that led to a "vacuum of responsibility and an entirely avoidable loss of life" (Strik 2012). The report's author, Tineke Strik, described the tragedy as "a dark day for Europe" and suggested that it exposed the continent's double standards in valuing human life: "we can talk as much as we want about human rights and the importance of complying with international obligations … but if at the same time we just leave people to die – perhaps because we don't know their identity or because they come from Africa – it exposes how meaningless those words are" (*Guardian*, 28 March 2012).

The Mediterranean has tested the fundamentals of state sovereignty to the limit (Moreno-Lax 2012). But it is not only in the Mediterranean that lives are being lost. Refugees from Afghanistan, Sri Lanka, and Iraq are perishing while attempting the hazardous journey in ramshackle boats from Indonesia or Malaysia to Australia.

One particular act of exclusion drew the response of Australia to international attention and conveyed the image of a country that was extremely hostile to refugees. In August 2001, a twenty-metre wooden fishing boat, bearing 438 asylum-seekers, set off from Indonesia for Australia. It was soon in serious distress. Responding to an alert by Australian coastal officials, the MV *Tampa*, a freighter from Norway, rescued the passengers and took them on board. The *Tampa,* now itself dangerously overloaded, headed for Christmas Island, where its new passengers would be able to claim asylum from Australia. But rather than seeing the *Tampa* asylum-seekers as bearers of rights, the government saw the issue as one of border control. Prime Minister Howard was adamant that none of the "rescuees" would set foot on Australian soil. So government officials telephoned the captain and warned him not to enter Australia's territorial waters. The captain, more concerned with rescuing people from the sea than with Australian politics, ignored these requests and entered Australia's waters. The *Tampa* was then boarded by troops who refused to let the ship land. After several days, the asylum-seekers were forcibly removed and transferred to the small Pacific island of Nauru. Strong public support for the government action was based on the premise that these asylum-seekers were "queue jumpers," and the thin end of the wedge, but in view of the relatively small numbers that have followed since 2001, this is hard to justify (Gibney 2004: 188–193). The government reaction to the MV *Tampa* affair was swift. Under tough new strategies of prevention, processing centres were set up on Nauru and on Manus Island in Papua New Guinea, and in return, the governments of the two nations received millions of dollars in aid. The Australian Navy diverted all boats carrying asylum-seekers to those camps, where many were detained for months – sometimes years – under high security. Eventually, Australia was accused of failing to meet its obligations under refugee conventions, and the "Pacific Solution" was abandoned in 2007. The government then pushed instead for the "Malaysia Swap" deal, under which Australia would send 800 asylum-seekers who arrived by boat to Malaysia and receive 4,000 "processed" refugees in return over four years. But on 31 August 2011, the High Court found (High Court 2011) that a country of destination must be bound by international or domestic law to provide protection for asylum-seekers, and further, that a minister has no power to remove from Australia asylum-seekers whose claims for protection have not been met. Following 9/11, the arrival of boats passed from an immigration issue to a defence issue, and "leaky boats" became known as "Suspected Illegal Entry Vessels". There is a state of hysteria in public discourse about immigrants in Australia (Gibney 2003: 19–45), and in the meantime, men, women, and children continue to hazard their lives in the attempt to reach Australian shores.

The people-smuggler: a racketeer or a friend in need?

The measures adopted by governments to intercept boat people and prevent them from setting foot in their country are often linked to a desire to control people-smuggling. Yet many people owe their lives to this very private enterprise. A Refugee Council report (Crawley 2010) refers to "a 'migration industry' of agents ... upon whom asylum seekers must rely in order to secure access to protection". Approximately two-thirds of those who participated in the research indicated that they had used an agent to travel to the UK. Of the poorest people, who cannot afford an agent, a number lose their lives in the journey to a new country. Less than one-third of those surveyed were in a position to pay for themselves. The majority stated that their families or a family friend either paid for the journey or contributed towards it. In return for a person's life savings, the agent will provide a range of services: from stolen identities, forged papers, and counterfeit documents to accompanying the respondent to his or her destination; the travel documents are then retained for "recycling" by the agent. Many people, however, are abandoned by the agent mid-route, and most experience the journey as threatening and difficult. It may involve a complex itinerary by land and sea. They are not given any opportunity to choose their country of destination; in some cases, they only find out where they are on arrival. Should people-smugglers be praised for their humanitarianism or censored for preying upon those desperate people whom they rescue? "Agents are both the villains and the heroes of the piece", the Refugee Council suggests. "If it were not for the services that agents provide, many asylum seekers would simply not be able to escape from situations of conflict, political repression and human rights abuse. On the other hand, most agents are involved in making arrangements for an individual's journey for reasons of financial gain and do not necessarily have the interests and safety of individuals at the forefront of their considerations" (Seabrook 2009: 196–204).

Nor indeed, it could be said, do governments. Donald Galloway (2003) instances ways in which government responses to people-smugglers may blur the edges of political morality. In April 2000, four ramshackle boats reached the shores of Canada, carrying around 600 exhausted passengers from China. The conditions on the boats were horrendous. There was some evidence that those on board had been treated harshly by smugglers, but they were alive and able to claim asylum. In an attempt to relieve the resulting political pressure, the Canadian Minister of Citizenship and Immigration made a visit to China. In a speech in Beijing to the Canada China Business Council, on 25 April 2000, she expressed her intention "to seek cooperation with" her "Chinese counterparts to prevent human trafficking operations in the future". Despite the fact that the majority of asylum claims from China had been accepted by Canada, the Minister declared herself willing to collaborate with the Chinese authorities to prevent people from being helped to leave the country. In her concern to curtail the spontaneous arrival of asylum-seekers, she appeared oblivious to the fact that if smuggling operations had been closed down, a significant number of people would then have had no means of escaping entirely predictable ill-treatment.

Non-refoulement *and national security*

While international law deals primarily with inter-state relations, it is left to domestic legislation to deal with relations between states and individuals. Since 9/11, there has been an increasing emphasis in most countries in the EU on sovereignty and security concerns. When this happens, humanitarian principles can take a back seat. The principle of *non-refoulement* has emerged as a key issue in cases where there are implications for national security. The first paragraph of Article 33 of the Refugee Convention, which forbids the expulsion of a refugee when his or her life or freedom would be placed at risk, is qualified by Article 33(2), which allows a refugee to be deported if he or she poses a threat to national security. The provision of *non-refoulement* "may not ... be claimed by a refugee whom there are reasonable grounds for regarding as a danger to the security of the country in which he is, or who, having been convicted by a final judgement of a particularly serious crime, constitutes a danger to the community of that country".

But what if such a person were to be at risk of torture on return? Since the Refugee Convention was drafted in 1951, there has been a rapidly evolving understanding of the rights of the individual, helped by the principles set out in the Universal Declaration of Human Rights. This has given rise to some important jurisprudential developments. The European Court of Human Rights found (Ahmed 1997) that a person who loses their refugee status because they have committed a serious crime in their country of asylum is protected from deportation under Article 3 if they would face a real risk of torture, or inhuman or degrading treatment or punishment upon return to their country of origin. The UK proposed to deport Karamijit Singh Chahal, an alleged Sikh militant, to India in reliance on diplomatic assurances from New Delhi that he would not be tortured (Chahal 1997). Mr Chahal applied for asylum, but his application was rejected. The refusal was quashed by the High Court, but the Home Secretary decided to proceed with deportation. Further legal challenges were unsuccessful. The European Court of Human Rights, however, in a landmark decision, affirmed the absolute nature of prohibition against torture or inhuman or degrading treatment or punishment "irrespective of the victim's conduct". For Mr Chahal to be deported, it suggested, would be a violation of Article 3 of the Refugee Convention: "Article 3 enshrines one of the most fundamental values of democratic society. The Court is well aware of the immense difficulties faced by States in modern times in protecting their communities from terrorist violence. However, even in these circumstances, the Refugee Convention prohibits in absolute terms torture or inhuman or degrading treatment or punishment, irrespective of the victim's conduct". There could be no "balancing act" between a person's national security risk and the risk that he or she might be tortured on return to their country of origin.

In 1998, the Human Rights Act was incorporated into British law and with that came an absolute obligation on the state to refrain from inhuman or degrading treatment. This created a potentially wide-ranging extension of the principle of *non-refoulement* beyond what might have been envisaged under Article 33 of the Refugee Convention and limited the sovereign power of the British state to exclude aliens (O'Sullivan 2009: 228–280). In an attempt to revisit the *Chahal* decision, the British government argued that the right of a person to be protected from ill-treatment abroad should be balanced against the risk he or she posed to the deporting state (Saadi 2009). But the Grand Chamber of the European Court of Human Rights upheld the reasoning in *Chahal*.

The matter came to prominence again in 2012 (Othman 2012). Mr Othman, known as Abu Qatada, a Jordanian national suspected of having links to al-Qaeda, had made a successful claim for asylum on arrival in the UK in September 1993. On the basis of his claim to have been detained and tortured by Jordanian authorities in 1988 and again in 1990–1991, he was recognized as a refugee and granted leave to remain for four years. In 2002, however, he was detained and in August 2005 served with notice that he was to be deported to Jordan to face retrial for alleged terrorist offences. Given the risk of torture if he were returned, the UK made special efforts to obtain assurances from the Jordanian authorities that were sufficiently detailed to satisfy the Special Immigration Appeals Commission (SIAC), though not the Court of Appeal. The House of Lords upheld the SIAC's findings, but the Strasbourg Court overruled the decision of the Lords. While it accepted the assurances of the Jordanian government that Abu Qatada would not be tortured, it also recognized that evidence against him was likely to have been obtained by the torture of third parties. To allow the use of evidence obtained by torture during a criminal trial would be a violation of Article 6 and amount to a flagrant denial of justice. The situation was finally resolved in June 2013, when Jordan and Britain ratified a special treaty that promised fair legal treatment and Mr Othman returned to Jordan for trial. In the UK, however, the battle continues between claims for national sovereignty and the international protection regime provided by the Refugee Convention.

In 1951, the language of national security was primarily concerned with the threat posed by an individual to the state. With *Othman v UK*, however, the emphasis has shifted. Here, the rights of the individual are upheld in the face of the actions of the state. Where such actions implicate a denial of rights, a refugee's international status entitles him or her to protection.

Human rights and refugee protection

Before 1951, states were already committed in general terms to protecting the human rights of refugees: the Preamble to the United Nations Charter reaffirms "faith in fundamental human rights, and the dignity and worth of the human person" (United Nations 1945). The need to define these rights further was in direct response to the depths of brutality revealed by the Second World War:

> The world bore witness to a country systematically oppressing, subjugating and then slaughtering its own citizens ... After the defeat of Nazi Germany, when the concentration and extermination camps were publicly exposed, there was an obvious need to ensure that such acts could never happen again. A first step towards "never again" was the Universal Declaration of Human Rights (United Nations 1948). In 1948, countries from across the world boldly and loudly set out the rights of all humans, all persons, all men, women and children irrespective of race, religion or the colour of their skin.
>
> (Freedman 2014: 31)

These rights enable people to live a fully human life; they are the due of every human being, just in virtue of being human. Justice, predicated on the moral equality of all human beings, "consists in giving each his due" (Dummett 2001: 26). The Preamble to the Declaration affirms "the inherent dignity and ... the equal and inalienable rights of all members of the human family (as) the foundation of freedom, justice and peace in the world". This moral grounding is echoed by the slimmed-down European Convention on Human Rights (1953). The Declaration affirms human dignity and challenges in law those who would infringe it. It has the potential to challenge the power of state sovereignty.

How did the right of the state to exclude aliens arise? Although the proposition is often cited as axiomatic, the notion only arose during the late 19th century in the context of American and European settled territories. As James Nafziger explains, it was then that, in common-law countries of Anglo-Saxon heritage, the right to exclude aliens assumed pre-eminence over the right of aliens to seek admission in a foreign country (1983: 808). Governments began to systematically deny admission to particular kinds of aliens.

The flowering of human rights legislation since 1951 has meant a change in the particular conception of the state as provider of refugee protection. A new emphasis on the possible risk to an individual if they are sent back to their country of origin has led to a questioning of the adequacy of the definitions in the Refugee Convention, particularly in cases of persecution of women, gay men, and lesbians. These are not included in the five identified "reasons for persecution", but can they be regarded as "members of a particular social group"? The phrase has always been hard to define in practice (Walker 2003: 251–277): it was introduced in 1951 by the Swedish delegate, Mr Petren, as an amendment to the initial draft on the grounds that "such cases existed, and it would be as well to mention them explicitly" (UN DOC A/CONF.2/SR.19: 14). Hathaway's argument (1991) that "membership in a particular social group" should be interpreted consistently with the other Convention grounds for persecution has helpfully allowed the meaning of "social group" to develop along with developments in human rights law. This was illustrated in 1999, when a landmark case in the UK recognized that while "persecution" may not create a social group, "discrimination" may do so. In a closely argued judgement in the House of Lords, which overturned the previous findings of the Court of Appeal, a claim to asylum status was upheld on the grounds that "women in Pakistan, who are suspected of adultery and lack protection", are a social group in Convention terms. The joined case concerned two women from Pakistan who had been forced by their husbands to leave their homes. They were at risk of being falsely accused of adultery, abused, and possibly killed should they return to Pakistan. They could not rely on being protected by the authorities (Islam & Shah 1999).

Members of a particular social group: abused women

There is an assumption that international refugee law is gender neutral (Crawley 2001), yet, as the now defunct United Kingdom Border Agency recognized (UKBA 2010), women are subject to harm which is gender specific. Women refugees are particularly vulnerable (Dorling *et al.* 2012). More often than not, sexual violence is a component of the political, religious, or ethnic persecution women have experienced, and it has become glaringly obvious over the past few years that there is a need for sex and gender to be included in the grounds for persecution that qualify one to be a refugee.

One well-publicized case in the UK illustrates this need very well. Mary, not her real name (Moorehead 2006), worked with Alex in Kampala for the opposition political party. They put up posters and canvassed door to door. One day, they left by car to visit her father who lived in the north of Uganda. Two hours into the journey, they found the road blocked; soldiers of the Lord's Resistance Army surrounded the car, dragged them out, and took them to a camp. Mary was enslaved. She prepared food and collected water by day, and by night she was raped. Alex tried to escape and was caught. His ears and lips were cut off; it took him two months to die. Then the camp was liberated by the Ugandan army. Mary, however, was accused of supporting the rebels; the soldiers kept her for several months, raped and tortured her. Finally, she managed to escape and realized that she was pregnant. A friend in Kampala hid her for a time and then paid a trafficker to bring her to the UK. Mary was refused asylum. In June 2003, she gave birth to a baby girl known as "Ella". After several refusals and a dismissed Tribunal appeal, they were finally granted indefinite leave to remain in February 2008 after a successful Judicial Review application in the High Court. The Home Office consistently refused to recognize them as refugees, despite overwhelming evidence. The grant was on compassionate grounds "outside the rules".

Can abused women be considered – "within the rules", in Convention terms – as members of a "particular social group"? Take Rody Alvarado Peña (*The Washington Post*, 18 July 2009). Nobody disputes the facts of this case. Aged sixteen, Alvarado Peña married a career soldier in Guatemala. She suffered daily violent abuse. On discovering that she was pregnant, her husband kicked her until she miscarried, and when she tried to run away, he beat her until she lost consciousness. With divorce impossible without her husband's consent, and no shelters or support available, Alvarado Peña fled to the US in 1995. Initially, she was granted asylum, but because there was a dispute over whether gender-based violence could be a basis in law for asylum, the Immigration and Naturalization Service appealed the case. And a few years later, the Board of Immigration Appeals, the nation's highest immigration court, denied her refugee status. The judges did not dispute what had happened to Alvarado Peña, and they recognized her husband's violence as "deplorable". Still, they found no basis in law to grant Alvarado Peña asylum. Over a period of fourteen years, three presidential administrations and countless judges deliberated, appealed, and ultimately deferred decisions on her case. In 2009, in a separate case involving a Mexican woman known as "L.R.", Department of Homeland Security attorneys under the Obama Administration had unexpectedly filed an amended brief, asserting that women who have suffered domestic violence may qualify for asylum based on membership in a particular social group if they meet certain clearly defined criteria. The brief in L.R. provides a roadmap in cases of domestic violence for how to establish eligibility for asylum based on membership in a particular social group. It served as a template for the legal memorandum in the August filing of the Alvarado case, and a recommendation was issued in October 2009 that finally opened the door to making Ms. Alvarado Peña a legal US resident.

Following the recognition of women's rights within international rights law, the UNHCR has recognized the need to interpret the Convention in a way that is sensitive to sexual violence; courts in the UK and other countries are beginning to develop the law around asylum in a way that takes women's experiences into account (Gonzaga 2003: 233–250).

Female genital mutilation (FGM)

Canada was the first country to argue that FGM is a form of persecution and to acknowledge the protection rights of women and girls threatened with FGM. In the first case of its kind in 1994, Khadra Hassan Farah was granted asylum status on fleeing Somalia with her ten-year-old daughter Hodan because she feared that Hodan would be subjected to cruel, inhuman, and degrading treatment.

Other grounds for asylum in FGM cases were allowed. In the US, the Ninth Circuit Court of Appeals ruled that an Ethiopian couple, Almaz Sayoum Abebe and Sisay Mengistu, who feared that their young daughter, Amen, would be subject to FGM if forced to return, were eligible for asylum. A "well-founded fear" was enough – they were not required to prove that the child was likely to undergo FGM (Abebe & Mengistu 2005).

But numerous cases in the UK have been refused chiefly because of uncertainty as to whether women and girls who come from a particular country or ethnic group, and who are especially at risk of undergoing FGM, constitute a "particular social group" in Convention terms.

Members of a particular social group: homosexuals

In "Protecting Refugees: Questions and Answers" (UNHCR 1996: 12), we read: "it is the policy of UNHCR that persons facing attack, inhumane treatment, or serious discrimination because of their homosexuality, and whose governments are unable or unwilling to protect them should be recognised as refugees". This is a clear basis for a discussion of the issue, though the pronouncements of the UNHCR are not binding on domestic courts, and in consequence what the UNHCR says and what the domestic courts say might not be the same thing (Walker 2003: 252). As far as US asylum law is concerned, Immigration judges and the Board of Immigration Appeals have accepted that homosexuals are to be regarded as a "particular social group" in terms of the definition set out in the Refugee Convention. The first case, involving a gay Cuban man, was Matter of Toboso-Alfonso 1990, and in 1994 the Attorney-General Janet Reno elevated the decision to the status of precedent.

However, the practical and legal difficulties didn't end there! This was a new development in refugee law. In 1951, same-sex activity was illegal in many countries, and homosexuals were widely considered to be deviant or mentally ill. "Sexual deviation" was a basis in law for refusing an alien entry to the US until 1990. So how, in the case of such a "social group", was "persecution" to be defined? The significant Canadian Supreme Court judgement (Ward 1993) enabled "membership of a particular social group" to be interpreted consistently with the other grounds for persecution listed in Article 1A(2) of the Refugee Convention. In linking "membership of a particular social group" with human rights law, *Ward* allows the meaning to develop with the development of human rights law (Walker 2003: 266). Accordingly, once sexuality was characterized as fundamental to human dignity, a person could be protected from persecution if it occurred because of his or her sexuality.

Concluding remarks

The principle that each and every individual has a duty to assist those in great distress is a principle that holds between strangers, those who have only their humanity in common (Gibney 2004: 231). It has implications also for state behaviour towards foreigners and particularly so for relations between states and refugees (Shacknove 1985). Until relatively recently, international refugee law, in itself a relatively new legal system, dealt primarily with inter-state relations and the respective rights and duties of states to protect. It was left to domestic legislation to deal with the relations and rights and duties between states and individuals, and those between individuals.

International human rights law is a departure from this in that it looks at the rights of individuals in the face of states and their actions. Few international human rights treaties have the mechanisms for individuals to enforce their rights through the courts, though this is a developing area. What is particularly encouraging about the Refugee Convention of 1951 is that governments which ratify the document in their domestic legislation are giving that measure of domestic enforcement to individuals. In the UK, The Human Rights Act of 1998 has taken it one step further and given a regional court structural power to further uphold the rights of individuals. Although this may be seen as a "wholly positive development within the tradition of natural law" (Sagovsky 2003: 75), it will lead to tensions until a larger body of case law is developed and narrow views of sovereignty are in some way overcome. In common-law jurisdictions like the UK, it is all the more important to uphold moral principles and affirm the values of humanity, justice, and decency in dealings with refugees and those who are seeking asylum. The following chapter will attempt to weigh up the extent to which these values and principles are being upheld by current asylum practice in the UK and in the US.

3

ASYLUM

This chapter raises moral and ethical questions about our societies and the ways in which we situate and construct the stranger: What practices are permissible? Against what standards are they to be judged? It looks at the tension between the requirement of a state to uphold the rights of its citizens and the moral claims of the non-citizen to asylum protection, acknowledging the extent to which public opinion is readily manipulated and xenophobia is easily fostered. The chapter then goes on to consider the hurdles that are encountered by the refugee before and during arrival in the UK. It considers decision-making by case-workers and tribunal judges, and highlights issues of credibility confronted particularly by abused women, by homosexuals, by Christian converts, and by unaccompanied children. The moral insensitivity associated with indefinite administrative detention is illustrated, and so too are the circumstances surrounding deportation. The erosion of the law of humanity is further exemplified by the situation of many refugees who are caught in a poverty trap, unable to access legal help, refused the right to work, and forced into destitution.

Citizens and asylum

How do we reconcile the moral claims of non-citizens in desperate need with a meaningful political democracy which privileges the claims of its citizens over others? This is a question for which there is no easy answer. The obligation to grant asylum continues to be guarded by Western states as a sovereign privilege: they control the laws and procedures that determine refugee status. Despite considerable developments in international law, there remains a tension between universal human rights and sovereignty claims. This raises philosophical and ethical problems with no easy solutions.

Seyla Benhabib (2004) examines the boundaries of political community. She explores the principles and practices for incorporating aliens and strangers, refugees and asylum-seekers, into existing polities. Taking as her point of departure the fact that boundaries define some as members, and others as aliens, she identifies types of boundaries within the civil community. On the one hand, there are those who could be considered second-class citizens of the state, but who might at the same time be seen as members of civil society through their cultural, family, or religious attachments. She instances women and non-propertied males before universal suffrage. On the other hand, there are people who do not fall into either category, who are considered to be neither second-class citizens nor members of civil society. A classic example of this is African-American slaves before 1865, when the declaration of the 14th Amendment to the US Constitution conferred US citizenship on Black peoples. And then there is a third group – residents "who do not enjoy full citizenship rights, either because they do not possess the requisite identity criteria through which the people defines itself, or because they belong to some other commonwealth, or because they choose to remain outsiders. These are the 'aliens' and 'foreigners' amidst the democratic people" (Benhabib 2004: 47). Their status is different from that of second-class citizens or slaves. They live amongst citizens, but their rights and claims are to be found in that "murky space" defined by respect for human rights on the one hand and international law on the other. In a world where ideas of national citizenship are unravelling, Benhabib sees that the boundaries of the political community as defined by the nation-state are no longer adequate to regulate membership. She advocates porous boundaries, recognizing both the rights of refugees and asylum-seekers to be admitted and also the rights of democracies to define the terms by which they might be admitted. Her strategy is to reject the claim of a sovereign people to bar the eventual citizenship of aliens and to incorporate citizenship claims into a universal human rights regime.

But these issues also raise insistent ethical and moral questions (Gibney 2004). Are states justified in privileging the claims of their own citizens over the protection needs of refugees and asylum-seekers? It is indeed the prerogative of the state to set some criteria of incorporation – but what practices are permissible from a moral standpoint? What practices are morally indifferent? And against what standard are they to be judged? Where it is held that there are objective standards of truth and morality which transcend political communities (Boucher 2009), political communities are not the arbiters of the moral universe in which they act. In the light of this, refugees and asylum-seekers will be treated with dignity. This may be instanced by Article 16a(1) of the German Constitution, which states simply: "persons persecuted on political grounds shall have the right of asylum". But where there is a common understanding that political order or stability is the primary principle with ordinary morality taking second place, there is room for political expediency. Ordinary morality may even be suspended in pursuit of political ends. And when that happens, the door is wide open to cruelty and inhumanity. The way in which a state treats refugees is a crucial test of moral conscience. In an attempt to ensure the protection of borders, governments around the world have become distanced from the humanitarian concerns which undergird the Refugee Convention, and they have become cynical about the human experiences of those who seek international protection. Where the will to adhere to the spirit of the Convention is lacking, those who have already suffered greatly are likely to be treated with callous disrespect, even cruelty.

It would appear (Gibney 2003: 32) that when the interests of asylum-seekers are seen to conflict with those of citizens, most citizens would consider the state justified in prioritizing their own interests over those of others. In order to win electoral support, the state needs to convince its members that this is what it is doing. And so, in most Western governments, Sweden and Germany to date being notable exceptions, there has been a rise in restrictionist measures driven primarily by electoral politics. Yet, when fuelled by populist concerns, the will of the people may be legitimate but unjust. Democratic rule and the claims of justice may conflict with one another (Benhabib 2004: 44).

Public opinion

Public perception of refugees, media reporting, and government attitudes are closely linked. Refugees are an easy prey (Türk 2012b: 5). In seeming to address concerns about asylum, governments fan the flames of public opinion – the process feeds itself (Hargreaves 2014). This is recognized in a Parliamentary report which recommends "that Ministers recognise their responsibility to use measured language so as not to give ammunition to those who seek to build up resentment against asylum seekers, nor to give the media the excuse to write inflammatory or misleading articles" (PJCHR 2007). Yet, the fact remains that press stereotypes of refugees which are "frequently biased, inaccurate, inflammatory and hostile" continue to shape the perceptions of many people in the UK (McIntyre 2011). In 2012, Morgan Odhiambo was interviewed by the *Guardian*. He had fled Kenya in 2003 and was granted asylum status in the UK. But he found people unfriendly and suspicious: "people get their views from the newspapers," he said. "People look at you like you're a scrounger. They think you're just 'one of them'. They think you're just here to take their money or their job" (*Guardian*, 8 December 2012). In the early 2000s, there was a sustained and brutal media onslaught against refugees. Public opinion was manipulated by a series of mendacious press reports which were often carried to the point of fantasy (Newman & Ratcliffe 2011: 132–133). This may briefly be illustrated by two particularly sensational stories which, in 2003, entered the popular imagination in the UK and were quoted in public debate. On 4 July, *The Sun* carried the banner headline, "Callous Asylum Seekers steal the Queen's birds for Barbecue". Despite representations to the Press Complaints Commission, the story was cribbed by the *Daily Mail* and repeated by both papers with variations in 2008. On 21 August 2003, the *Daily Star* also carried the headline "Asylum Seekers Eat our Donkeys", a story which received wide coverage on the radio and in other papers. In each case, the stories were deliberate fabrications. The newspapers concerned, all popular daily newspapers in the UK, were finally constrained to publish apologies, but these did not appear on their front pages: "by the time these and other stories had been taken apart, 'asylum' had appeared week-in week-out in every newspaper in the country as a proxy for foreign brutality and alien values impinging on British life" (Hargreaves

2014). In 2003, *The Sun* set a virulently anti-asylum agenda which the UK government did nothing to refute. Indeed, in one notorious instance, at the Conservative Party conference, 2–5 October 2011, the Home Secretary publicly reinforced a story that had circulated in a number of press articles, but which bore little resemblance to reality or law. She claimed that the Human Rights Act was responsible for blocking the deportation of an "illegal immigrant" because he had a pet cat (*Guardian*, 4 October 2011). Although the ensuing controversy forced her to retract her statement, the story received further circulation.

The *Guardian*, *The Independent*, *Red Pepper*, and *The South Manchester Reporter* all carry regular investigations and reports of injustice against asylum-seekers and refugees. But in other sections of the press, statistics are frequently manipulated and articles with a whiff of brimstone fuel public hostility. This is well instanced by an article in *The Sun* published on 31 May 2011 (JCWI 2011). "Third of rapists and killers 'are foreign'" screams the headline. And the article continues: "IMMIGRANTS make up a THIRD of murder suspects and alleged rapists in a string of areas, shock new figures reveal". Already, the use of the words "suspects", "alleged", and "a string of areas" nuance the headline. And the next sentence nuances it further: "and one in seven of all people accused of these crimes in the UK as a whole is a foreign national". The journalist then goes on to cite murder statistics – "four forces each had 33 per cent of non-UK murder suspects" – and helpfully provides an illustrative table. From this, it can be seen that Kent had two such murder suspects, and Lincolnshire, five. The other two police forces are not mentioned. Cambridgeshire, however, had four out of seven murder suspects of foreign origin, which translates to "an astonishing 57 per cent". And in what he says about rape, the journalist continues to bolster his sensational headline by deriving meaningless statistics from small samples.

In his inquiry into the culture, practices, and ethics of the press, Lord Justice Leveson (2012) has this to say: "although the majority of the press appear to discharge this responsibility with care, there are enough examples of careless or reckless reporting to conclude that discriminatory, sensational or unbalanced reporting in relation to ethnic minorities, immigrants and/or asylum seekers is a feature of journalistic practice in parts of the press rather than an aberration". And he observes: "the inquiry heard sufficient evidence to conclude that some sections of the press have deliberately invented stories with no factual basis to satisfy the demands of a readership".

Yet, if we assume that journalists will run stories that work for them, there are some indications that in certain circumstances a fragile public sympathy for refugees is retained (Hargreaves 2014). On 20 February 2013, *The Sun* carried the headline "Afghan refugee wins scholarship to Eton College" (Ross 2013), and the story went viral. Rohid Amani, who at the age of three fled Al-Qaeda from Afghanistan with his family and who was given asylum in the UK, had won a scholarship to David Cameron's old school. Fabrice Muamba, who had fled "from the bullet-flecked battlefields of Zaire to the pristine pitches of the Premier League" (Liew 2012), received sympathetic press coverage following his heart attack in March 2012. And the double Olympic gold medallist, Mo Farah, a Somali-born refugee, had a huge amount of positive coverage as a person who had brought honour to the UK. How much weight may we give to this?

Natascha Klocker and Kevin Dunn have analyzed "unrelentingly negative" media releases in Australia between 2001 and 2002 and the language used by the federal government in portraying asylum-seekers (Klocker & Dunn 2003). Following 9/11, the Australian government asserted that there was an "undeniable link" between "illegal immigrants" and terrorism. Asylum-seekers from Afghanistan were particularly suspect; they had "strange identities". Rumours were circulated that asylum-seekers "threw their children overboard" or sewed their children's lips together in detention centres – all were found to be baseless. But these were decisive in the media portrayal of asylum-seekers as inhumane barbaric "others". *The Advertiser*, *The Sunday Mail*, and government pronouncements dehumanized those who were seeking asylum, and constructions of illegitimacy, illegality, and threat worked together to justify detention. Teun van Dijk observes that "the official panic of the political elites about what they saw as a deluge of poor third world peoples arriving at their door-steps soon led to a corresponding media panic. Before long, this barrage of negative media coverage ... also affected large parts of the public, which ... was easily persuaded to resent the 'threatening presence'". He continues: "the government, which appeared to be responsible for producing these constructions, used the resultant negative public opinion towards asylum seekers as legitimation for the continuation of stringent anti-immigration policies" (Dijk 1991: 2).

Klocker & Dunn find, however, that while the media "largely adopted the negativity and specific references of the government", they "departed somewhat slightly from the government's unchanging stance following some key events" such as the *Tampa* affair (2003: Abstract; see p. 22). They conclude that there may be some scope for disrupting the vicious circle of negativity between government, media, and general public and that "the constructions surrounding asylum seekers may be shifted in a positive direction if the political will to do so exists" (2003: 89).

Statistics are regularly used by UK politicians to give the impression that immigration is "under control". The United Kingdom Border Agency (UKBA), whose functions were returned to the Home Office in March 2013, has been described as "target-driven". Government rhetoric about the limitation of numbers of those seeking asylum means that men, women, and children are treated as ciphers not people, degraded to the status of objects. Evidence suggests that preoccupations with time-scales and targets cloud judgements (Refugee Council 2007). After a prolonged investigation of the UK asylum system, the Independent Asylum Commissioners found it "incredible that 'targets around the number of returns ... do not affect the way in which an individual application is decided'" and found it "a noble but unrealistic aspiration that they 'should not'" (IAC 2008a). The Director of the UNHCR Division of International Protection affirmed starkly that "the success of today's asylum policies seems to hinge more on keeping numbers down and people out ... rather than ensuring access to safety, the management of the asylum systems in a spirit of solidarity, or crafting solution-oriented arrangements" (Türk 2012b). Refugees are widely viewed not so much as people needing protection, as threats to national well-being, like a force of nature that floods, swamps, or engulfs. They are dehumanized (Lynch & O'Brien 2001: 215).

The relatively high level of general immigration into the UK since the year 2000 and the tabloid and popular response to this have entangled asylum-seekers in this general resentment. In a time of economic uncertainty, high unemployment, and spiralling recession, they are perceived to be competitors for already scarce economic benefits (Gerwen 1995). There is a widely held belief that asylum-seekers have a sufficiently detailed knowledge of opportunities for employment, access to health care, and welfare benefits to choose their final destination on these grounds. However, in the light of clear evidence that most asylum-seekers are primarily concerned with escaping from persecution or war (Crawley 2010), the need is obvious for politicians, policy-makers, and the media to challenge the assumption that asylum-seekers come to the UK to improve their economic prospects. Research confirms that few have any choice (Crawley 2010). Even if they had, what amount of decline in welfare is permissible before it can be seen as grounds for refusing entry to the persecuted, the needy, and the oppressed (Benhabib 2004: 36)?

For Benhabib, the way we perceive aliens is intimately linked with the ways we define and renegotiate our own identity as people (2004: 178). Our collective identity as Europeans and as nations is evolving, and this can make us feel uncomfortable, bewildered, and insecure. We cherish conservative utopias: the nation, the people, the culture, the flag. In the light of this, many citizens are reluctant to see refugees and asylum-seekers as anything other than aliens, a threat to their socio-cultural identity. Where an indigenous population feels under threat, an encounter with another culture can feel risky; assimilation or apartheid are always easier to cope with than the slow process of getting to know the other (Kristeva 1989; Todorov 1982).

Volker Türk declares: "the real test of our commitment to protection and asylum comes in times of uncertainty. Opposing extremist views and addressing xenophobia requires political leadership. It will also continue to be critical to condemn strongly violence and discrimination against refugees, asylum-seekers and migrants, to stand firm and not to yield to anti-foreigner sentiments". And Türk reaches the sober conclusion that "the UNHCR alone cannot change such sentiments or attitudes" (2012a). We can only achieve an attitude to refugees that is ethically adequate if we are prepared to do something about the much broader problem of our attitude to foreigners in general.

Arrival

External sanctions

In the UK, as in the US and Australia, the increased number of refugees generated by conflicts is seen as a threat to what has been described as "the orderly form of managed migration flows" (Flynn 2005: 463; Snyder 2012: 106–108). Increasingly, severe barrier measures have been introduced to deter the unwanted settlement of people who are fleeing life-threatening situations.

Visa restrictions close down asylum options. While "non-visa nationals" – mostly from White Commonwealth countries or countries deemed friendly at the time – can arrive in the UK without a visa and have permission to stay for six months, more and more countries do require visas. For someone who is seeking asylum, often fleeing situations of conflict, this is normally out of the question. The situation is recognized in Article 31(1) of the 1951 Refugee Convention, which stipulates that receiving states should not "impose penalties" on those who arrive in "their territory without authorisation" (UNHCR 2010). Yet, the UK Asylum and Immigration Act of 2004 made it a crime punishable by two years in prison to fail to produce a valid travel document on arrival in the UK. Eighteen months later, over 200 asylum-seekers, including children, elderly people, and victims of torture, had gone to prison under the section (Webber 2012). Although a ruling in 2006 should have brought an end to such prosecutions, widespread ignorance of the asylum defence still caused many refugees to be wrongly convicted. In a key case in 2010, two Iranian dissidents and a Somali woman who arrived without a valid passport were detained on arrival, charged, prosecuted, convicted, and sentenced to between eight and fifteen months' imprisonment; but their convictions were overturned by the Court of Appeal. Immigration officers, police, duty solicitors, and judges in the magistrates' or crown court were severely castigated by Lord Justice Leveson for their apparent unawareness of the legal exemption (R 2010). A mapping exercise carried out in 2014 by the Centre for Criminology and Criminal Justice at The University of Manchester in conjunction with the Migrants Rights Network reviewed the position for undocumented migrants in the UK, argued that a "law and order" approach to irregular migration is not an effective policy response and called for a restructuring of the immigration system in order to uphold core principles of justice and fairness that conform to those used within the criminal justice system. A key finding was this: "irregular migration status is not just a law and order issue and cannot be solely tackled by criminalizing undocumented migrants" (Spencer *et al.* 2014).

Airlines and shipping companies face substantial fines if they transport people who have no legal right to enter the UK; their overseas personnel are instructed to verify the credentials of all passengers. As a result, refugees are forced to travel irregularly, and dangerously, often without passports or with false papers supplied by an agent. As Frances Webber observes:

> Thousands have died trying to reach Spain, Malta, Lampedusa or the Canary Islands in small boats from Africa, or as stowaways thrown overboard on discovery by ships' captains unwilling to pay the fines they would incur if they allowed them to land. Others have been killed by landmines as they tried to enter Greece, shot by border

> guards at the Spanish Moroccan enclave of Ceuta, frozen to death in the wheel arches of planes, electrocuted trying to get into the Channel Tunnel, fallen from or crushed by trains.
>
> (2012: 32)

Those who survive encounter the same stringent border controls at ports and airports as other irregular migrants. The possession of false documents, even if for "understandable and non-criminal reasons" (IAC 2008d: 22–23), undermines the credibility of an asylum-seeker's account, particularly if they then claim to come from a different country from that indicated on their travel document. They will almost certainly be sent back.

Internal sanctions

If refugees manage to surmount all the obstacles facing them and make a claim for asylum in the UK, their refugee status then has to be determined. If their application seems uncomplicated, in rare instances, they may be granted asylum. Otherwise, they will be assigned to the Detained Fast Track (DFT) process. An asylum claim "may be considered suitable for DFT … processes where it appears, after screening (and in the absence of suitability exclusion factors) to be one where a quick decision may be made" (Home Office 2012). In practice, the majority of those claims are refused. Referral to DFT is made following a screening interview in a public area, lacking in privacy and often noisy, where officers use a standard questionnaire to record information about the applicant. Discretion is allowed to individual officers in weighing this basic information. In the light of all this, John Vine, the Independent Chief Inspector of Borders and Immigration, concludes that "there is currently too great a risk of the survivors of torture or trafficking being placed in DFT due to the way screening is carried out" (2011b). Rule 35 of the Detention Centre Rules 2001 is designed to ensure that asylum-seekers who have been tortured are not held in detention. But the government is not implementing its own policy (McGinley & Trude 2012; IAC 2008c: 48–50). A growing body of evidence notes that, despite debates in both Houses of Parliament and several internal audits by the UKBA, victims of torture are still being "routinely detained" (Tsangarides 2012). A history of sexual violence makes it hard for women to disclose personal information to a stranger in a public area. Often showing signs of Post-Traumatic Stress Disorder (PTSD) and acute shame, they tend during interviews to become detached from their surroundings and from their emotional and physical experiences (Bögner *et al.* 2007). In these circumstances, women are particularly vulnerable to being assigned to DFT (Girma *et al.* 2014).

The policy is shaped to facilitate the refusal of claims and to do so as rapidly as possible. It has been strongly criticized by the UN. Roland Schilling, UNHCR representative to Britain, says this:

> Asylum-seekers who come to the UK have often experienced extremely distressing circumstances. To be led off to a detention centre – sometimes in handcuffs – as soon as they arrive is a far from humane way of being treated for persons who did nothing else than ask to be protected. There is a presumption by UKBA that most asylum claims can be decided quickly, but in UNHCR's view, the process of determining whether someone has a well-founded fear of persecution is not only very complex but an extremely important procedure.
>
> (*Guardian*, 23 February 2012)

In addition, Vine is of the view that there are insufficient safeguards in place to prevent people from being incorrectly allocated to DFT in the first place (2011b). In short, "misrecognition of refugees due to the inappropriate use of accelerated procedures involves the risk of returning the very people who have the right to protection from further persecution" (Wilson-Shaw *et al.* 2012). This view is affirmed by Mr Justice Ouseley in a significant High Court judgement where, having outlined at some length the deficiencies of the scheme, he concludes:

> I am satisfied that the shortcomings at various stages require the early instruction of lawyers to advise and prepare the claim, and to seek referrals for those who may need them, with sufficient time before the substantive interview. This is the crucial failing in the process as operated. I have concluded that it is sufficiently significant that the DFT as operated carries with it too high a risk of unfair determinations for those who may be vulnerable applicants.
>
> (Detention Action 2014)

While, as we have seen, there can be injustice where interviews and decisions are made too quickly, there is also undoubtedly injustice in overlong delays. Sometimes there are delays in getting an appointment in order to make a claim in Croydon. Currently, there are reports of long delays, of around six months, after the screening interview before the substantive interview. And frequently, there are long delays, in some cases, of well over a year between the substantive interview and a decision.

Decisions

Credibility

In January 2014, the *Guardian* reported that UK Home Office officials who hit a target of winning seventy per cent of their tribunal cases were given high street vouchers to "recognise positive performance over a short period of time" (*Guardian*, 14 January 2014). Predictably, this caused controversy. It was criticized by lawyers as a "clear incentive to bad practice". It undermined any sense that those who are seeking sanctuary would receive a fair hearing. It suggested that the Home Office was biased against individuals being granted refugee status.

At best, decision-making is not easy. The official who interviews the claimant at the stage of the screening interview or the subsequent asylum interview has usually no corroborative evidence at his or her disposal, although he or she may draw on evidence that relates to the current situation in the claimant's country of origin. Decisions are based on little more than a claimant's story and an assessment of credibility in the context of a "culture of disbelief" (IAC 2008b). Many have pointed out the subjectivity of this approach. It relies on assumptions about human behaviour, judgements, and attitudes, as well as assumptions about how a truthful account is presented (Herlihy *et al.* 2010). Jane Herlihy and Stuart Turner instance a US survey of state determinations where biases are much in evidence and where there are widespread inconsistencies according to which court hears the claim, the country of origin and gender of the claimant, and the gender of the judge (2013).

There are certain expectations about how people think, remember, and behave. Authorities in Britain and America conflate credibility with "truth" and allow concerns in one aspect of an applicant's story, even if not directly pertinent to the case, to undermine his or her claim for protection (Griffiths 2012; Chen 2006). To be deemed credible, asylum applicants "need to present a coherent, consistent and prompt account of their claim" (UKBA 2011). There is a common assumption that experiences of severe violence will be so important that they will be etched clearly in a person's long-term memory. If applicants change their account of such experiences, it is taken to be a fabrication. But this is challenged by the scientific evidence. The ability to recall with consistency details of traumatic experiences over repeated interviews has been shown to be impaired by PTSD, a severe anxiety state that can develop after exposure to any event that gives rise to intense negative feelings of fear, helplessness, or horror. Long-term symptoms are maintained by flashbacks or nightmares and cause significant impairment in social function.

An important study (Herlihy *et al.* 2002) of Kosovan and Bosnian refugees points to the danger of concluding that asylum-seekers are fabricating their histories solely on the basis of discrepancies between interviews. Discrepancies are common in people with high levels of PTSD, and these increase with the length of time between interviews. The authors conclude that "such inconsistencies should not be relied on as indicating a lack of credibility". Assessment of PTSD requires specialist experience, yet the judgement as to whether or not to apply for a medico-legal report is usually made by people who are not professionally qualified in this area, and in reality independent reports are rarely requested. A recent survey of lawyers, for instance, noted that they attempt "quasi-diagnoses of common mental health problems. They nonetheless demonstrate stereotypical understanding of post-traumatic stress disorder and other possible diagnoses and the role of subjectivity" (Herlihy *et al.* 2002). Yet a failure to identify mental health difficulties impacts the asylum interview.

Narrative variations are generally associated with lying. But the deduction that a person is not telling the truth can be insensitive to the many reasons why people forget or do not provide details: "British decision-makers tend to assume that truthful asylum seekers have a good recall of events, provide 'plausible' accounts, present their stories in a consistent and unhesitating manner" (Griffiths 2012). But initial recall of traumatic events does not usually involve normal narrative memory. Survivors struggle to find words that speak of the unspeakable. This is exemplified particularly well by a study (Lijnders 2012) which explores the ways in which Eritrean asylum-seekers en route to Israel seek to articulate their experiences of suffering. Held hostage by human traffickers for indefinite periods of time during their journey, they suffered or witnessed torture, kidnapping, extortion, rape, or organ removal. When encouraged on a voluntary basis to talk about their experiences, words failed them. They had to find an alternative idiom by which to express the inexpressible. Scars as an embodied expression of violence were used symbolically, and women conceived of pain as through another body. In the context of an asylum interview, is there time for a severely traumatized person to build up the necessary trust to begin to talk about such experiences with a stranger? Would that stranger necessarily have the cognitive imagination to grasp the truth of what he or she is being told? Yet, "failure to understand these issues could mean a decision to return someone to further persecution and even death" (Wilson-Shaw *et al.* 2012).

The following case illustrates the difficulties very well (R 2012b). AM, an Angolan national, was detained pending removal following an unsuccessful appeal from the refusal of her asylum claim. The Asylum and Immigration Tribunal had found her to have "no credibility whatsoever" and rejected her evidence that she had been raped and tortured. She later launched a fresh asylum claim on the basis of new evidence, in the form of an expert report by a wound and scar specialist, which linked the various scars on her body to torture. The claim was refused again, but AM won on appeal. The Tribunal this time found that she had been raped and tortured as she had claimed, causing the scars on her body.

In a subsequent claim for false imprisonment, AM argued that when the expert report was received, she should have been released from detention in accordance with official guidance. The Home Office denied that the report constituted "independent evidence" of torture, arguing that the report relied on AM's own vague account of how the scars came about. In a letter to AM's representatives, the Home Office expressed its scepticism of her inability to recollect exact dates and causes of her scars, when "the precise circumstances of these events would have been so searing as to have engraved themselves including the date and period of detention upon your client's memory".

Lord Justice Rix, who gave the unanimous judgement of the Court of Appeal, strongly disagreed with this. He ruled that the independent expert was expressing her own independent views. It was evident from her assessment that she believed that AM had suffered torture and rape which had left her "grossly traumatized" with intense feelings of shame. Yet this "expert opinion" and "honest belief" had previously been refused the status of independent evidence. What then of the policy whereby independent evidence of torture makes the victim unsuitable for detention?

Not all are so fortunate. A Sri Lankan man told the Upper Tribunal how he had been arrested by the authorities in 2009 and surrendered to the army. Detained in an army camp until 2011, he was ill-treated and tortured by heated bars being applied to his back and right arm. Despite the evidence of seven specialist doctors in the field and a GP, his appeal to remain in the UK was dismissed on asylum/human rights grounds. The claim to torture, it was alleged, "did not stand scrutiny". The only alternative explanation of the deep "tiger scars" had to be "self-inflicted injuries by proxy". The scarring had to have been inflicted by a third party with the man's consent (KV 2014).

An institutional emphasis on truthfulness exists alongside an endemic image of asylum-seekers as liars and opportunistic cheats. So all-embracing is that perception that expert witnesses have found that "frequently little weight was given to (their) testimony based on a personal knowledge of the appellant gained over months and sometimes years" (Smith 2008). A research study goes so far as to suggest (Griffiths 2012) "that the 'truth value' of UKBA representatives is considered far greater than those subject to the asylum and detention systems, allowing the former to insist on particular versions of the 'truth', and threaten individuals who resist it with immigration detention or even persecution".

In judging whether or not a person is in law a refugee, authorities must also judge whether a certain risk can be conceived of as persecution. And here again, credibility is an issue. In the US, the law states that an immigration judge's perception of an applicant's ignorance is not a proper basis for an adverse credibility finding (Cosa 2007). For a claim for asylum in the US to be upheld, under the US Code, an applicant must have been persecuted in the past and show a well-founded fear of future persecution if returned to his or her country of origin (US Code: Title 8). But this claim has to be evaluated. The immigration judge must assess whether the applicant's claim is credible. If the judge believes that the applicant is not credible, they must then explain their reasons for that finding – they must "provide a legitimate articulable basis for challenging an applicant's credibility, and must offer a specific, cogent reason for any stated disbelief" (Zi Lin Chen 2004). An adverse credibility finding will typically lead to a denial of the claim for asylum. There is a grey area between refugee law and human rights law, and the link between them in practice is not always obvious. What is the link between persecution and human rights? What does it mean to be persecuted? Who bears the ultimate responsibility to protect? (Noll 2006). Norms of human rights have multiplied over the last few decades, and more and more states have accepted human rights obligations. These have become ever more precise. Might we not expect that increasingly detailed human rights legislation would lead to asylum obligations becoming more closely defined and more widely binding upon states? Yet, in practice, it isn't quite so simple. Some human rights violations do not necessarily meet the refugee definition of persecution. The onus is then on the claimants to give an account of their experiences and to explain why they have a "well-founded" fear of what might happen to them on return to their country of origin. Here again, decision-making is based largely on a subjective view of the claimant's credibility. This is more evident in some categories than in others: issues have arisen around gender and persecution, sexual orientation and persecution, and in cases concerning converts to Christianity.

Women

Though law, policy, and practice are fast evolving in this field, advances in international refugee law and policy regarding gender-related claims are still "nascent, contingent and fragile" (Edwards 2010), and decisions as to what constitutes persecution in these areas often hinges on subjective choices made by judges and decision-makers.

In illustration, I refer to a case that attracted much publicity at the time. In 2002, the UK Home Office accepted that Rose Najjemba had been raped by soldiers in Uganda because of her alleged complicity with rebel groups, but it was not prepared to accept that this constituted persecution. Court of Appeal judges concurred, concluding that the rape was "not a matter of persecution. This was simple and dreadful lust". In the ensuing public outcry, the Immigration Minister intervened, and Rose Najjemba was subsequently given leave to remain in the UK. Evidence suggests that judges may now be more ready to see how rape or sexual violence may amount to persecution. In 2005, Lady Hale ruled that "sexual violence and rape may be an actual weapon or a strategy of war itself, rather than just an expression or consequence. In the context of armed conflict or civil war, the rape of women is also about gaining control over other men and the group (national, ethnic, political) of which they are a part" (R 2005).

But in spite of these legal developments, women who are fleeing persecution often struggle to convince authorities that their claims for protection are credible: "prejudices around gender and race make for a toxic alchemy, especially when mixed with a culture of disbelief which so often permeates border control agencies" (Dorling *et al.* 2012). Despite the UK government's commitment to ensure gender sensitivity (Home Office 2011), the Independent Asylum Commission (IAC) concluded that guidelines on gender are inconsistently observed and implemented (IAC 2008c: 42–45). All too often, officials show scepticism in their failure to accept histories of rape and sexual abuse from women who are fleeing from conflict zones. They often ignore cultural inhibitions and fear, and are prone to misunderstand a woman's shame at having to recount such personal degradation to a stranger, particularly so if this is a man in uniform (Muggeridge & Maman 2011). In the belief that "every woman seeking asylum in the UK should be treated fairly and with dignity and respect" – but in the awareness that they are not – Asylum Aid launched in 2008 The Charter of the

Rights of Women Seeking Asylum. Now this is endorsed by more than 330 organizations, from the smallest refugee groups to large charities like Amnesty International, Oxfam, and the Red Cross. It outlines simple measures that are needed to make the asylum system decent and safe for any woman who turns to it for help. It has had significant impact. Women seeking asylum will now be interviewed by another woman, and their children will be looked after; their case will be handled by someone with specific training: "campaigning through the Charter gathers strength from a multiplier effect, as each action draws on and amplifies the role of all the charities lined up behind it. This, and the unceasing persistence of all the Charter's endorsers, means that gender is now clearly on the agenda for lasting, meaningful reform of the asylum system" (Charter 2008).

Sexual orientation

Cases on sexual orientation offer further illustration of the discretionary vacuum between human rights law and asylum procedure. Compared with a seventy-three per cent initial rejection rate for refugees in general in the UK, there was in 2010 a ninety-eight to ninety-nine per cent initial refusal rate for gay and lesbian applications (UKLGIG 2010). A Stonewall report (Miles 2010) found that gay and lesbian applications were often refused because policy and case law are incorrectly applied. Homosexual applicants have been sent back to their country of origin on the premise that if they are "discreet" about their sexual orientation, they will not evoke persecution (Millbank 2012). Yet, this logic of discretion is particularly invidious. It affirms the perspective, if not the conduct, of the persecutor and reverses the onus of protection under the Convention. The obligation has been displaced from the state to the individual; the individual is being compelled to protect him or herself. But this is clearly absurd. As Gregor Noll indicates, under the logic of human rights law, it makes no sense to "oblige" an individual to protect him or herself. The choice is not a legal one (2006: 496).

In 2010, seven years after a landmark judgement in the High Court of Australia (Appellant S395/2002), the Supreme Court of the United Kingdom issued a unanimous adjudication by five judges. This condemned in forceful terms all legal reasoning based on assumptions about the ease with which a person who was lesbian or gay could conceal their identity, and in so doing advanced significantly the development of refugee jurisprudence (HJ & HT 2011). The decision was endorsed with public approval by the UK government (*Guardian* 2010; UKBA 2011). However, a new research report in September 2013 says this: "whilst the quality of decisions greatly improved following HJ and HT, case-worker training and the issuing of Policy Instructions, the analysis of recent material shows that old problems are creeping back in" (UKLGIG 2013). Dispensing with the "voluntary discretion" policy has led to more and more claimants having to prove their sexuality in response to inappropriate questions without a clue as to what evidence a case-worker may require. An analysis of refusal letters reveals that case-workers still cite minor discrepancies to doubt a claimant's credibility; fail to act in accordance with Home Office guidelines on sexual identity; and use out-of-date country information.

Christian converts

In cases involving Christian converts from Islam, such "discretion reasoning" has until recently led courts in the UK to refuse the appeals of applicants. Although these are regarded as apostates by authorities in Iran and Afghanistan, they have regularly been told by the courts that if they exercise "discretion" they will not suffer harassment or persecution. The judgement in *FS Iran* (2004) was confirmed in *SZ & JM* (2008), which ruled, despite a well-documented deterioration in the situation, with increasingly repressive measures by the state, that "conditions for Christians in Iran have not deteriorated sufficiently to necessitate a change in the guidance". On 13 November 2009, however, the UK Immigration Appeal Tribunal ruled in the case of a Christian convert from Islam that "in the light of the evidence of the appellant's commitment to the Christian faith, in our view he cannot be expected to modify his behaviour on return to Afghanistan and it is not reasonable to expect him to tolerate living his life in a manner which would involve a significant suppression of his religious belief" (NM 2009). The return of a Christian convert to Afghanistan, it was decided, would involve a risk of inhuman or degrading treatment which would violate his rights under Article 3 of the Convention. And this decision was reinforced by a decision of the UNHCR published on 19 January 2010 (ZNS 2012) in respect of a refugee from Iran who was in detention in Turkey. The court ruled that to deport back to Iran a refugee who had converted to Christianity would be in violation of his or her rights under Article 3.

The claim of a person who converts to Christianity once he or she has arrived in the UK is seldom believed. Such applicants are invariably assumed to be manipulative, despite the fact that many are people who are believed by churches in the UK to be genuine in their faith. A lack of credence is given by adjudicators to the informed opinion of Christian clergy. The genuineness of the applicant's Christian faith is tested by inappropriate questions, and unsupported distinctions are made between active proselytizing and "mere" faith practice; between church leaders and "ordinary" Christians; or between an "evangelical" Christian who cannot be expected to conceal his or her beliefs and a member of a mainline church, who can. Following meetings between the Churches Main Committee and relevant government authorities, clear guidelines for decision-makers were published by the UKBA (Home Office 2010), but adjudicators in the asylum process continue to exercise a wide discretionary margin.

These findings are exemplified in a carefully argued High Court judgement (R 2012a). SA had made an unsuccessful claim for asylum in December 2007 on the grounds that as an apostate she would be at risk of persecution on return to Iran. Her appeal was rejected on 20 May 2010. It was a decision where the judge "formed a strongly adverse view of her credibility". He found that there were "lies and discrepancies" in her evidence. He disbelieved her account of her husband's conduct; he rejected her account of how she had come to the UK; he disbelieved her claim to have converted to Christianity; and he did not accept that she would be in danger on her return to Iran. In short, he rejected her asylum claim.

On 28 September 2011, a fresh claim was launched. Her son was showing signs of acute anxiety at the prospect of returning to Iran. Despite corroborating medical evidence from two behaviour therapists and a consultant psychiatrist that this amounted to PTSD, this claim too was rejected. So too was a subsequent appeal.

On 15 October 2012, the claimant challenged the previous decision of the Home Secretary that her claim for asylum had been unfounded. And the High Court judge who heard the claim allowed her case to proceed. His Honour Judge Gilbart QC made three compelling observations. First, "the Home Secretary simply had no evidential basis upon which she could safely and conclusively exclude the effect of earlier events on the son's exhibited symptoms and presentation. Expert psychiatric and psychological evidence cannot simply be set aside in the manner adopted by the Home Secretary". Second, the judge "had a concern" about the Home Secretary's assessment of the risk to apostates in Iran, given her own current Operation Guidance Note on Iran, published in November 2011. "It puts a notably different complexion on the level of risk endured by an apostate convert in Iran to that taken by the Immigration Judge, who relied on now rather elderly country guidance". And third, he continued:

> It is a dangerous thing for anyone, and perhaps especially a judge, to peer into what some call a man or woman's soul to assess whether a professed faith is genuinely held, and especially not when it was and is agreed that she was and is a frequent participant in church services. It is a type of judicial exercise very popular some centuries ago in some fora (*the reference is to the Inquisition*), but rather rarely exercised today. I am also uneasy when a judge is bold enough to seek to reach firm conclusions about a professed conversion, made by a woman raised in another culture, from the version of Islam practised therein, to an evangelical church in Bolton within one strand of Christianity. I am at a loss to understand how that is to be tested by anything other than considering whether she is an active participant in the new church. But that is not the only point. There must be a real risk that if she has professed herself to be a Christian, and conducted herself as one, that profession, whether true or not, may be taken in Iran as evidence of apostasy. On the basis of the Home Secretary's now stated position, that amounts to a potentially different circumstance from that addressed by the Immigration Judge.

While it is regrettably possible for an immigration judge to ignore the law and deny the claim for asylum on unjust premises, it is also possible that a refusal on credibility grounds may be overturned. Li, a Christian convert, originally came from China and claimed asylum in the US on the basis of persecution on the grounds of his Christian observance. On 26 January 2005, an immigration judge found that Li had "failed to demonstrate credible evidence that he is a Christian" and dismissed his claim on the grounds of adverse credibility. The basis of the judge's decision was that Li claimed that Thanksgiving was a Christian holiday and that he knew little about the difference between the Old and New Testaments. Five years later, the Board of Immigration Appeals upheld this decision. But in 2011, it was overturned by the Ninth Circuit Court (Li 2011). The Court found that, with regard to Thanksgiving, Li was in good company, from the Pilgrim Fathers to President Washington to President Lincoln. Then, in their consideration of his knowledge of the Bible, the judges had totally disregarded his eloquent testimony of conversion to Christianity and the power of his Christian faith. And, finally, the Ninth Circuit found a procedural flaw: "Reviewing the January 26, 2005 merits hearing, it seems that Li was not provided a translator fluent in English. Confusion throughout the hearing record, that at first glance, may be ascribed to Li, may in fact be confusion in translation". And so seven years later, a blatant disregard of the law and due process was finally corrected.

Cultural factors

Cultural matters are often a vital component of the claim of persecution. Yet, a Western perspective which fails to appreciate the meaning of unfamiliar cultural practices can affect consideration of the truthfulness of stories of persecution and influence assumptions as to the safety of an asylum-seeker on return to his or her country of origin. These practices are often imperfectly understood by decision-makers, who will tend to uphold their own particular understanding (Noll 2006) – sometimes in the teeth of strong evidence to support an applicant's claims. A classic example of this is the case in the UK of Anselme Noumbiwa, an asylum-seeker from Cameroon who claimed that his tribe tried to force him by torture to become chief on the death of his father and to engage in animist practices rejected by his Catholic faith. Despite evidence to support his claim for asylum, including testimony given by a Mill Hill missionary in Cameroon and a medico-legal report which stated that the scars on Noumbiwa's body were "highly consistent with his account of maltreatment during his time at his father's village", it was decided that it was safe to send him back to Cameroon, and he was deported. In this case, it appears as if the Home Office's inability to recognize the importance and inexorability of chiefdom issues in a tribal culture overruled other considerations (Tulloch 2009).

Unaccompanied children

One of the biggest hurdles faced by young people seeking asylum in the UK is that they are usually unable to produce documentary evidence of their date of birth. An "undocumented" child cannot prove that he or she is under eighteen; he or she, assumed to be adult, may be detained for deportation. Having fled from their homes in traumatic circumstances, unaccompanied refugee children face a particularly complex process of assessment with the potential for further disorientation and distress. And these unaccompanied refugee children are granted refugee status at a substantially lower rate than adults. In 2011, twenty-five per cent of asylum applications were granted, but only eighteen per cent of unaccompanied children were accorded refugee status (Pinter 2012). In the case of a further 354 new arrivals, officials challenged the assertion that the asylum-seeker was under eighteen (Dennis 2012). Asylum Aid sees this situation as concerning: "the UKBA routinely and inappropriately refuse asylum applications by children on 'credibility' grounds. Many of these refusals are then overturned on appeal. Although the Asylum Policy Instruction on 'Assessing an asylum application from a child' is strong, children are left vulnerable because of how often officials depart from their own policy in practice" (2012). Instances are given where UKBA officials routinely dispute a child's credibility by applying "standards and norms which take little account of the child's age, maturity, and cultural background". Although the UKBA is "obliged under the policy instruction to apply the benefit of doubt more generously when dealing with a child … officials regularly burden children with far too high a standard of proof, including children as young as twelve to thirteen years old".

The Independent Inspector noted, however, that during the inspection period – February to June 2013 – there had been no forcible removals and that officials had exercised sensitivity in their dealings with these children. Yet, there was room for improvement. He cautioned the Home Office to "ensure that in this sensitive area where children's futures are involved, performance targets do not adversely affect the quality of decisions on their applications" (Vine 2013).

Comparison may be made with the announcement made in Washington, DC on 15 June 2012 by the Secretary of Homeland Security, Janet Napolitano. With immediate effect, young people who were brought to the US as young children, who did not present a risk to national security or public safety and who could demonstrate that they met certain key criteria, would be eligible to receive leave to remain for a period of two years, subject to renewal, and would be eligible to apply for work authorization: "our nation's immigration laws must be enforced in a firm and sensible manner", said Secretary Napolitano. "But they are not designed to be blindly enforced without consideration given to the individual circumstances of each case. Nor are they designed to remove productive young people to countries where they may not have lived or even speak the language. Discretion, which is used in so many other areas, is especially justified here" (Napolitano 2012). This "Deferred Action for Childhood Arrivals" (DACA) process has been widely welcomed by church leaders even as they deplored Arizona Governor Jan Brewer's executive order denying state and local welfare benefits to young undocumented immigrants who are eligible for deferred action.

The impact of bureaucracy

The bureaucratic insistence on administrative detail can be problematic. The UKBA works with a general assumption that people know the dates of significant events in their lives, including their own date and place of birth, or that spellings of names remain consistent despite being transcribed from different alphabets. In response, Melanie Griffiths suggests, "people may guess or invent identifiers rather than admit ignorance or risk producing discrepancies. In so doing, they adapt their narratives and identities to fit the system … most bureaucracies encourage at least a massaging of the truth" (2012).

Asylum-seekers are held to much higher standards than those who are making decisions about their claims. There is ample evidence of a bureaucratic system unable to handle complexity fraught with error, inconsistency, and poor decision-making. In a devastating inspection report, Vine critiqued ways in which he found the UKBA to be economical with the truth (2012). No attempts had been made to trace "archived" applicants, despite assurances given to the Home Affairs Select Committee that 124,000 cases were only archived after "exhaustive checks" to trace the applicant had been made. One hundred and fifty boxes, containing correspondence from applicants, their lawyers, and MPs, lay unopened in a Liverpool office. For those who are seeking sanctuary, the consequent blunders may be of life or death significance: "there is an irony in a system, that is itself imbued with error and confusion, placing such great primacy on the truthfulness of asylum seekers that narrative inconsistencies can undermine the chances of a person receiving refugee protection" (Griffiths 2012).

No man's land

Administrative detention

The widespread use of the term "illegal immigration" is identified in the popular mind with crime: "if it is illegal, it must be criminal, and 'illegal immigrants' must be criminals" (Bouman & Deffenbaugh 2009: 58). The perception that asylum-seekers are associated with illegality, even criminality, is enhanced by the widespread use of detention. In the US system, under the 1996 anti-terrorism laws, persons seeking asylum without proper documentation are held in immigration detention facilities while their claims are adjudicated (Bouman & Deffenbaugh 2009: 65).

Fr. Peter Balleis, International Director of the Jesuit Refugee Service in Rome, visited a federal detention centre in southern Arizona in 2009. He described what he saw:

> Three hundred men dressed in yellow, orange and blue prison jumpsuits had gathered under the shade of the open air sports facility. A six meter high double fence with several rolls of razor wire encircled the

> confines of the detention center that is located in southern Arizona, not far from the Mexican border. The center holds up to 1,500 non-citizen detainees, many of whom are awaiting deportation to their home countries.
>
> When asked where they were from, many answered "California", "Arizona" or another US state. When I asked how long ago they had lived in the US, many said five, ten or fifteen years. Most had families with children who were going to school in the US. Most had been picked up by the police or the border patrol and, without documents or with expired visas, were being processed for deportation. While current law claims that those without documents are illegal and subject to deportation, the law does not weigh the human cost for families pulled apart or for children separated from their parents. Hard-working men, who for years had contributed their labor to the nation's economy and had raised children (many of whom will be the next generation of US citizens), had been torn from their loved ones.
>
> (JRS/USA 2012)

Many of those detained will be resettled refugees who had not adjusted their legal status in time. This is often simply because they do not understand that after one year in the US they are required to adjust their immigration status by applying to become lawful permanent residents. There is no expiry date on the I-94 card that resettled refugees receive upon entry to the US, so refugees often assume that they already have permanent permission to live in the US. Even those refugees who do know that they should apply for lawful permanent resident status, a "green card", may not realize that they must apply exactly after one year of being in the US. Minimal English language skills increase the likelihood that refugees will fail to understand the need to apply for adjustment. Moreover, the government does not remind refugees of the need to adjust and in fact will even issue travel documents to refugees who have not adjusted, thus allowing them to travel outside the US. Prior to their arrest and subsequent detention, none of the refugees interviewed by Human Rights Watch in 2010 had been aware of the potential consequences of not applying for a green card. Most were upset that the same government that selected them for resettlement in the US and gave them a future and hope would then place them in federal detention.

Unadjusted refugees receive no warning before being placed in indefinite detention (Myers & Colwell 2012: 107–121). Emily Butera, Program Officer at the Women's Refugee Commission, said that the focus of Immigration and Customs Enforcement (ICE) is misplaced: "ICE needs to take into account the pressing humanitarian needs of individuals not held on criminal charges … In addition to poor conditions in detention facilities, our immigration and enforcement policies are needlessly endangering the well-being of vulnerable people and tearing apart families" (Women's Refugee Commission 2009). For those with young children, the experience can be devastating. This is particularly so in the case of women. Mothers may be taken to detention facilities hundreds of miles away without being given the opportunity to make the most basic arrangements for the care of their children. While in detention, they are denied access to telephones and are unable to communicate with lawyers or family courts. "ICE took me from my home while my children watched in fear", said Marlene Jaggernauth, a single parent who was separated from her four children, all of them US citizens. "Had I not experienced a year in immigration detention, I would never have believed that such inhumanity existed" (Women's Refugee Commission 2009).

In an attempt to deal with this, Congress directed that ICE should stop separating families and either place them in alternative programmes or detain them together in non-penal, home-like settings. But instead, ICE chose to develop a penal detention model. The T. Don Hutto Residential Center, a former medium-security prison, was pressed into service for family detention following the expansion of Expedited Removal and the implementation of the Secure Border Initiative along the US–Mexican Border. Faced with compliance measures to bring Hutto up to standard, ICE ceased to use it for families in 2009. But for ICE, alternative models of provision had still to demonstrate a concern for security and enclosure.

Every year, several hundred thousand people in the US are arrested for possible deportation by ICE and are held in administrative detention. Despite this large number, the immigration system lacks meaningful safeguards for people throughout the process of arrest, detention, deportation hearing, and removal. The current immigration system violates US and international human rights standards of protection against arbitrary and indefinite detention, and puts vulnerable people at risk of wrongful deportation.

The UK has maintained many forms of administrative detention over the years, and the use of detention is widespread for those whose claims to asylum have been refused. These are either people whose rights in law have been exhausted and who are waiting to be deported, or those who are waiting for the outcome of an appeal. After refusal at first instance, a high number of cases do indeed go to appeal and a number of these are successful; twenty-five per cent of appeals were won in the year ending June 2013 (Home Office 2013). Asylum-seekers are held in immigration removal centres and prison cells (Vine 2012). Those who are held in prison cells are usually foreign ex-offenders, a category that may include asylum-seekers, refused asylum-seekers being particularly prone to criminalization through illegal work or petty theft when forced into destitution by government policies. Those who are held in immigration removal centres are a mix of ex-offenders and non-offenders – both categories include asylum-seekers.

In the eyes of the public, asylum-seekers are tainted with criminality; they may even be associated with terrorists. Under the provisions of the 2001 Anti-Terrorism, Crime and Security Act, immigrants who are suspected of being terrorists could be interned. This was followed by a further act in 2006 which specified that asylum was to be denied to terrorists. As Susanna Snyder points out (2012: 112), an association of asylum with national security permits the state "to introduce otherwise unacceptably illiberal and pernicious policies". While the Refugee Convention already granted powers to deny refugee protection on grounds of national security, the UK's broad interpretation of what offences should exempt a person from refugee protection is highly problematic. When Parliament voted in 2008 to detain terrorist suspects without charge for up to forty-two days, the debate was charged. The fact that a significant minority of asylum-seekers were then – and still are – detained solely for administrative reasons for one or two years, or longer, passed virtually without comment.

It might not be an exaggeration to say that asylum-seekers are regarded as humans who are not humans (Butler 2006), exceptional people whose lives are devoid of value (Agamben 1998: 136–143). Although they are considered to be part of the human community through national and international laws, practices in various states reduce them to "a bare, rightless existence" (Fitzpatrick 2005: 65). Where a Western government detains asylum-seekers for an indefinite period for administrative purposes alone, it is abusing emergency measures. This is an illegitimate exercise of power, which can be seen as part of a wider tactic to neutralize the rule of law in the name of national security (Butler 2006: 67). Powers intended to be exercised on an exceptional basis in times of political crisis have been established as the norm since 9/11 in the open-ended and indefinite "war on terror". In deciding what will or will not constitute a "state of exception", government sovereignty constitutes a "paralegal universe that goes by the name of law" where political rules have the force of laws (Butler 2006: 61).

Refugees who are detained indefinitely live a "suspended life". Some may have played an active role in the community for many years, but in detention they are deprived of basic, let alone universal, human rights; they are neither living in the community, bound by law, nor dead; this is what Agamben refers to as "bare life" (Agamben 1998: 83–86). A documentary film entitled *How Long is Indefinite?* (Wood 2011) explores the detention of three people trapped in limbo with no apparent end to the situation. The director decided to make this film "to emphasise the stories of detainees as human beings and not just news sound bites or statistics". Fouad, an Iranian political activist, was detained for one year and eighteen months. He came as a refugee to the UK in 2000; the Iranian embassy wouldn't accept him back, and the UKBA refused to release him. His friends and fiancée describe the impact of his incarceration on their lives. Saleh, an asylum-seeker from Darfur, was torn from his children after twenty years in the UK and detained for around two years, unable to prove his nationality. Aissata speaks of her twenty-eight-day hunger strike in response to six threats of deportation, which the Home Office did not carry out. How, the film asks, can such treatment be accepted in a society that prides itself on upholding civil liberties and human rights?

In continuing to detain people like Fouad, Saleh, and Aissata, the UK Home Office is faced with the eventuality that it may not be immediately able to remove a failed asylum applicant. Power to detain under Schedule 3 of Immigration Act 1971 "pending deportation" is apparently unfettered. Britain and Denmark are the only EU members who have chosen to opt out of the EU returns directive, which implements a time limit of eighteen months for detaining individuals. But the courts have developed jurisprudence to limit the exercise of power. According to Article 5 of the Convention, detention must not be "arbitrary"; arbitrariness is usually avoided by compliance with what are known as the "Hardial Singh" principles, taken from the judgement of Woolf J (R 1984). These are common law requirements that detention must only be for the purpose of deportation and that it must only be "for a reasonable period under the circumstances". Detention should be regularly reviewed (R 2011). One unintended consequence of this is that people who are detained but cannot yet be deported may be released back into the community for a period of weeks, months, or years before being detained once more. As this cat-and-mouse activity can happen several times, there is invariably a negative impact on these persons' psychological and social well-being and on their capacity to integrate if they are ultimately given leave to remain.

While the construction of what might be meant by "reasonable period under the circumstances" may be debated, it is clear that the practice of holding asylum-seekers in custody – while they are awaiting a decision on their claims or enforced removal from the UK after refusal – impacts adversely on the mental health of adults and children. A landmark High Court judgement (R 2014a) ruled that the depressive illness suffered by a claimant, amounting to PTSD, was precipitated by her experience in detention. The psychological distress caused can be acute. Refugees from the conflict in Syria, for instance, may already have spent long periods of time in state detention facilities, during which they were tortured, raped, or sexually humiliated (Nasar 2013). Immigration detention may activate fears of further torture. Detained asylum-seekers in general have higher levels of depression, anxiety, and PTSD than asylum-seekers in the community (Cleveland *et al.* 2012). Psychiatrists in Australia have identified a new syndrome unique to asylum-seekers who had their applications rejected and have had to continually press claims for protection. They "demonstrate clinical features that we haven't seen before and certainly seem to characterise a unique, or distinct, syndrome from other people who have been through similar types of traumas. We've coined the term [Asylum Seeker Syndrome] to best describe this subgroup of asylum seekers who've had this protracted and difficult refugee determination process" (Behavior and Law 2012).

Children in detention

Children in detention are particularly vulnerable:

> The thundering knock came early in the morning. It was 6.30 am. Without waiting for an answer, the security chain was smashed from

> its fittings. Feet thundered up the staircase. The five children, all under the age of ten, were alarmed to be woken from their sleep by the dozen burly strangers who burst into their bedrooms, switched on the lights and shouted at them to get up. This is not a police state. It is Manchester in supposedly civilised Britain in the 21st century ... And Britain's deportation police have launched another of their terrifying dawn raids on sleeping children.
>
> (Vallely 2010)

This is how a well-known journalist begins to document a forcible arrest. The facts are well known. The children's parents, Hany and Samah Mansour, are Coptic Christians who fled to the UK in 2005, leaving all their belongings behind. In Egypt, Hany had been detained in solitary confinement for seventeen days and tortured by the secret police. His claim was corroborated by the medical evidence of a doctor in the UK who examined him on arrival in Dover. But the British government decided not to believe him. Four years passed, during which the family became well integrated into the community of Moss Side. They were liked and respected. The younger children were born in the UK. Then, on a morning like any other, they were snatched from their beds, bundled into vans, and taken away. They were held in Tinsley House near Gatwick for twenty-four days with a view to being deported to Egypt. Ten minutes before their plane was due to take off, they were driven back to the detention centre. Lawyers had obtained a judicial review. A week after this, a judge directed that the family should be freed and allowed to return home. Five months later, the parents and children were seized once more. At 6.15 am, UKBA officials entered the Mansour home. With belongings packed into a few laundry bags, the family was taken to Yarl's Wood Detention Centre, where they were held for a week. Hours away from deportation, they obtained a judicial review and were once again sent home. Finally, many months later, with huge support from the local community, they were granted leave to remain in the UK. Commenting on the case, the Regional Director of the UKBA said: "our asylum and immigration system is humane and compassionate. We would much rather those families found not to need international protection leave the UK voluntarily. Where an enforced removal is necessary these are undertaken with extreme care, treating those to be removed with courtesy and dignity" (*South Manchester Reporter*, 10 December 2009). The children's teachers were very clear about the impact of all this. The traumatic effect on the children was "massive". And Paul Vallely observes that "when a family is ripped so brutally from their home it is not just those who are carted away by the police to whom an injustice is done. Something is rent in the very fabric of the community" (2010). The commissioners of the IAC heard testimony about the effects that the removal of a child had on the community and the child's peers: "when a child is removed and does not turn up at school one day it is like a ripple in a pond – it affects all the people around them. Some pupils in Glasgow are now receiving counselling to help them overcome the trauma of losing a fellow pupil. It is an emotion very similar to bereavement" (IAC 2008b: 107).

The traumatic effect of such practices on a community, and especially a community's children, is vividly illustrated by the immigration raid in Postville, Iowa, on 12 May 2008: 389 workers at the US's largest kosher meat-packing plant were detained, and more than 300 of them were subsequently charged with using improper social security numbers. Bishop Steven L. Ullestad, of the Lutheran North-Eastern Iowa Synod, described what happened:

> That morning, schools and computers were shut down. All the roads into and out of Postville were blockaded by people with guns and guard dogs. Government trucks crashed through the gates of the local meat packing plant. Hundreds of ICE officers and other police officers in flak jackets with guard dogs and guns surrounded the place. Everyone with Latino background was brought out in handcuffs, whether they were documented or undocumented, while Black Hawk helicopters with machine guns visible circled overhead. Our little town of 2,300 was in shock ... I need to emphasise the number of people – 389 individuals arrested in a town of 2,300 – that are simply gone. You can imagine the impact on families, schools, downtown businesses and everything else. Why do this to towns and why do this to children?
>
> (Bouman & Deffenbaugh 2009: 68)

The whole community was traumatized. Half the town's schoolchildren were absent from classes the next day, chiefly, it was claimed, through fear.

Studies in the UK confirm that administrative immigration detention causes significant harm to the physical and mental health of children and young people. This is the conclusion of a briefing paper from the Royal College of General Practitioners, the Royal College of Paediatrics and Child Health, the Royal College of Psychiatrists, and the UK Faculty of Public Health (Significant Harm 2009). In the face of overwhelming evidence that almost all detained children suffer injury to their mental and physical health as a result of their detention, sometimes seriously, it argues that such detention is unacceptable and should cease without delay. These findings were based on the first study of its kind in the UK into the mental and physical health of twenty-four children, aged between three months and seventeen years, held in a British immigration detention centre (Lorek *et al.* 2009). Many of these showed signs of deep disturbance. The study speaks of "state-sanctioned neglect" and continues: "the traumatic experience of detention itself also has implications for the sizeable proportion of psychologically distressed children who are eventually released from detention and expected to successfully re-integrate into British society, while those children who are deported are returned with increased vulnerability to future stressors". These findings were confirmed a year later by a report (Burnett *et al.* 2010) commissioned by Medical Justice using a larger sample of children.

The Children's Commissioner, Professor Sir Al Aynsley-Green, continued to urge that "the detention of all children should cease". He highlighted concerns over the trauma children experience when being arrested, transported, and separated from their parents, and he affirmed that Yarl's Wood Detention Centre was "no place for a child" (2010). Some children were being detained far longer than the average fourteen days, and many were not being adequately prepared for their return to their home countries. His report states that "there was evidence from our visit and audit of records that children in detention have emotional and psychological needs that are not always being met". It also found that the Centre's policy for assessing children's well-being was inadequate. In a further highly critical report, published on 24 March 2010, the Chief Inspector of Prisons, Dame Anne Owers, added to growing pressure on ministers over Yarl's Wood by questioning the need to detain families and children in immigration removal centres. And while the UKBA Chief Inspector was of the opinion (Vine 2010) that "the removal of families who do not have permission to remain in the UK is one of the most challenging and sensitive areas of work undertaken by the UKBA", he nonetheless considered it "unacceptable that the UKBA has no system or process in place to capture and publish with confidence data on families". He said that "given the potential stress experienced by families who are detained, together with the significant cost to the taxpayer both of detention and of supporting families in the community, (he) would expect to see more comprehensive information collected, analysed, produced and published by the UKBA". With the overwhelming evidence of these reports, the consequent public outcry, and considerable political pressure, there have been significant improvements since the 2010 general election.

Cedars, a "family-friendly" holding facility at Pease Pottage, Crawley, opened in August 2011. Here, families are held for up to a week before they are forcibly removed from the UK; this has "largely replaced" the use of Yarl's Wood. Inspection (HMIP 2012) found conditions and treatment that exceed by some distance what families have previously experienced before removal – it is judged to be "an exceptional facility", unlike the "degrading and disgraceful" (Independent Monitoring Board 2014) conditions in which children are regularly held overnight at Heathrow. Visitors noted, however, a "sense of dissonance" between the attractive environment and caring ethos and the inevitable fear and uncertainty of the families. It is a place which "precedes traumatic dislocation for children who have, in many cases, been born in this country or been here for much of their lives". The main causes for concern were the initial arrest, point of removal, and use of force to effect removal rather than to prevent harm. Force had been used against six out of thirty-nine families, including a pregnant woman, where "non-approved techniques" were used that were an "unacceptable risk to the health of the unborn child".

Alternatives to detention

> While acknowledging that irregular entry or stay may present many challenges to states, detention is not the answer.

This is how the UNHCR begins its report "Beyond Detention" (2014). This launches a five-year initiative which aims to "support governments to end the detention of asylum seekers and refugees" by systematic analysis, advocacy, and raising awareness. The Jesuit Refugee Service in Europe published a report, "From Deprivation to Liberty" (2011), which presses the European Parliament for a strong presumption against the detention of asylum-seekers to become enshrined in EU legislation. In encouraging constituents to explore alternatives to custody in line with Article 15(1) of the EU Returns Directive (Directive 2008), it urges the governments of Belgium, Germany, and the UK to take seriously the recommendation that it is important to link alternatives to detention to larger systemic change. In the UK, the first ever all-party parliamentary inquiry into the use of immigration detention was launched in July 2014.

Departure

Deportation

When detainees are deported, this can be in ways that are brutal or inhumane in contravention of international guidelines. A report (Birnberg Peirce & Partners *et al.* 2008) describes a number of injuries sustained by asylum deportees at the hands of escorts contracted by the UK Home Office. The dossier of 300 cases reveals "widespread and seemingly systemic abuse" of vulnerable people who have fled their own countries seeking safety and refuge in the UK. This, the report suggests, is "frightening state-sponsored violence". A short time before, The IAC expressed concern "that the use of contracted out services has resulted in incidents of unacceptable restraint being used in instances that do not constitute 'the last resort'. We believe that further measures are required to ensure that unwarranted force is not used in the first place" (IAC 2008a). The warning was portentous.

Jimmy Mubenga, who suffocated on British Airways flight 77 from Heathrow to Angola on 12 October 2010, was so heavily restrained by security guards that he lost consciousness and died. Twenty-one months later, the Crown Prosecution Service found that, while there were "shortcomings" in the training provided to the guards, there was insufficient evidence to bring a charge of corporate manslaughter against the security firm, G4S Care and Justice Services UK (*Guardian*, 18 July 2012). Yet, a mere three months before Mr Mubenga's death, a special investigation report published by *The Independent* on 5 July 2010 pointed to cases where escorts had used excessive force.

The Crown Prosecution Service's decision not to bring charges against the guards was reviewed following the inquest in 2013 where the jury returned a verdict of unlawful killing, and on 20 March 2014 it was announced that the three G4S guards were to be charged with manslaughter. The coroner's powerful report exposed pervasive racism in the escort organization; pointed out the dangerous and unlawful practices used for deportations; and expressed concerns over the financial incentives offered to guards to keep detainees quiet. Following Mr Mubenga's death, the recommendation that escorts should be trained in non-pain-based restraint techniques as used in high-security prisons and mental hospitals was urged by the National Independent Commission on Enforced Removals (NICER 2012).

A further instance of gross inhumanity occurred on 10 February 2013 with the death of Alois Dvorzak, a frail eighty-four-year-old Canadian citizen, in transit from Canada to Slovenia to see his family. He was removed from his flight at Gatwick Airport and, although he was not seeking UK residence, was taken to Harmondsworth Detention Centre. No explanation has to date been forthcoming. But there he died three weeks later, detained in handcuffs until his heart stopped.

What happens to those who are deported on their return? The IAC notes (IAC 2008b: 107) that there is no systematic monitoring by government agencies of people who have been removed from the UK. Once removed, they are no longer considered to be the responsibility of the government. Yet, if the safety and security of those who are removed is not monitored, how can the UK be sure that its policies do not amount to *refoulement*? (Podeszfa & Manicom 2012). A number of organizations have compiled reports of human rights violations in particular countries. These typically include arbitrary detention at an airport, mistreatment, and torture. The report "Unsafe Return" (Ramos 2011) documents the harassment and torture of failed asylum-seekers on their return from the UK to the Democratic Republic of Congo; Human Rights Watch has evidence that at least three Tamils forcibly returned to Sri Lanka were subsequently tortured. In one case, the Immigration and Asylum Chamber accepted that a woman who made her way back to the UK in late 2010 after having previously been deported had been tortured and raped following her forcible return to Sri Lanka (*Guardian*, 1 & 6 June 2012). Some states view the very act of applying for asylum in another country as an act of treason (Amnesty International 2009; Iyodu 2010; Ramos 2011). But coordination of such monitoring is lacking. The Fahamu Refugee Programme has launched an initiative to provide channels of support for failed asylum-seekers on arrival in their country of origin and build a body of evidence to inform policy in countries that deport failed asylum-seekers (Podeszfa & Manicom 2012).

Stay

Destitution

A particularly disturbing feature of the UK asylum system is the effect of driving large numbers of asylum-seekers into destitution. Whether or not such destitution may be considered to be a "deliberate policy" (IAC 2008a: 19, 21), the Parliamentary Joint Committee on Human Rights does not mince words. In a report published in 2007, it states: "we believe that all deliberate use of inhumane treatment is unacceptable. We have seen instances in all cases where the government's treatment of asylum seekers and refused asylum seekers falls below the requirements of the common law of humanity and international human rights law" (PJCHR 2007). The phrase "the law of humanity" was first used in the context of destitute "foreigners" by the then Lord Chief Justice, Lord Ellenborough, in a case concerning the liability of the parish of Eastbourne to maintain a foreigner. This is what he says: "as to there being no obligation for maintaining poor foreigners ... the law of humanity, which is anterior to all positive laws, obliges us to afford them relief, to save them from starving" (R 1803). And this statement of the responsibilities of a civilized state has formed the basis for a succession of UK cases ever since. Following the introduction in 1993 of new welfare regulations which excluded most asylum-seekers, Neill LJ had this to say: "Parliament cannot have intended a significant number of genuine asylum seekers to be impaled on the horns of so intolerable a dilemma: the need either to abandon their claims to refugee status or alternatively to maintain them as best they can, but in a state of utter destitution. Primary legislation alone could in my judgment achieve that sorry state of affairs" (R 1997: 293; R 2003). His words were prophetic. That "sorry state of affairs" was achieved when Parliament passed the Asylum and Immigration Act of 1996.

Three years later, in an attempt to remedy the situation, the Immigration and Asylum Act of 1999 introduced a national system of asylum support. This takes two forms. While those who are waiting for the outcome of an asylum appeal are not allowed to work, they are provided with support under S.95 of the Act. Eligibility for S.95 support starts with the original asylum claim and continues through the wait for a decision and until appeal rights are exhausted. However, it may be refused, and often is, if asylum is not claimed at the very earliest opportunity or if the claimant has had some support from friends or relatives which cannot continue. Those who receive S.95 support are allocated a no-choice offer of accommodation outside London, and they receive a living allowance which in 2014 was £36.62 a week (about US$52.50). This is fifty-one per cent of the rate of income support (welfare) and clearly inadequate. For several years, Refugee Action, a charity established in the UK to facilitate the successful resettlement of refugees and asylum-seekers, had with other groups sought to persuade the Home Office that these cash payments were insufficient for an individual's basic living needs; but they did so in vain. Finally, they resorted to legal action. The case was heard in the High Court (R 2014b), and although the Home Secretary was ordered to remedy the situation, a solution has not yet been found.

Those who have exhausted opportunities for appeal lose the right to accommodation and support twenty-one days later. If, however, they can show that they are taking steps to leave the UK, they qualify for interim support under S.4 of the 1999 Act. The living allowance is less than S.95 support and is delivered in the form of a plastic card which has to be exchanged for food in specified shops; these shops may not be the cheapest, and they may be some distance away. The asylum-seeker has to live in a cashless economy, unable to use public transport to see a legal advisor or to visit a hospital, unable to buy phone cards, and, because inadequate administration often means that the card is refused at the check-out till, often even unable to buy food. The measures are humiliating; they emphasize a degree of separation between the asylum-seeker and mainstream society (Snyder 2012: 115). Qualification for S.4 support is not in itself a guarantee against destitution. A "large number" of applicants who seek the help of the Red Cross are destitute because of delays in dealing with their S.4 support pending consideration of further "fresh claim" submissions (MK 2012). The statement by Mr Hugh Tristram, the Development Officer for Refugee Services, British Red Cross, describes some of the circumstances in which such people find themselves:

> Many of our street homeless clients report sleeping at bus stops, on night buses ... in train and bus stations. People can only get on night buses if they have been able to obtain a bus pass or ticket (which means that it is not an option for the overwhelming majority of street homeless asylum seekers). They also tell us they feel vulnerable and unsafe sleeping rough. Some report being attacked whilst sleeping rough and it is not uncommon for them to be subjected to racist abuse ... The overwhelming majority of the people who are street homeless find the experience of being in that position frightening and hugely distressing. Most of them have never experienced being homeless and lack the necessary survival skills to cope ... Many of them will not be sufficiently proficient in the English language. A lot of them, even if they speak English, are educated and from professional backgrounds. The distress and humiliation they report feeling at being homeless is particularly acute given their unfamiliarity with such a way of life. They find it particularly difficult to deal with the encounters with established groups of rough sleepers (often drug and alcohol users) which are unavoidable when someone is homeless.
>
> (MK 2012)

Governments have long held the position that refused asylum-seekers should leave voluntarily or should expect to be removed. S.4 support is only available for those who have fresh claims for asylum or who agree to voluntary return. The IAC notes drily that "for those with a continuing fear of persecution on return it is a starkly unattractive option" (2008a: 119). Many come from places of conflict. They may have fled serious human rights abuses in their own country including torture, sexual violence, and forced conscription by government or militia. They fear the danger of return; they may feel that the Home Office decision was incorrect; they are unable to access legal advice. Others who have no identity papers cannot be repatriated, since some of the countries to which they would be deported will not accept them on UK government-provided papers. A survey carried out over one week by the Scottish Poverty Information Unit at Glasgow Caledonian University published in June 2012 on behalf of the Scottish Refugee Council, the Refugee Survival Trust, and the British Red Cross found one person who had been destitute for more than six years, eleven persons who had dependent children, and five women who were pregnant. Around one in four had mental health problems. Study author Morag Gillespie said that a substantial number of people had "absolutely nothing". "The fact we managed to find one hundred and forty destitute people in one week is a big worry", she said. "I think there is a government position about refused asylum seekers which accepts this is the situation people are going to get into, if they are not returning home. In some cases what people are arguing is that it is very hard – if possible at all – for them to return home, so they are stuck in limbo. They have got nothing here, but nor can they get home either" (*The Herald*, 11 June 2012). Refused asylum-seekers are more likely to be destitute than others. With no access to government support or permission to work, they have few options other than street homelessness, begging, or sex work, which exposes them to further violence and exploitation in the UK (McIntyre 2012).

Mr Justice Foskett makes the point that

> recourse to statistics must never be allowed to divert attention from the fact that there are human beings behind each application made and that some (including single men) may be extremely vulnerable at the time of making the application for support, the vulnerability being exacerbated by being destitute and homeless at the time. Whilst it would probably be unrealistic to expect that any policy or practice, however tightly drafted and conscientiously observed, would always ensure that every deserving case was dealt with properly and efficiently, that can never be a justification for not endeavouring to set in place a policy that does try to achieve this objective.
>
> (MK 2012)

This pointed critique, however, has not formed the basis of a fairer, more humane, or more effective system. The significant changes in asylum procedures since 2007 have been accompanied by an increase in destitution. The Red Cross report "Not Gone but Forgotten" "tells us things about ourselves we would rather not know. It confronts us with the case histories of people who came to Britain for sanctuary and find themselves destitute on our street" (2010: 3). The depth of suffering is immeasurable.

This is the context for an event which, to quote Archbishop Mario Conti, "initially sounds too unlikely, too horrendous, to be true" (McIntyre 2012). Put briefly, around 100 refused asylum-seekers had been housed in the Red Road Flats in Glasgow. The housing was substandard – Glasgow City Council had declared it unfit for habitation in 1980. Nonetheless, after the 1999 Immigration and Asylum Act, asylum-seekers were housed there. Tower blocks were surrounded by anti-suicide netting. That did not deter Serge Serykh, his wife Tatiana, and her son from jumping to their deaths in March 2010. The final trigger for their decision to take their own lives appears to have been the eviction notices served on them and other inhabitants of the Flats when the contract for housing them passed to another provider (*Guardian*, 11 March 2010). Archbishop Conti concluded: "it seems utterly inconceivable that a country with such strong traditions of welfare provision, fairness and social cohesion could allow innocent persons to be evicted, banned from working, left without food and shelter, and effectively eliminated from society".

Destitute children

Under international and domestic law, the UK is prohibited from returning unaccompanied children to their countries of origin unless there are safe and adequate reception facilities for them. Even if these children are refused refugee status, they may be granted discretionary leave to remain until they are seventeen and a half. But once they are eighteen, their choices are limited. They may return voluntarily or abscond into a life of destitution. For many, the outcome will still be detention and forced return. A study of unaccompanied children from Afghanistan in the UK confirms that there is very little official awareness of what happens to them on return, although the indications are that life for them there is "anything but safe" (Gladwell & Elwyn 2012). Increasing numbers of children also lack access to the basic necessities of life. The Children's Society (Pinter 2012) has identified an "alarming rise" in the number of destitute children and young people in desperate need of help. Many of these are at great risk from having nowhere to live and no support. The Society points out that a lack of regular access to food, clothing, toiletries, medicine, and a place to live has a huge impact on these children's lives and prospects. Zach Adesina reports an estimate by charities that around the UK about 120,000 children "do not exist". At least half of these are thought to be in London. Although many of them have come into the UK legally, they have never been officially recognized and have as a consequence no access to education or social housing. Some are forced into sex work in order to buy food (Adesina 2012).

Unable to meet basic needs for food, shelter, or health care, destitute men, women, and children are forced to rely on handouts supplied by friends, charities, or churches. In the telling words of an aid worker with the International Red Cross, "giving food to destitute asylum seekers here is not very different from handing out food from the back of lorries in the Sudan. The humanitarian need is the same" (IAC 2008a: 7; IAC 2008c: 32–34; IAC 2008b: 91–94; Asylum Matters 2008; Pinter 2012). The campaigns of Church Action on Poverty (Living Ghosts 2007; Still Human Still Here 2009) have brought together a coalition of around fifty organizations to protest against "inhumane and ineffective practices". On 1 October 2012, the Scottish Refugee Council and the Refugee Survival Trust, on the basis of research by Glasgow Caledonian University, launched a campaign to end destitution that was supported by the National Theatre of Scotland, which collaborated in the production of a documentary film entitled "Destitution" with the award-winning director Chris Leslie.

This extreme poverty gives rise to higher rates of physical and mental health problems than those found in the population at large. In order to survive, destitute men and women may have to engage in illegal, often exploitative, work or prostitution, or be forced to endure street homelessness. It is ironic that in so doing, the public perception that such people are criminals is enhanced. Benhabib comments on

> the extent to which refugees and asylum seekers are still denied the "right to have rights". They are completely dependent on the will of the sovereign state which grants them temporary sojourn; the transitional nature of their stay is accentuated by restrictions on their employment capacities; they are often segregated in housing blocks, denied the right to employment, easy targets for xenophobic outbursts, retained in a "state of exception", treated as quasi-criminal elements.
>
> (Benhabib 2004: 162)

Those who are caught in a poverty trap are also caught in a legal trap. Legal aid has been slashed. It has become increasingly difficult for those who are fleeing persecution – but whose claims for asylum have been refused – to find a solicitor to access legal aid, unearth new evidence, and submit a fresh claim. The Law Society has expressed grave concern as to the likely impact of cuts in legal aid (2014). Michael Mansfield QC writes: "access to justice ... encompasses a recognition that everyone is entitled to the protection of the law and that rights are meaningless unless they can be enforced. It is about protecting ordinary and vulnerable people and solving their problems. Yet the law is complex such that most ordinary people with small or even moderate means cannot access the law without help" (Robins 2011: 5). There are "legal deserts" where it is impossible to find publicly funded access to justice. Asylum specialists have closed down, including the legal charity Refugee Migrant Justice, leaving some 10,000 cases in limbo. The largest remaining provider of publicly funded legal representation for asylum-seekers, the Immigration Advisory Service (IAS), was also controversially placed in administration in July 2011. The closure of the IAS had considerable impact. Contracted, for instance, to provide ninety-seven per cent of the legal aid cases in Leeds, its demise meant that the majority of the city's asylum-seekers had no access to justice (*Guardian*, 5 August 2011). The independent commission of inquiry appointed by the Law Society to survey the situation took "a dispassionate look at the facts and reported on their findings". They concluded that legal aid is vital to ensuring that everyone is equal before the law; that it protects the needs of vulnerable people and upholds the rule of law; that it is essential to holding the state to account; and that the proposed cuts are not a fair and effective way to reduce unnecessary litigation (Robins 2011). The House of Lords pronounced the cuts to be "ill-conceived and unfair", and on 5 March 2012 affirmed, against the government, that legislation must state "that people must have access to legal services that effectively meet their needs". Without legal help, people with a right to stay in Britain may get turned away. Without legal help, bad decisions will go unchallenged, putting people's lives at risk.

Integration

The right to work

If an initial decision is not made within a year of an asylum claim, or a fresh claim, there is a right under European regulations to ask for permission to work. In the UK, this is always given, but the request is only granted to those on a shortage acceptance list of highly skilled professions. Very rarely can asylum-seekers take advantage of this. It is a deeply unjust and cynical approach to those who are waiting and in breach of European legislation.

The right to work is granted in numerous international and regional legal instruments, including the European Social Charter. While the right to work for refugees is granted under the 1951 UN Refugee Convention, the right to work for asylum-seekers is usually only provided for after a certain period of time. Under Directive 2013/33/EU of the European Parliament and of the Council, member states of the EU must give the right to work to asylum-seekers after nine months of waiting for a decision on their applications.

It is well known that work enhances a person's dignity, self-respect, and feelings of self-worth. The point is well made by an influential UNHCR report: "irrespective of the particular right at issue, it makes enormous economic and social sense to allow asylum-seekers, whatever their mode of entry or particular circumstances, to work. Being able to participate as productive members of society is fundamental to individual self-esteem and dignity, and it can equally contribute to improving relations between asylum-seekers and the local community" (Edwards 2006).

Many examples of good practice can be found in the Refugee Integration Capacity and Evaluation (RICE) Project, which identifies factors that hinder or enable refugee integration (UNHCR 2013). For instance, due to Sweden's generous welfare system, high employment rates are necessary. Those who apply for asylum are allowed to work immediately, and they receive a daily allowance sufficient to pay for clothes, medical care, and leisure activities. If their asylum application is successful, they are offered free language, culture, and labour market integration classes. Research has shown that such policies help to reduce unemployment among refugees in their first twenty years in Sweden. However, it still needs to be taken into account that the employment rate for refugees lags behind that for natives, essentially for the duration of their time in Sweden, and it varies by country of origin and the age of refugees at the time of arrival (Lundborg 2013).

In the US, refugees and asylum-seekers have the right to work indefinitely, and they are allowed to receive social security cards, without employment restrictions, on an equal basis with US citizens (OSC). Research has shown that this, in itself, is no guarantee that they will find work. The "New Immigrant Survey" found that this depended on a range of factors which included language ability, education experience, different forms of family support, mental and physical health, and the type of housing and neighbourhood in which they lived. Yet, even after accounting for these differences, there was still a disparity in earnings and occupational attainment (Connor 2010). Nonetheless, the study found that the disparity decreased with the length of time spent in the US and with increases in education levels. Although little is known about the effectiveness of policies and resources that are invested in integrating refugees into the labour market, these findings suggest that it is not sufficient simply to give refugees the right to work. A UNHCR report concludes that "countries must also invest in labour market activation policies specifically designed for refugees" (Ott 2013).

A difficult transition

In the UK, the award of refugee status brings happiness followed by bewilderment (Doyle 2014). Twenty-eight days after notification of their new status, they are no longer entitled to accommodation or cash support. During this time, they must find a means to support themselves and their families and find somewhere to live. They may not speak good English; they will not have had access to employment and savings; and they will find themselves having to make a rapid transition from passivity and dependency to being responsible for negotiating the complex housing, health, and welfare systems in the UK.

Restrictions on employment for asylum-seekers are seen as contributing to the risk of poverty on gaining refugee status. Once a person's claim for protection is recognized by the UK government, and they have leave to remain, the restrictions on employment are lifted and the majority of refugees are keen to enter the labour market. However, they may have become de-skilled over the period of enforced unemployment, and they will certainly have diminished self-confidence; the difficulty in obtaining recognition of their qualifications has also been recognized as a barrier to employment as is providing proof that they have been awarded such qualifications in the first place (SPIU 2010). In addition, administrative difficulties frequently mean that a person's Biometric Residence Permit and National Insurance Number are delayed, these being the main sources of identification for welfare, bank, landlord, and doctor's surgery. Where a new refugee is forced to sleep in hostels, on the streets, or on park benches, it is left to charities and faith groups to plug the gaps; even then, voluntary organizations are limited by a lack of funding.

A comprehensive integration programme can make a huge difference in the well-being of refugees. Yet policy changes and funding cuts in the UK have had a severely negative impact. The punitive nature of asylum policy means that charitable resources tend to be taken up with meeting the immediate survival needs of asylum-seekers rather than being available for the longer-term integration support needs of those who become refugees (SPIU 2010). And this can make all the difference between life and death. Some fall through the gaps. In 2012, a baby boy starved to death in Westminster as his seriously ill mother who had had her claim for asylum approved struggled to obtain food, proper housing, and welfare. She died two days later. A serious case review pointed "to weaknesses in the support system for asylum seekers whose applications are granted, which means they can wait weeks before they are transferred to a new benefits [welfare] system" (*Guardian*, 5 October 2012).

Where political agendas take precedence over ordinary morality, the door is left wide open to cruelty and inhumanity. A callous indifference towards the fate of those who are seeking asylum may be seen in the target-driven policies of many Western governments and the often brutal ways in which these policies are implemented. Referring to accounts of people who had died without adequate food or with untreated medical conditions, Judith Butler writes:

> Of course, it is still possible to hear such statistics, and not to deny them, but to insist that they do not finally matter – it may be a matter of indifference, or it may be that such suffering is understood as deserved, or it may be something else: a form of righteous coldness cultivated over time by local and collective practices of nation-building, supported by prevalent social norms as they are articulated by both public policy, dominant media, and the strategies of war … Righteous coldness is … what is required to look on the destruction of life with moral satisfaction, even moral triumph.
>
> (Butler 2010: xxiv)

But that is not the whole story. Refugees themselves can be powerful agents for change and outspoken advocates for the vulnerable. Zrinka Bralo, Director of The Migrants and Refugee Communities Forum in London, says of the winners of the 2013 Migrant and Refugee Woman of the Year Awards that

> their communities recognise them … as women who are willing to take risks not only in speaking out, but also in standing up to those who have control over their lives. They live in the limbo of exile, with unimaginable losses and traumas and yet they find the strength not only to help themselves but to support and inspire others and to be the drivers of integration for their families and communities. And

> they don't stop there – they work to change policies and the hearts and minds of our politicians and the public. These women are essential for how modern Britain is and should be – just, fair, hard-working and respectful of difference and diversity.
>
> (Migrant and Refugee Woman of the Year Awards 2013)

Remzije Sherifi trained as an electrical engineer, but radio was her passion. She was one of the first female radio journalists in Kosovo. She lost her job in 1992 as a result of the political persecution of Albanians at the time of the fall of Yugoslavia. As the war in the Balkans spread, and at the beginning of the Western military intervention in Kosovo, Remzije and her family were forced to flee their homeland and took refuge in a refugee camp in Macedonia. She says: "as a consequence of ethnic cleansing during the war in Kosovo in 1999 more then 90 per cent of Kosovan Albanians became refugees in different parts of the world. I was one of the lucky ones, with my three sons and husband to be evacuated by British troops to Scotland as a medical evacuee. When we got to Glasgow, it was amazing to find people with smiles who were welcoming us. I didn't speak any English but I could read the expressions on people's faces".

This is how Remzije remembers the early days:

> On arrival in Glasgow we immediately felt freedom for the first time ever. It was our second chance for life, especially for our children to have their childhood back, to be able to have education and build their future. Immediately, I started setting up activities for young people and for Kosovan women, to celebrate and share the richness of our culture as a way of making links and building bridges with our Scottish neighbours. Integration should come from both sides; it is the only way to promote harmony and equality and respect. My passion was to build bonds between communities to encourage and celebrate cultural diversity.
>
> (The Forum 2013)

Remzije now runs Maryhill Integration Network (MIN), where three staff and sixty volunteers operate a diverse programme of weekly activities in health, learning, and creativity to support and improve the lives of people from overseas as well as those from Scotland. She believes that the arts and storytelling are a powerful way to reach out and change attitudes, culminating in MIN publications, theatre productions, and events at local, city-wide, and national levels, including the Scottish Parliament. Remzije's community work has had a long-term impact on the lives of hundreds of people who have needed a helping hand at starting their new lives in the UK. She is able to understand the traumatic experiences they have been through, and her support and example has inspired others who in turn have made new lives and passed on the lessons they have learned. One of her supporters said:

> I can testify personally to the difference that this support has made to me, my husband and children. I experienced the threat of deportation after being in the UK for seven years, and that fear made me so terribly depressed. Remzije worked to challenge the UKBA decision. If I am here today enjoying my life with my family and granted leave to remain it is the result of the campaign and support that Remzije was part of. Her support continued after my family and I were granted leave to remain and it helped us to move on. I have now completed my college course, and am training as an adviser and counsellor, working with the Scottish Refugee Council. She has enabled me to support others in turn, passing on the skills and confidence I gained.
>
> (The Forum 2013)

Remzije offers hope for the future to the people she deals with, supporting individuals facing violence, homelessness, racism, and destitution.

Those who work alongside refugees in NGOs, charities, and voluntary organizations testify to the tenacity, determination, and faith of volunteers, staff, and refugees. The International Care Network (ICN) in Bournemouth has seen "very many people rescued from complex legal asylum situations, destitution, poverty, unemployment, entangled bureaucracy, separation from family members, hopelessness, loneliness, isolation, marginalisation, disempowerment, danger and fear". The same could be said of the Jesuit Refugee Service, RESTORE in Birmingham, ASSIST in Sheffield, the BOAZ Trust in Manchester, and other organizations in major cities of the UK. Many volunteers are dedicated, compassionate people with a common sense of the injustices of the asylum system and the evil of destitution. Although many of these organizations face an uncertain future because of funding cuts, in the middle of all the hardship, they foster mutual relationships and a sense of community. In times of turmoil, uncertainty, and despair, they keep hope alive.

Faced with glimpses of a world where there is justice and compassion, where men, women, and children are treated as persons with dignity, not objects or ciphers, we are confronted with the following question: can an affirmation of the moral claims of people in need be reconciled with instances where societies violate human worth and treat refugees and asylum-seekers with indignity, even cruelty, as if they did not matter? As the following chapters make clear, the Bible has light to shed on the issue.

4

THE STRANGER IN YOUR MIDST

Throughout the Old Testament, we find Israelites and non-Israelites fleeing from their homes to a place of refuge. They fall broadly into two categories: Israelites who flee to another country, or who are displaced internally, and "sojourners", non-Israelites who come to live in Israel. In this chapter, we look first of all at provisions for the sojourner, which are prominent in the law books, and then we consider those narratives which feature named individuals who are fleeing from Israel. In each case, we take into account the ethical norms and values which are conveyed.

The sojourner

In the Covenant Code (Exod. 20.22–23.33) and Deuteronomy, we have a vision of what it means to be a community living before God. Such a community exercises special care for the socially marginalized. Injunctions deal with the status granted to the "stranger" who is resident in Israel and is governed by the internal regulations of the Israelite community. The Hebrew term used to allude to such a person, *ger*, is always masculine. He is variously described as "the *ger* who is 'among you' or 'in your midst'" (Deut. 16.11); the *ger* "in your towns" (Exod. 20.10; Deut. 5.14; 14.21, 29; 16.14; 26.12; 31.12), "in your land" (Lev. 19.33), "in Israel" (Lev. 22.18), or "in your land in one of your towns" (Deut. 24.14). This stranger is faceless: he has no name; there is nothing to tell us of his hometown; and no reasons are given for his presence in the land. If he has a wife and children, these are not mentioned. He and his ancestors could have been there for many generations or they could have come quite recently. Nothing is ever said about him having fled his home country, and there is no reference to an eventual return. He is consistently designated as *ger*, a term which defines him from the point of view of the Israelites. To be a *ger* is to be perceived as a *ger* (Ramirez Kidd 1999: 32). We may note in passing that there are no functional equivalents for *ger* (Ramirez Kidd 1999: 28). None of the nouns used to refer to "foreigner" in the Old Testament are ever used as a synonym for *ger*; the noun, consistently found in the singular, is "used as an anonymous figure in theoretical situations" (Ramirez Kidd 1999: 16). Because of the different understandings of the noun in English – the NRSV has "alien" (Exod. 20.10), "resident alien" (2 Sam. 1.13), and "stranger" (Jer. 14.8) – I shall for simplicity from now on use the Hebrew word.

But who is this mysterious person? What can we say about him? It has been generally assumed that the *ger* is a non-Israelite living in Israel (Houten 1991: 107), and this view is supported by Exod. 12.48, Deut. 14.21, and many other places in Deuteronomy and Leviticus. There have, however, been attempts to qualify this. Walter Houston indicates that, "in a lineage-based agrarian society the immigrant from another tribe or even the next village is just as much of an outsider" (2008: 108), and Reinhard Achenbach, along the same lines, offers as a working definition of the *ger*, "a person, who, in order to protect his life and family, looks for a new home. *Gerim* may have their origin among related or non-related ethnic groups" (2011: 29). Christophe Bultmann argues more specifically that the *ger* is not a "foreign immigrant", but one of a subclass of free, landless people, temporary workers for farmers from whom they receive charitable support (1992). Although this view is contested (Houtman 2000: 224), Houston suggests that it is quite possible that this might have been the original meaning, "but that with the urban decline of the lineage-based system and the development of a sense of popular national identity (these tendencies are clearly observable in Deuteronomy) the term does come to be applied mainly to foreigners" (2008: 108). He adds that "in their social marginality and economic need there is no difference".

If we accept the general understanding that the *ger* is a non-Israelite living in Israel, can we associate the emergence of the term with specific political developments? Again, because there is no firm evidence, scholars differ on this question. Christiana van Houten, for instance (1991: 156), sees the *gerim* as Israelites who remained in the land and joined those exiles who returned from Babylonia, whereas Bultmann (1992: 216) associates them with persons who, coming from outside, want to become part of the religious community. Achenbach (2011: 29) finds an explanation in the fact that the inhabitants of Judah added the *ger* to the traditional listing of poor widows and fatherless children (Exod. 22.20a, 21; 23.1–9). And he links this to the dramatic changes that occurred in Judah following the fall of the northern kingdom of Israel to the Assyrians in 720 BCE, following a three-year siege of its capital, Samaria (2 Kgs 17.5.6; 18.9–11). This precipitated a population movement on a grand scale and led to an increase in those who were poor and landless. Though Biblical sources are silent on the matter, archaeological evidence (Burke 2011: 47–54) indicates that there was a sudden influx of refugees into Judah during this period. The spectacular growth of Jerusalem, far beyond what one might expect from natural population growth, correlates with the abandonment of hill sites in the northern hill country of Israel. Approximately fifty-three per cent of the city's population arrived in the late 8th century. Aaron Burke argues (2011: 48) that it was the landlessness of these refugees from the north that determined their resettlement in Jerusalem. Many were probably employed in labour projects such as the Broad Wall and the Siloam Tunnel with its inscription in Israelite Hebrew (Burke 2011: 51). But interestingly, there is no evidence for increased morbidity and mortality associated with refugees at this time. Burke argues that this points to the relatively successful integration of these refugees from the north with their basic needs being met (2011: 52).

However, while these people, refugees from the northern kingdom, would certainly be "foreigners" in a political sense, the *ger* in Deuteronomy and in Exod. 12.48–49 is clearly a "non-Israelite". The simple presence of resident aliens is not sufficient to account for the emergence of the *ger* – this is a new phenomenon. Given the fact that there is no precise historical evidence (Awabdy 2014: 36), where can we go from here? The insights of Eckart Otto are helpful (1994: 85–86; cf. Houston 2008: 113). Against the background of the cataclysmic social changes of the 8th century BCE, he shows how, in Deuteronomy, the laws for the protection of the *ger*, the fatherless child, and the widow are no longer based on genealogical but on religious principles. This enables solidarity between the native-born and the *ger*, which is not possible when the relationship is seen exclusively in ethnic and kinship terms.

Let us look now in more detail at references in the Covenant Code and Deuteronomy that are concerned with the protection of the *ger* and with material provision for the needy.

Fair treatment of the ger

Laws in themselves cannot establish a just society unless members of society want to behave justly (Houston 2008: 107); law is of little use without moral education, and in Exod. 20–23, illustrations are given of how ethical behaviour might take shape.

The *ger* is not to be "wronged or oppressed" (Exod. 22.21). The word for "oppression" used here implies depriving a person of what is his or hers by right. We may note in passing that the second verb in this verse is more regularly used to describe the oppression of one nation by another (Houten 1991: 52), and there may be some sense here of the *ger* as a foreigner, an alien in the ethnic sense (Houston 2008: 109). The exhortation is directed to the average reasonably well-to-do Israelite who may be tempted to abuse their privileged position in the way they treat weaker members of society (cf. Ezek. 18.7–8). Their conscience is appealed to; they are to be just and merciful, especially with regard to those like the *ger*, the fatherless child, and the widow who have no-one to care for them (Houtman 2000: 217).

An offender contends, not with juridical sanctions as we know them today, but with YHWH. This section concludes with an explicit threat: if an Israelite abuses the *ger*, and if the *ger* cries out to YHWH, then the Lord "will surely hear his cry" as surely as he heard the cry of the Israelites in Egypt; and, as YHWH is the guardian and avenger of those who lack human protection, there will be consequences for the oppressor (Propp 2006: 258). But a closer look at the text in Hebrew leaves one wondering who exactly the oppressor is and who exactly is being oppressed. There appears to be a direct connection between the first half of v. 21 and v. 23: in each case, the verse is addressed to a singular person (the AV translation for v. 21a makes this clear: "thou shalt neither vex a stranger, nor oppress him"). Here, the *ger* is also singular, and the same happens in v. 23. It is therefore possible, as Otto points out (1994: 85–86), that vv. 22 and 24 have been added because they address a plural "you" and are speaking not about the *ger*, but about the widow and the fatherless child. But having said this, if we take Exod. 22.20–23 as a whole, are we not justified in understanding the verses to refer not only to the *ger* but also to the widow and the fatherless child? And is it also possible to come to an ethically significant understanding of v. 22 as it stands, with its fluctuations in number? Houtman cites Ibn Ezra, who sees that the oppressor is not just the individual who does wrong, but "also the person who witnesses oppression and does nothing about it ... ; in consequence, a community in which there is oppression is collectively guilty; the judgment is upon the entire community" (2000: 225).

Exploitation in law

It would appear that the *ger*, along with other socially disadvantaged people, was vulnerable to a particular type of oppression: exploitation in law (Houten 1991: 55, 97). Protection in Exod. 23.1–9 explicitly includes judicial procedures. Exod. 23.9 echoes Exod. 22.21. These two verses bracket a section that deals, amongst other things, with the exploitation of the poor and vulnerable. According to Achenbach, "it was clearly necessary to put legal barriers up against the activities of the powerful who may have exploited sojourners and tried to intervene when they attempted to get justice at the gates" (2011: 30). Judges are exhorted (Exod. 23.6) not to pervert justice. They are not to pervert justice through deceit (Exod. 23.7), making an indictment on the basis of false testimony or insufficient evidence (cf. Deut. 19.18–19). This can condemn an innocent person to death. It is judicial murder, and the person responsible is answerable to YHWH (Exod. 23.7). Corruption in the judicial process causes truth to be violated and makes it impossible for the innocent to get a fair hearing (Exod. 23.8; cf. Isa. 1.23; Houtman 2000: 250). All these admonitions are addressed to the Israelite citizen, whether testifying in court as accuser or witness, or acting as judge (Houtman 2000: 238). Finally, Exod. 23.9, in an emphatic climax to the series of prohibitions against injustice, singles out the *ger* – the *ger* is not to be oppressed.

The verse is pivotal. The *ger* is not to be oppressed; he is also to be treated well. The verse may be taken as an introduction to the humanitarian provisions in Exod. 23.10–12 (Houtman 2000: 224). Although the *ger* is not mentioned here specifically (cf. Deut. 24.19–22) as being amongst the "poor" who benefit from gleaning, the final reference to the *ger* in Exod. 23.12 provides for rest on the seventh day. The concern here "that you may be refreshed" is purely humanitarian (Houten 1991: 52). To underscore this, attention is narrowly focused on the association between the ox and the donkey, typical work animals, and those whose work is burdensome, the slave and the *ger*. None of these are to be required to work on the day of rest (Houtman 2000: 257).

These prescriptions for proper ethical behaviour suggest that the *ger* was not being treated fairly either in the courts or in the community. This is also one of the core themes of Deuteronomy, where the opening section of the narrative sets the scene for what follows and establishes a juridical framework for the bearing of the law upon the community life of the Israelites (Deut. 1.9–18). To deal with the problem of case overload, Moses, with the agreement of his hearers, appoints wise, discerning, and reputable leaders (cf. Exod. 18.13–27; Num. 11.11–17). By implication, these are the judges referred to in Deut. 1.16–18 (Nelson 2002: 20) who are to give members of the community "a fair hearing" and adjudicate fairly, irrespective of whether the disputants are "citizens" or "*gerim*" (meaningless in the hypothetical situation in the wilderness!). As a further guarantee of equity, there is the possibility of appeal to Moses himself (Deut. 1.17). The *ger* is seen here as being entitled to the same impartiality in law as the citizen.

The principle is reinforced in Deut. 16.19a, a general prohibition against perverting justice which would in practice particularly benefit those who are most vulnerable, the *ger*, the fatherless child, and the widow (Deut. 24.17). And the point is driven home in Deut. 27.19, where the Levites declare to the Israelites that "anyone who deprives the *ger*, the orphan and the widow of justice" shall be cursed.

The fact that such injunctions are considered necessary conjures up an image of a sinful Israel who is failing to deal justly with the *ger* in particular. The very fact that it is considered necessary to instruct the Israelites not to "withhold the wages of poor and needy labourers, whether other Israelites or aliens who reside in your land in one of your towns" is indicative of employment practices that are immoral and unjust (Deut. 24.14). And the day labourer, whether *ger* or Israelite, can cry out to YHWH against their Israelite employer who will be held to account. Similar injunctions against oppressive behaviour recur in late prophetic writings; Jeremiah advises the King of Judah to "do no wrong or violence to the *ger*, the fatherless child and the widow" (Jer. 22.3); Zechariah records how the people "stopped their ears" when he exhorted them not to "oppress the widow, the fatherless child, the *ger* or the poor" (Zech. 7.10); and Malachi excoriates "those who thrust aside the *ger*" (Mal. 3.5). The words are clearly ethical in intent and are capable of being applied in many ways to present-day situations.

As we have seen, the injunctions against the oppression of the *ger*, particularly in the courts of law, are accompanied by positive recommendations for humane behaviour in social life. He is a "protected stranger" (Smith 1927: 75–79).

Humane treatment of the ger

Typically in Deuteronomy, the *ger* features as part of the formula "*ger*-fatherless child-widow" (14.29; 16.11, 14; 24.17, 19–21; 26.12–13). This is a striking innovation. In Mesopotamian texts, "widows and fatherless children" tend to be associated with "the poor, the humble, the hungry" (Ramirez Kidd 1999: 114), but in Deuteronomy they are specifically associated with the *ger*. The collective triad "*ger*-fatherless child-widow" may be taken to refer to the helpless, marginalized group of people who were emerging in the late monarchy (Houston 2008: 176) and with whom the Deuteronomic Code was particularly concerned: the widow and the fatherless child with no man to support them and the landless *ger;* and the prominence of these three categories indicates an awareness that their suffering has no place in a stable and harmonious community; it is contrary to the will of YHWH (Houtman 2000: 223) and ethically unacceptable. We should note that most of these references in Deuteronomy extend also to the Levites, possibly seeking to alleviate the negative effects upon this group of the elimination of the use of the tithe to support the local sanctuary (Nelson 2002: 186). The majority of references deal with the theme of food. In Deut. 16.11–14, religious and social practices are integrally related. The harvest festivals of Weeks and Booths are in each case celebrated by the whole community, inclusive of the "*ger*-fatherless child-widow" triad.

Tithes (Deut. 14.22–29) are seen as a way of securing means for those who have no property of their own in Israel (McConville 2002: 252). The poor tithe (Deut. 14.28–29) appears to be an obligatory produce tax collected every three years in a local centre. The regulations are addressed to free, land-owning citizens, not to the state or the temple (Nelson 2002: 183). Deut. 14.29 and 26.12–13 instruct the farmers to bring the tithes of their produce in the third year to give to the *ger*, the fatherless child, and the widow so that they "may come and eat their fill". Rejoicing at the generosity of YHWH, the Israelite farmer responds with generosity; this involves sharing the gifts of YHWH with, amongst others, the *ger*. In a further three instances (Deut. 24.19–21; Lev. 19.10; 23.22), the farmer is commanded to leave the surplus of his barley or wheat harvest, the fruit of his olive trees, and the grapes of his vineyards for the "*ger*, the fatherless child and the widow". In fostering social mechanisms to protect those in need, all these provisions articulate an awareness of YHWH's blessing that is expressed in the nation's life, worship, and ethical behaviour.

The provision of food is also a feature of one of the non-triad references where Deuteronomy (14.21) provides for the disposal of the carcase of a food animal for humanitarian ends. The Israelite may not himself eat carrion, but rather than leave it to go to waste, he may give the carcase to the *ger*. Although the Israelite is bound by the law on carrion, which does not affect the *ger* (McConville 2002), the donation of food is consistent with the humanitarian ethos of Deuteronomy as a whole. It also points up, interestingly enough, the distinction between the status of the *ger* and that of the *nokri* ("foreigner"). The carrion is given to the *ger*, but is sold to the *nokri*. When the *ger* appears alone, he is included in the community and there is the understanding that he will live within a household on the same sort of basis as an impoverished (Israelite) dependent relative (Lev. 25.35); when the *nokri* appears alone, he is excluded from communal benefits. The law of remission does not apply to him (Deut. 15.3), neither does the loan without interest (Deut. 23.20).

Love the ger*!*

One of the functions of a ruler in the Ancient Near East, as illustrated by the epilogue to the Code of Hammurabi (Richardson 2000), was to execute justice for the fatherless child and widow. In Deut. 10.17–19, it is YHWH who does so. He commands that the fatherless child and widow be treated fairly and humanely; and he himself provides food and clothing for the *ger* (cf. Ps. 146.7–10) whom he loves. The transition in Deut. 10.19 to the unconditional command to "love the *ger*" is as sudden as it is remarkable. The emphasis now is not so much on the poverty and need which the *ger* shares with the fatherless child and widow, as on his particularity as a stranger. As perspective moves from the *ger*-fatherless child-widow in their collective need to the *ger* who is singled out in his distinctiveness, "royal" responsibility extends to the people of Israel (McConville 2002: 201). Just as YHWH does justice to the *ger* and loves him, so Israel too must treat the *ger* justly and love him – with the love of Abraham for Isaac, the love of Isaac for Rebekah, the love of Ruth for Naomi, and the steadfast love of God to the thousandth generation of those that love him.

The command to love the *ger* is explained theologically in the motive clause "for you were *gerim* in the land of Egypt" (Deut. 10.19b). The appeal in the narrative is to Israel's own experience of being alien settlers experiencing oppression in Egypt from harsh and xenophobic people. But for readers of the text, the experience of being an alien is coloured by the experience of exile in Babylon, which gives Israel a new awareness of "the heart of an alien" (Exod. 23.9b). The awareness applies by extension to the people as a whole. Having been themselves *gerim*, they know what it feels like; they can identify with the *ger* because they have themselves been *gerim*. This is the central issue. The four references in the motive clauses to being *gerim* in Egypt (Exod. 22.21; 23.9; Lev. 19.34; Deut. 10.19) appeal to the principle of reciprocity – you know what it is like to be oppressed, so see to it that you do not in your turn oppress the *ger*; love him!

The language is emotional; it resonates with the use of the term "brother" in contexts of social justice where the Covenant Code and Holiness Code have "neighbour"; "as your brother" occurs at Deut. 15.2, 3, 7, 9, 11, 12; 17.15; 23.19–20; Lev. 25.25, 35, 36, 39. (The NRSV, in an attempt to be inclusive, loses the intimate force of the word in its rendering as "a member of your community"; it loses also its specificity: the *ger* is also a member of the community!)

All these draw attention to what the addressee has in common with the person being addressed; they are fellow members of the same family. The *ger* has the same claim to concern as the brother (Deut. 24.14). The relationship of all Israelites to one another as brothers reflects the law's appeal to treat one another as such (Houston 2008: 183). Brothers should act towards one another with generosity, not harshness.

It is worth noting here the distinction between these motive clauses which refer to the *gerim* and those where Moses exhorts his hearers to remember "that they were *slaves* in Egypt" (cf. Deut. 5.15; 15.5; 16.12; 24.18; 24.22). In these, the principle is gratitude for the memory of what YHWH has done for them in saving them from slavery. In consequence, they themselves are exhorted to look to the needs of those who are needy – chief amongst whom are the *ger*, the fatherless child, and the widow (Ramirez Kidd 1999: 94; Awabdy 2014: 127–129).

A different type of motivation is spelt out in Deut. 28. In a series of blessings, Moses recounts the consequences of obedience to the precepts of the law and, in an excruciating, lengthy sequence of curses, of disobedience. Moshe Weinfeld has pointed out the striking similarity between these maledictions and the Assyrian treaties, particularly the Vassal Treaties of Esarhaddon II 528–533, which are virtually identical both in subject matter and sequence of curses (1972: 121) and which would have been familiar to scribes working in Judah in the 7th century. This is "a scribal reworking of borrowed political curse material for theological purposes" (Nelson 2002: 327); the curses come into effect as a punishment for breaking the Covenant. But there is a respect in which the Deuteronomic curses differ from the Assyrian imprecations and that is in the reference to the *ger*, which is new. The last curse of the nightmarish sequence, rhetorically the most significant, is the threat of social reversal (Deut. 28.43–44). As a culmination of the curses that rain down upon a disobedient Israel, the *ger* rises in status over the Israelite; furthermore, "they shall lend" to the Israelite, in sharp contrast to the prophecy at Deut. 28.12b. The "lending" is presumably a consumption loan (cf. Exod. 22.25) not a commercial loan to build up capital. It illustrates the depths of poverty to which the people of Israel will have sunk when they are forced to borrow (cf. Neh. 5.10–11), presumably to tide them over until the next harvest, and thereby to incur debt to the *ger*. The unrelenting sequence of curses concludes with the phrase "they shall be the head and you shall be the tail" (Deut. 28.44), a definitive and unwelcome reversal of the conditional promise in Deut. 28.13a. Although the threat of "foreigners" possessing the land of Israelites is a common warning used by prophets (Amos 5.11; Mic. 6.15; Jer. 5.17), this is the only occasion where the *ger* is evoked in this context. In this image of social reversal, the author conveys a pointed awareness of where the *ger* is currently situated: at the bottom of the social scale and forced into debt-bondage.

While Deuteronomy does envisage a certain amount of judicial and political authority (16.18–20; 17.8–20), no particular function is assigned to the king.

The Israelites are bound to YHWH by covenant and committed to ordering their lives accordingly in justice and righteousness. No other nation has "statutes and ordinances as just as this entire law" (Deut. 4.7–8), for these statutes are ordained by YHWH, and YHWH and his statutes are in a different league from the deities and laws of other nations (Nelson 2002: 65). YHWH is the authority and enforcer of the law; the blessings and curses of Leviticus 26 and Deuteronomy 28 make that clear. This is not "the law of a polity. It represents the standards to which the people as a whole and every individual is supposed to be committed" (Houston 2008: 172). The statutes mark the reciprocal responsibilities of the relationship between the people and YHWH. They are the statutes of a covenant. Every member of the people of the Covenant is charged (Deut. 27.1; 31.12) to "pursue justice" (Deut. 16.20) and to display the wisdom and discernment that typify the wise ruler (Deut. 1.13; 4.6; Isa. 11.2). At a narrative level, Moses' appeal is addressed to the nation as a whole, to "all who are assembled" (Deut. 29.10) on the Plain of Moab, the leadership cadres, the men of Israel, their children, women, and the *gerim*. But within this universal, inclusive address there is a particular identification of the addressees with those who employ the *gerim*, who are described here as "those who cut your wood and those who draw your water" (Deut. 29.11; cf. Josh. 9.23). Landowners, lower officials, who are able to give loans, who may own slaves (Houston 2008: 176), these have a particular responsibility to behave justly towards the landless *ger*.

The assembly in Moab is a new act of covenant-making, building upon the previous promises made on Mount Horeb and extended to future generations. The exhortation is widened to "those here and those not here" (Deut. 29.15). The inclusion is in space and time. Moses' fictional hearers and subsequent generations of readers are exhorted to do "what is good and right in the sight of the LORD your God, you and your children after you forever" (Deut. 12.28). They are instructed to "keep the statutes for your own well-being and that of your descendants after you" (Deut. 4.40). No other great nation has a god "so near to it as YHWH whenever we call to him". The nearness of YHWH in Deuteronomy becomes one with the nearness of his word, which is "in your mouth and in your heart, in order to do it" (Deut. 30.14). Loving YHWH and obeying him becomes second nature.

Holy living

We have seen how in Exodus and Deuteronomy the *ger* is treated to the same impartiality in law as the citizen and how in Deuteronomy in particular the *ger* is singled out for humane provision in straitened circumstances along with the fatherless child and the widow. There is a strong relational emphasis in Deuteronomy in particular; the landowner, following the example of YHWH, is to love the *ger*.

In the Holiness Code (Lev. 17–26) and priestly writings, we change perspective. In these, we find provisions which are addressed to the community as a whole – Israelites and *gerim* together. They take the integration of persons of non-Jewish origin for granted (Ramirez Kidd 1999: 69). Both native and *ger* are required to rest on the Day of Atonement (Lev. 16.29), and both have a right to make use of cities of refuge (Num. 35.15; cf. Deut. 19). And if the *ger* observes certain Jewish cultic practices, he is regarded as a "native of the land". Neither he nor his Jewish brother are to eat leaven for the seven days of Passover (Exod. 12.19), and if the *ger* then wishes to celebrate the feast, he may do so as long as he and the males in his family are circumcised (Exod. 12.47–48). The injunction concludes: "there shall be one law for the native and for the *ger* who resides among you" (Exod. 12.49; cf. Num. 9.14; 15.15–16; Lev. 24.22). Some read this statement as "a general principle applicable to all rules for all time" (Houten 1991: 150, 156), marking the fact that the *ger* is fully integrated into the community of Israel, but Jacob Milgrom (2000: 1496) argues more cautiously that the references are to be taken on a case-by-case basis and do not necessarily mean that the *ger* is yet fully integrated into civil and religious matters.

There is a desire to secure cultural and religious identity by attempting to define the rules which preserve the holiness of the land and Israel's identity as a people of YHWH. To violate these leads to pollution both of the sanctuary and of the land, for the land belongs to YHWH (Lev. 25.23). Consequently, there are sanctions. Neither citizen nor *ger* is to commit abominations – in either case, the perpetrator will be "vomited out" by the land (Exod. 18.26). Both the Israelites and "the *ger* residing amongst them" come under the same legislation for atonement when they have erred unwittingly, and both alike, in the case of deliberate fault, are liable to be "cut off from the people" (Num. 15.29–30). Israelite and *ger* alike are subject to regulations as to the sacrificial offering (Lev. 17.8; 22.18), and both are subject to the prohibition against eating blood (Lev. 17.10–13). The priestly tradition allows for purification by Israelite and *ger* in the event of the eating of carrion (Lev. 17.10–16) or of corpse impurity (Num. 20.10). Under penalty of death, neither Israelite nor *ger* is to sacrifice a child to Molech (Lev. 20.2) or, as exemplified by an interesting case, "blaspheme the Name" (Lev. 24.16). No person, whether or not they are of full Israelite parentage, whether he or she be a *ger* or a citizen, may use disparagingly the revealed name of YHWH; for this offence, justice is presented in both religious and secular terms. The offender is brought to Moses and imprisoned until the will of YHWH is clear. Then the sentence is reiterated three times. He is taken outside the camp and stoned to death, and it is emphasized once more that the prohibition applies equally to citizen and *ger* alike (Lev. 24.22). This case exemplifies the awareness in the Holiness Code of the active role played by human beings in their relationship with YHWH (Milgrom 2000: 2145). The administration of law sustains YHWH's close relationship with Israel: "only through the ongoing, dynamic interweaving of YHWH's law with Israel's story can Israel assure itself of a meaningful future" (Milgrom 2000: 2145).

Although the *ger* is bracketed with the poor and landless, dependent and living in the household of a landowner (Lev. 25.35), at least in theory, he may prosper. The day may come when he acquires wealth and slaves (Lev. 25.47). We should acknowledge that in Lev. 25.45 landowners are permitted to acquire *gerim* as slaves. But the very fact that this is the only place in the Torah where the *ger* is to be treated in a different manner to the Israelite underscores the generally egalitarian nature of the relationship.

The cities of refuge

There is no reference to the provision of asylum in the documents of the Ancient Near East. The Biblical accounts of the cities of refuge relate to fugitive homicides. The stipulations in Exod. 21.12–17 show undifferentiated liability: a murderer, a man who strikes or insults his father or mother, a kidnapper – all shall be put to death. But the qualifications in vv. 13, 14, and 16 hint at the beginnings of a more nuanced jurisdiction. A homicide may under certain circumstances find sanctuary. The "place" to which the murderer can flee is not detailed, but the "altar" is specified at v. 14. This may mark the beginnings of a change from the concept of asylum at the altar to the concept of asylum in the city (Hagedorn 2014). In Deuteronomy, where the chief concern is to protect the killer from the avenger of blood, the reference is clearly to the city. Cities of refuge are appointed so that fugitives, who are accused of homicide, "might flee there and live" (Deut. 19.4), safe from "the avenger". Distinction is made between premeditated and accidental homicide as grounds for asylum. Joshua elaborates further: the slayer is to "stand at the entrance of the gate of the city, and explain the case to the elders of that city; then the fugitive shall be taken into the city and given a place" (Josh. 20.4). The six cities are "designated for all the Israelites, and for the *gerim* residing among them, that anyone who killed a person without intent could flee there" (Josh. 20.9) pending "trial before the congregation" (Num. 35.12). The cities of refuge provide a "pause" to permit due process for Israelite and *ger* alike. Individuals accused of murder are protected from those who are seeking rough justice; their cases are heard, and justice is seen to be done.

The cities of refuge may appear utopian, but some things are clear. They are an integral part of the just society ordered by YHWH, where the vulnerable are protected and treated with equity. The spaces involved are not "states of exception"; the Israelites have jurisdiction over them. Nor could those who take refuge there be said to exemplify "bare life" (see p. 52). Israelite and *ger* have equal access to the law; their cases are heard and judged justly. These provisions can still challenge us today (Marfleet 2011).

The narratives

How do the law books relate to the narratives? What light do they shed on one another? The Torah is an integral part of the narrative account of the wandering of the Israelites with Moses in the wilderness. This is not law in the sense that we understand it today, namely, legislation intended to be applied by the courts. It is neither precise enough nor comprehensive enough for this, and it often warns of the judgement of God rather than of human beings: "The purpose of the written torah text is to teach the people what God requires of them … Its function is to teach them how they should behave, to develop a moral conscience, to teach them the essentials of their religion, and to create a sense of community. Slavish adherence to the letter of the law was not required" (Houston 2013: 60). The Torah, then, presents a vision of the way people ought to live their lives: they are to live up to ethical ideals. The same principle undergirds the narratives. For Gordon Wenham, the Bible narrators work with "an ideal of godly behaviour that they hoped their heroes and heroines would typify" (2000: 3). If so, the attainment of this ideal is erratic. Most characters in the narratives have a mix of virtues and vices. The original readers would have been able to identify with them easily enough; so too can readers of today, for despite differences of context, these characters remain convincing as human beings. Through storytelling, we come to understand what it is to be human (Barton 2003). John Barton helpfully builds upon Wenham's argument. He suggests, following Martha Nussbaum, that the aim of the narratives is not to develop moral qualities by encouraging the reader to follow the example of Biblical characters, but to grow ethical perception through entering the complexity of a particular situation. Although God is absent from many of the narratives, the reader is nonetheless aware of the divine perspective; when things are not as they should be, either in the Bible or in our world, he or she is aware of that. God, if present at all, is hidden behind processes of human history, but in these we also discern the outworking of divine promise and blessings.

Flight from danger to a place of safety is part of the human predicament. The narrative, non-legal texts of the Bible testify to the existence and plight of refugees in the Levant over a long period of time; people who are forced to leave their homes for specified reasons, usually connected with famine or drought, war, political danger, or personal threat. These are described in realistic terms. Typically, they have names and a voice. They are set in a specific context. They are forced to flee to another country where they usually receive protection. While there is some indication of long-term settlement (2 Sam. 4.3) and the formation of refugee communities abroad (Jer. 29; 40.11; 42–44; 2 Kgs 25.26), it is clear that many choose to return when the danger is past, sometimes after many years (Jer. 40.11–12).

Famine

Famine is a major precipitating factor. Because of famine, Abraham and his family are forced to leave Canaan for Egypt (Gen. 12.10); Isaac in like circumstances settles in Gerar in Philistine territory (Gen. 26.1–2), while Jacob and his sons also seek refuge in Egypt (Gen. 47.4–5). It is famine that drives

Elimelech and his family to leave Bethlehem for Moab (Ruth 1.1) and drought that drives Elijah by stages to Zarephath in Sidon (1 Kgs 17).

War

Individuals or groups of people flee because they are caught up in war or implicated in dangerous political situations. In the aftermath of the war between coalitions of kings, the kings of Sodom and Gomorrah flee to the hill country (Gen. 14.10). Seventy of Jotham's brothers have been massacred on the instigation of their brother, Abimelech, in an effort to secure his claim to the throne; Jotham flees to Beer, where he remains for fear of Abimelech (Judg. 9.21). David flees from Saul to King Achish of Gath (1 Sam. 21.10) and then, in fear of Achish, escapes to the cave of Adullam, where he is joined by a motley crew of malcontents, some of whom are seeking asylum on account of debt (1 Sam. 22.1–2). Hadad, an Edomite, later viewed as a threat to Solomon, flees as a child to Egypt in order to escape the slaughter of Edomites by David and Joab. The Pharaoh of the time gives him generous hospitality; on learning of the deaths of David and Joab, Hadad subsequently returns to Edom (1 Kgs 1.14–18). When Jeroboam rebels against Solomon, he is forced to flee for his life to King Shishak of Egypt, who gives him sanctuary until the death of Solomon makes it safe for him to return (1 Kgs 11.40).

Sometimes, too, people are compelled to flee for religious reasons. 1 Kgs 18.4 tells how, when Jezebel was killing off the prophets of YHWH, Obadiah hid one hundred of them in two caves, fifty to a cave, and supplied them with bread and water.

The narratives convey the difficulty involved in making decisions where the people involved are not in control of their circumstances. War and civil unrest cause population displacement. In Jer. 42–44, we read of the regrouping of remnants of the Judaean community following Gedaliah's assassination. They are tottering on the brink of annihilation. They fear retaliation by Babylon. Should they risk staying in Judah? Should they flee to Egypt? Jeremiah's prophetic word is unambiguous. If they stay in Judah, they will have a future, unlikely as that seems. Flight to Egypt would be fatal. In Egypt, "they shall die by the sword and by famine". There will be no survivors. But they decide to ignore his advice, and Jeremiah himself is taken with them into Egypt. Certainly in this instance, Jeremiah got it wrong; whereas Jer. 44.27 envisages total annihilation of the "people of Judah who are in the land of Egypt". Jer. 44.28, presumably a later editorial addition to the text in the light of historical experience (Carroll 1986: 743), foresees a time when "those who escape the sword shall return ... to the land of Judah" (cf. Lam. 4.15).

A story may convey graphically the awful urgency of the need to flee pending disaster and the uncertainty of those involved. In Gen. 19.12–22, Sodom is about to be destroyed: the messengers give Lot advance warning of imminent catastrophe and urge haste. Lot makes an attempt to mobilize his family, but his sons-in-law think he is joking. He dallies until the next morning, uncertain of what to do. But the messengers insist: "Get up, take your wife and your two daughters" (Gen. 19.15) … "Flee for your life, do not look back or stop … flee to the hills" (Gen. 19.17). There is no time to lose. They seize him and lead him out of the city. And "fire and brimstone" rain down on Sodom (Gen. 19.24).

Moral tensions of the ancestral family

The narrative texts in the Old Testament allow the reader to develop an understanding of human behaviour that is responsive to actual situations. The narrators do not comment on what is happening; they usually leave events to speak for themselves. But they do leave us with a pretty clear sense of whether a specific way of behaving is good or bad. They raise moral issues that are not dealt with in the legal texts, issues which arise from the complexities of human conduct and motivation (Barton 2003: 172). This is particularly evident in the patriarchal narratives.

The curious narrative trio Gen. 12.10–20; 20.1–18; 26.6–11 shows us how Abraham and Isaac behave in ways that are morally reprehensible, when as refugees they are in fear for their lives. The relationship of the three variants to one another is not clear. While commentators disagree as to which of these is the oldest, some (e.g. von Rad 1961) favouring Gen. 26.6–11 and others (e.g. Westermann 1985) favouring Gen. 12.10–20, the fact that these stories are told three times in distinct settings has to indicate that they were held to be significant, probably sustained in oral tradition (Van Seters 1975: 168–183).

In Gen. 12.10–20, Abram is fleeing a "severe" famine in Canaan. On the borders of Egypt, he fears that in Egypt he may be exposed to other risks; his fears may or may not be well founded (Wenham 1991: 268), but he clearly thinks he may be murdered because his wife is irresistibly beautiful. So Sarai is to be introduced as his sister. The plan backfires; Sarai is taken into Pharaoh's house; and Pharaoh discovers her true identity and has an angry face-to face confrontation with Abram, who is ignominiously sent on his way. Here, Pharaoh has the moral high ground. Considering that Abram's dishonesty has led to Pharaoh's adultery, he is lucky to escape with deportation and with vast wealth!

In Gen. 20.1–18, Abraham, "residing in Gerar as an alien", puts it about that Sarah is his sister. The story, however, has a new twist. King Abimelech takes her, but is warned in time in a dream that she is Abraham's wife. There is an angry and sorrowful exchange where Abraham justifies himself, almost as if he were answering the questions raised in Gen. 12.10–20, and is handsomely vindicated by Abimelech (Westermann 1985: 319).

In Gen. 26.6–11, a later famine causes Isaac to take refuge in Gerar. He misleads his hosts in much the same way as Abraham. He too is afraid that he might die because of his wife's beauty. He tells the "men of the place" that Rebekah, his wife, is his sister. No-one commits adultery. King Abimelech discovers by chance that she is Isaac's wife and reproaches Isaac angrily. His behaviour has brought the people into a dangerous situation. The King decrees that anyone who molests Isaac or Rebekah will be put to death, and Isaac prospers in the land.

The three narratives have the same basic storyline. Two men, fleeing famine, settle in a foreign country. They are each afraid of what will happen to them in their new context and use their wives as shields, claiming that they are their sisters. In each case, there are unintended consequences. The beauty of the women attracts the attention of the ruler of the land. When the truth is revealed, their husbands are exposed angrily and either deported immediately or, duly chastened, afforded protection so that they prosper in the land. Although neither woman has anything to say, their silence would seem to indicate complicity. After all, Sarah shows herself well able to overrule Abraham when she so desires (Gen. 21.8–15), and Rebekah can be dexterous in her deception (Gen. 27). Be that as it may, in none of these instances does Abraham or Isaac act honestly. Indeed, where the plan led Pharaoh unwittingly to commit adultery, Abram's behaviour is rightly seen as criminal. These foreign rulers know the law; they call the offenders to account. But they know too how to treat a sojourner in their land (Hoop 2001: 368). In each case, they deal with him justly. But these stories also illustrate a real ethical dilemma. To what extent might a person who is in fear for his or her life be justified in practicing deception in order to survive? How under such circumstances does a righteous ruler judge rightly?

Ruth, the Moabite: source of new life and blessing

The Book of Ruth illustrates the just and righteous behaviour, not this time of a ruler, but of a community towards a foreign widow. Most people would agree that the book is to be read as a short story (Campbell 1974); this allows for an interest in typical or ordinary people, dialogue, and a depth of purpose highlighted by literary artistry. On that basis, it has been further defined as a comedy (Trible 1982), a subversive parable (Lacocque 1990), and a legal legend (Daube 2003), and it has been interpreted along formalist lines as "folkloristic" (Sasson 1979). But if it is folkloristic, can we read it as a legal legend? Questions of genre matter because they determine what questions may properly be asked of the text (Larkin 1996). I propose in what follows to treat Ruth as a short story where the narrator draws on elements of folklore and makes allusions to customary legal provisions for the marginalized as a narrative device. The story is rooted in the world view of Deuteronomy, but the narrative transcends its setting. There is a particularity about the struggle for survival in a world marked by famine, death, patriarchy, and xenophobia (Trible 1976).

Most commentators now agree that it is impossible to date the book with any degree of certainty, and I do not propose to discuss the issue here. The opening phrase "in the time of the judges" (Ruth 1.1) is too imprecise to be more than a narrative claim to historicity.

Why Moab?

In the first few words of the book, we are plunged directly into the narrative of a family on the move; a man, his wife, and two sons are forced by widespread famine in Judah to migrate. But this is by no means a straightforward account of displaced people and their fortunes at a specific period in history. Twice in the first two verses, we are told that Elimelech and his family went into the country of Moab and remained there. The emphasis is clear. The author intends us to take note. The fact that they went to Moab has to be significant. But why?

In many respects, such a family would have felt at home. We know from King Mesha's inscription (ANET 320–321) that the inhabitants of Moab spoke and wrote a language that was very close to Hebrew and that there was a sanctuary to YHWH in Nebo. The inscription suggests in general that in the 9th century BCE Moabites lived in a state of material wealth, civilization, and culture, with a ruler who was just as capable of organizing and consolidating his kingdom as any contemporary monarch of Israel or Judah. Certainly, in fleeing to Moab, the family is breaking with tradition. According to Biblical convention, Egypt was the primary destination for Israelites who were "hungry for bread" (Jer. 42.14; cf. Gen. 12.10; 42.3–5). Yet there, on the other side of the Salt Sea, the family settles for around ten years.

The author makes no comment. But the relentless emphasis on the name invites us to consider Moab in a wider Biblical perspective. That perspective is consistently hostile. Moab was repugnant in the eyes of Israel. Its origins are recorded in a scurrilous etiological legend (Gen. 19). There is a long history of enmity between the two kingdoms. Sometimes one had the upper hand, sometimes the other. Israel held Moab in subjection for forty years following its conquest by Omri, exacting annually an enormous tribute of wool (2 Kgs 3.4; cf. Isa. 16.1) until the middle of Ahab's reign, when Mesha led a successful revolt (Driver 1890: lxxxv–xciv; 2 Kgs 3). It is recorded (Num. 22–24) that in extremity King Balak of Moab hired a prophet to curse the Israelites, but that YHWH intervened to turn the prophet's cursing into blessing.

Moab is the last place you would expect an Israelite to regard as providing sanctuary (Spina 2005: 121). By repute, Moabites were callous and hard-hearted; they had given no food or water to the straggling Israelites in the desert (Deut. 23.4). But were the Israelites any more hospitably disposed towards them? In Isa. 15–16, in the general context of anti-Moabite propaganda, there is a graphic evocation of the refusal of the inhabitants of Judah to give asylum to Moabite refugees. Against a background of devastation and disaster, the daughters of Moab are "like fluttering birds, like scattered nestlings at the fords of the Arnon" (Isa. 16.2). They need protection. Isa. 16.1–4a appears to describe a Moabite embassy to Jerusalem requesting asylum for the refugees. The language of the plea describes the ideal situation: "Give counsel, grant justice, make your shade like night at the height of noon; hide the outcasts, do not betray the fugitive; let the outcasts of Moab settle among you; be a refuge to them from the destroyer" (Isa. 16.3–4a). But the plea for humanitarian protection is refused (Isa. 16.7a), and the reader is told that "when Moab presents himself … he will not prevail" (Isa. 16.12). The grounds for refusal is Moab's "arrogance, pride and insolence" (Isa. 16.6). Though historical details are obscure, the language stereotypical, and the literary structure unclear (Childs 2001: 131–132), in these chapters there emerges a vivid picture of Moabite refugees in flight from devastation, seeking asylum in Judah and having their request for protection refused.

The narrative of the Book of Ruth, then, is played out in the wider context of the deep-rooted mutual animosity between Israelites and Moabites, and Israel's stereotypical attitudes towards the inhabitants of Moab. Yet, even in these highly unpromising circumstances, a "daughter of Moab" finds the security of a new life in Judah.

Why does Ruth "return"?

Elimelech and his family do not thrive in Moab. Elimelech dies, leaving his wife Naomi a widow with two sons. The names of the young men are inauspicious: Mahlon and Chilion, "Weakening and Pining" (Sasson 1979: 18–19). After their father's death, they marry Moabite women and also die childless. Naomi, now bereft of husband, sons, and prospects of grandchildren, is left alone, a sojourner in Moab, isolated from any family she may have in Israel. She sees in this "the hand of the LORD" (Ruth 1.13; 20–21). The Almighty has dealt bitterly with her. The narrative is sparse; no reasons are offered. Mahlon and Chilion had Moabite wives; did they also worship Chemosh? Speculation is fruitless. Whatever happened, about ten years after this little family settles in Moab, only Naomi is left to lament.

While Naomi is in Moab, she hears that "the LORD had considered his people and given them food" (Ruth 1.6). The famine in Israel is now over. She sets off to return to Bethlehem. The idea of "return" is crucial: the verb *shub* is reiterated twelve times in the first chapter with dramatic effect (Ruth 1.6, 7, 8, 10, 11, 12, 15, 16, 21, 22; cf. 2.6; 4.3). And the narrative begins a dynamic movement from death to life, from curse to blessing (Trible 1978: 166). Naomi is not alone. She is accompanied by her daughters-in-law – all three set off "on their way to go back" (Ruth 1.7) to the Land of Judah. But choices have to be made by Orpah and Ruth. They are, after all, Moabites. Still on Moabite territory, Naomi urges the two young women to "go back" to their mothers' homes, kisses them farewell, and calls down YHWH's blessing on them. They refuse to return. Three times, with passion and eloquence, Naomi insists, pointing out that their prospects in Israel are far from promising (Spina 2005: 123). Finally, Orpah tearfully kisses her mother-in-law farewell and returns "to her people and to her gods" (Ruth 1.15). But Ruth stands her ground and in a "stupendous expression of loyalty and love" (Ozick 1993: 208) cleaves not only to Naomi, whom she "loves" (Ruth 4.15), but also to her people and her God (Ruth 1.16–17). It is a dramatic crux in the narrative.

"To love" and "to cling" is the language of personal affection and loyalty. But when these words are used of a person's relationship with YHWH, they herald new life (Deut. 30.20). Ruth's words resonate with Moses' final appeal to the Israelites assembled on the Plain of Moab. YHWH has allowed other nations to chastize them; the curses of chapter twenty-eight have come about; but these need not be the end. Fortunes can be reversed. The verb *shub* is crucially important in Deut. 30.1–10; both YHWH and Israel "return", but it is Israel who turns first (Nelson 2002: 347). If the Israelites make a sincere return to YHWH in complete obedience, then YHWH will, in his compassion, turn everything around for them. The need for Israel to "return" is absolute, so too is YHWH's compassion. His compassion extends to every single person who has been driven from their home (Deut. 30.4). Loving YHWH and obeying will become second nature, and the ensuing blessings will lead to enduring new life (Deut. 30.6–10). Moses' culminating appeal to "choose life" is the high point of Deuteronomy and brings that life within the grasp of future generations (McConville 2002).

Will something similar happen in the case of Ruth? The scene is now set for the "return" of the two women to Bethlehem, though there is no reason to suppose that Ruth has ever been to Bethlehem before; a foreigner, she has come to live among Israelites. On arrival, Naomi is welcomed by her fellow townswomen who listen to her lament: a silent Ruth is greeted with silence. But just as the silence is being filled with suspicion, if not xenophobia (Gitay 1993: 182), Ruth is designated by the narrator not just as the Moabite, but as "Naomi's daughter-in-law who came back with her from the country of Moab" (Ruth 1.22; cf. 2.6). Ruth has clung to Naomi as a daughter to her own mother; this is affirmed in their return together to Bethlehem, and the Moabite is now seen to be integrated into Naomi's family. This is underlined by Naomi when she describes Boaz as "a relative of ours, one of our nearest kin" (Ruth 2.20). The two women lack food, husbands, and children, and the household faces a hard struggle for survival, but through the "Moabite who came back with her", Naomi finds new life.

The legal background: the sojourner

Given the many resonances between Ruth's situation and that of the sojourner in Israelite law, it is suggestive that (against Spina 2005: 127; Spencer 2004: 87; and Burnside 2001: 14) the *ger* is not mentioned. The noun does not occur in the Book of Ruth (Ramirez Kidd 1999: 24). It is not used of Elimelech and his family during their time in Moab: the term is not used of Israelites who emigrate. But neither is it used to designate Ruth when she comes from Moab to sojourn in Bethlehem: the term *ger* is restricted to men, and Ruth describes herself accurately as *nokriyah* (Ruth 2.10), a non-Israelite. Only with the *ger* does Israel enter into formal mutual relationships.

What may we deduce from this? We may choose to dismiss the provisions for the *ger* as irrelevant to Ruth; but we should not do that too hastily (Awabdy 2014: 81–83), for we may not forget that the legal obligations exemplify the ethical and moral ethos of the Israelites, chief amongst which has to be the protection of the vulnerable in the community: the *ger*, the fatherless child, and the widow. The widow faces a hard life. If she does not return to her parental home (Gen. 38.11), if levirate marriage is not possible, or if she has no son (2 Sam. 14.5–7), her prospects are bleak; she may be subject to oppression (Job 24.3, 9); and destitution is all too real a possibility (Job 24.5–12). We would expect problems to be compounded if she is a foreigner. But from the time Ruth arrives in Bethlehem with Naomi, she is gradually incorporated into the community. There is a decreasing emphasis on her foreignness. There are no references to her as a Moabite in chapter three and in chapter four; such references are only in the context of legal process. She is regarded by Naomi as family. With this incorporation into the community comes the consciousness that here in their midst is a widow in need of statutory protection. Whose consciousness are we talking about? In one obvious sense, that of the protagonists in the narrative as evoked by the author. But there is also the consciousness of the first hearers of the story and the consciousness of readers down to the present day. Through the narrative skill of the author, we too respond to Ruth in all her precariousness.

The legal background: gleaning

It was, we are told, the beginning of the barley harvest. The famine is over. And for the two widows, this marks a movement from lack to provision, from affliction to blessing. They are aware (Ruth 2.2) of the custom in Israel for landowners to leave a portion of the harvest crop in the corners of the fields. The gleaning provision probably reflects old agrarian customs (Milgrom 2000: 1627) whereby a portion of the harvest was left behind as an offering to gods of fertility (Ramirez Kidd 1999: 43, n.39), although the claim that this was "a votary offering to chthonic spirits in the hope of their beneficence during harvest time" (Fishbane 1985: 279, n.21) has to be speculative. In Deuteronomy, the custom is preserved and given a new meaning (Deut. 24.19–22; cf. Lev. 19.9–10; 23.22). It is now seen as an offering to YHWH in the persons of the "marginal triad" (Buis & Leclerq 1963: 163). This understanding is so well established that gleaning comes to be perceived as the special prerogative of the needy (Ruth 2) that should be distinguished from the legal right of all citizens to have access to grain in the fields (Deut. 23.25). When Ruth begins to glean, her entitlement is unchallenged by the workers, who see her as a Moabite who has come to live in Israel (Ruth 2.6); she describes herself as a "foreigner", and Boaz knows her to be a widow with neither father nor mother in Israel. The corn which she takes away is her due. But to see gleaning exclusively as a right is to miss the point. At harvest, landowners are exhorted to remember their obligation to the landless by making provision for them to glean on their fields. This provision is not almsgiving, it is seen as a service to fellow members of God's people. Making provision for gleaning is a religious and ethical duty, a reminder for those like Boaz who understand themselves to be blessed by YHWH that blessing is to be shared.

The emphasis on blessing now increases incrementally. Boaz knows of Ruth's kindness to Naomi and blesses her in the name of "the LORD, the God of Israel, under whose wings [she has] come for refuge" (Ruth 2.12). He instructs his young men not to touch her and invites her to drink water whenever she is thirsty (Ruth 2.9). He gives her food at mealtime along with his reapers and gives instructions to his workers that are designed to benefit Ruth in ways which are well beyond what is required of him (Ruth 2.14–17; cf. Deut. 24.19). So he continues to provide for Ruth and Naomi with overflowing generosity until the end of the wheat harvest.

But what happens to the widow and fatherless child when harvests come to an end and they are no longer able to glean for food? In a paternalistic social system, they need male protection.

The legal background: the go'el *and the* levir

Although Ruth is not a juridical document (Sasson 1979: 228), some would argue that we can deduce from this book information as to Israel's legal system, which is not attested anywhere else (Hubbard 1988: 48–63). For others, "this is a moot point" (Larkin 1996: 29). References to the law may be nothing more than a narrative device.

There are certainly points of connection with the law, parallels in vocabulary and motifs, but there are also a number of discrepancies. As early as the Targum, the issue of levirate marriage (Deut. 25.5–10) has been associated with Ruth 4 (Sasson 1979: 125). According to Deuteronomy, the law of levirate marriage obliges an Israelite to marry his dead brother's wife if she has not borne a son; she may not marry a stranger. The aim of this is to secure the family line: the first son of the marriage will perpetuate the "name" of the dead man in Israel. The surviving brother's responsibility is not mandatory (as in Gen. 38), and the sole available penalty is public humiliation (Deut. 25.8–10).

It is obvious that the precise conditions for levirate marriage do not obtain in Ruth. Chilion and Mahlon are both dead, Naomi has "no more sons" (Ruth 1.8–14), and Ruth is under no legal obligation to marry any Bethlehemite. Boaz recognizes that, where marriage is concerned, she is a free agent: although she might have "gone after young men, whether poor or rich" (Ruth 3.10), she comes to him. The comparison between Ruth and the provisions for levirate marriage in Deuteronomy is fraught with incongruities. But can we "exorcise the ghosts of leviracy from Ruth" so quickly (Sasson 1978)? At Ruth 4.10, Boaz clearly states the purpose of his marriage in terms of Deut. 25.6; he calls the elders to witness that he is "to maintain the dead man's name on his inheritance, in order that the name of the dead may not be cut off from his kindred". Perpetuation of the name of the dead is clearly linked to the issue of inheritance (cf. Num. 27.4), and in Ruth the issue of redemption of inherited land is a main feature of the plot. So we find fragments of the *levir* tradition interwoven with the *go'el*/redeemer tradition. According to this, if poverty forces you to sell your land, your relations are bound to redeem it to satisfy your creditor (Lev. 25.25–28). If you are ruined to that extent, the chances of recovery by your own efforts are slim. Your only hope would be that relatives would help you out (Daube 2003: 64). Naomi, a widow without any surviving sons, is in obvious need of a *go'el* to come to the rescue. The anonymous Mr So and So at Ruth 4.4 would probably have served as well as any other.

But the intervention of Boaz in the constitutional assembly by the gate confuses the issue, intermingling as it does allusions to the institutions of *go'el*, marriage, and redemption of a widow's land. We have already learned from Naomi's revelation to Ruth that Boaz is more than an ordinary benefactor – he is a relative of Elimelech's, a possible *go'el* (Ruth 2.20). We have seen how, at the end of the harvest season, Naomi outlined a plan by which she and Ruth were to find security. And we have noted that, in the great scene on the threshing floor, Ruth introduced herself as Boaz's "handmaid" and asked him to spread his cloak over her because he is a *go'el* (Ruth 3.9). As D.R.G. Beattie points out, the precision of statement expected of a legal textbook is not expected in a fictional narrative; Ruth may not be using the term *go'el* in a technical sense. But in the skillful interweaving of motifs, the author makes "Ruth offer herself to Boaz in return for his kindness, and in the same words, ask for protection on the basis of his kinship" (Beattie 1978b). We remember how, evoking the name of YHWH, Boaz then made a solemn promise to protect her and how he then sprung a surprise; there is another man, more closely related, who has to have first refusal. In the dramatic dénouement before the elders at the gate, Boaz reveals that the impoverished Naomi has some land that she wants to have redeemed (cf. Lev. 25.25; Jer. 32.6–13). The timing is right – the barley and wheat harvests are both over, and so any crops will now have been harvested. Naomi's nearer kinsman, Mr So and So, eagerly accepts to do so. Boaz then springs his trap, declaring that with the land goes "Ruth the Moabite, the widow of the dead man, to maintain the dead man's name on his inheritance" (Ruth 4.5). Faced with this unappealing prospect, Mr So and So, whose very name is dismissive, surrenders his rights of redemption and, possibly in oblique reference to the practice described in Deut. 25.8–10, confirms this by exchanging shoes with Boaz. Boaz then testifies before the assembled elders that he will become Naomi's *go'el* and marry Ruth "to maintain the dead man's name on his inheritance" (Ruth 4.9–10). The elders and witnesses "provide David's ancestor with a blessing worthy of a dynast" (Sasson 1979: 229).

But why does Mr So and So lose interest in the transaction so quickly, when Ruth's name is mentioned? This question appears to hinge on a syntactical crux which has been much debated. There are two variant versions of Ruth 4.5.

In the reading that is generally favoured, we find the second person singular of the verb: "you have bought". According to this, Boaz tells the next of kin that Naomi's land is available and the man agrees to buy it. But when told he must also take Ruth as well, he refuses. This is difficult to understand. In the alternative reading, we have the first person singular of the verb: "I have bought". With this reading, the meaning becomes intelligible (see Sasson 1979: 125–131; Beattie 1978a). Boaz confirms that he has become engaged to marry Ruth, and the next of kin would be very likely to assume that there might be an heir to Elimelech's remaining land. It would, under such circumstances, not be worth his while to continue with the purchase of the land.

Although in chapter four there appears to be an authoritative legal tradition in operation which was generally understood (Houten 1991: 30), there is no indication that what we have here is legislation intended, in the present-day sense, to be interpreted and applied by the courts. In the complex interweaving of the motifs of the next of kin, marriage, and the redemption of the land (Becking & Wetter 2013), any connections there might have been with the written provisions for the *levir* and the *go'el* are obscured or lost. None of the protagonists, Boaz, Mr So and So, and the elders at the gate, refers to any specific regulations, and the elders make no attempt to clarify the obfuscations. It is simply impossible to tell from Ruth what relationship there might have been between these written laws and legal practice (Houten 1991: 31). It has to be assumed that the court came to its decision according to traditional custom.

Why Obed?

The two women find personal security. Boaz assumes a kinsman's responsibility for Naomi and takes Ruth to be his wife. Naomi is blessed and her life restored. Ruth, no longer described as a Moabite, is "more to Naomi than seven sons" (Ruth 4.15b); the son whom she bears to Boaz is, as a surrogate, seen as assuring Naomi's future.

But the story is also played out against a wider horizon. In a chorus of ecstasy, the women of Bethlehem bless YHWH (Ruth 4.14–17); the God of Israel has been faithful to the woman who clove to him on the road from Moab to Bethlehem. They name the child Obed. The choice of name is significant. It resonates with the term *'ebed*. First, Deut. 23:16–17 makes the point that an *'ebed* who has escaped from his owner and seeks sanctuary amongst the Israelites is to be treated with humanity. The refugee is described as "slave" or "servant"; he is likely to be a foreigner rather than an Israelite (the word is avoided in the law of slave release up to Deut. 15.17). And he has permission to reside "in any of your cities", that is, he is free to live anywhere in the land (McConville 2002). This is highly unusual. Deuteronomy's law is unique in the Ancient Near East. Whereas vassal treaties require the giving up of political fugitives from the suzerain, and the Code of Hammurabi requires the return of fugitive slaves under penalty of death (Richardson 2000), here there is to be no *refoulement*. The refugee is not to be "oppressed" (cf. Exod. 22:20; Lev. 19.33), a provision not found elsewhere in Deuteronomy. No-one is to exploit the slave's precarious position and thus reduce him again to slavery (von Rad 1964; Nelson 2002). The "oppression" of the refugee that is forbidden here is like the oppression of weak Israelites by the rich and powerful. The force of the text is theological – the slave is to imitate YHWH in the free choice of a "place" and live fully integrated in Israel's midst ("among you"), just as YHWH does (Deut. 6.15; 7.21) (Nelson 2002).

This brings us to the second layer of resonance. The Hebrew term *'ebed* may also imply that this is a person of high status, subordinate to a master (cf. 1 Kgs 11.17, 23, 26); the noun *'ebed* can designate kings and their officials, who are perceived to be "servants" of YHWH (Sasson 1979: 177). In naming the baby Obed, the women are affirming that YHWH has assured not only the future of two vulnerable widows, but also the future of the people of Judah: as we are reminded in the genealogy (Ruth 4.18–22), Obed is to be the grandfather of King David and hence an ancestor of Jesus (Mt. 1.5; Lk. 3.32).

And third, as the birth of Obed assures the future of the people of Israel, the name stands as a reminder for generations yet to come of the injunction in Deuteronomy to "remember that you were a slave (*'ebed*) in the land of Egypt" (Deut. 24.18, 22). In these verses, the noun *'ebed* is used to accompany the commands to care for the "marginal triad" (Ramirez Kidd 1999: 80). The associations are clear. In naming the baby Obed, the women of Bethlehem are not only reinforcing the command to give humanitarian protection to the runaway slave who is seeking sanctuary in Israel, they are also affirming the ethical and religious obligation of Israelites present and future to care for the alien, the fatherless child, and the widow.

The Book of Ruth is a rich and multilayered narrative. At one level, it features a range of people on the move to a new homeland; it testifies to the difficulties of the ethical choices and tactical decisions people have to make in order to survive in lands other than their own. It hints at negative stereotypes of foreigners, especially foreigners from a particular country. But we are never allowed to forget that all this is set in the context of the providential power of YHWH. Religious and ethical duties are consonant with one another. Boaz, blessed by YHWH with land and wealth, shares that blessing with two impoverished widows; as a relative by marriage, he gives them security, and Ruth, the Moabite immigrant who cleaves to Naomi, her country, and her God, is a source of new life and blessing for them all.

Concluding remarks

In the law books, the people are told by Moses to love the sojourner and provide for him: he is not to be oppressed; he is to be treated well. This is especially important for the Israelites because they know from bitter experience what it feels like to be sojourners. This collective memory is part of their national identity. Concern for the sojourner is also part of a wider ethical vision that embraces widows, fatherless children, and the poor. Care for the sojourner may not be detached from other categories of social need. The narratives put flesh on these prescriptions: the Book of Ruth shows how religious and ethical duties towards the stranger are consistent with one another and how an immigrant, even from Moab, may be a source of blessing.

5

HOW TO SING THE LORD'S SONG IN A STRANGE LAND?

The two major Biblical sagas, the Exodus and the Exile, can be seen as exercises in collective memory. They give a vivid impression of oppression and its effects, both political and personal. The Exodus narrative invites solidarity with the oppressed. But when those who were formerly oppressed become oppressors, are their victims excluded from moral concern? The physical, psychological, and spiritual trauma suffered especially by women in warfare is evoked in poetry and prophecy. The suffering of forced migration and the challenges of resettlement have obvious human resonance with the plight of many refugees and asylum-seekers today.

The Exodus

The story of the Exodus from Egypt has been described as "a paradigm of lasting importance" which "expresses an experience that is closely related to one of the fundamental and lasting human needs, that of freedom and independence" (Iersel & Weiler 1987). It would appear from the narrative that the Israelites in Egypt had a "well-founded fear of being persecuted for reasons of race, religion, or nationality". It hadn't always been so. In Gen. 47, we are told how Joseph's father and brothers fled famine in Canaan to settle in Egypt. For at least a generation afterwards, Israelites and Egyptians seem to have enjoyed a harmonious co-existence. The Israelites were "fruitful and prolific" (Exod. 1.7). They possessed livestock and cattle (Exod. 9.4ff.; 10.9, 24, 26; 12.32). But then the Israelites fell on hard times. A new king, "who did not know Joseph" (Exod. 1.8), persuaded that the Israelites were a potential threat to national security, embarked on a ruthless process of genocidal exploitation. The political and economic independence of the Israelites was smashed in an attempt to transform them into a helot class of workers. They were set to hard forced labour, their lives "made bitter" through building projects and agricultural work (Exod. 1.13–14). Their male children were targeted: every newborn baby boy was to be thrown into the Nile (Exod. 1.22). They were refused time off for religious observance (Exod. 5.2). Their workload became intolerable; they had to produce the same daily quota of bricks while being forced to gather in the fields the straw that was needed to make them (Exod. 5.6–9). When the men could not keep up the supply, their Israelite supervisors were beaten (Exod. 5.14). The narrative describes an attempt, motivated by one man's phobic consciousness, to destroy, cripple, and degrade a whole people.

Reference to the oppression of the Israelites is entrenched in the Old Testament. Egypt is described as a "house of slavery" not just in Exod. 13.3 and 20.2, but also in Deut. 5.6, Josh. 24.17, Judg. 6.8, Jer. 34.13, and Mic. 6.4. Forced labour is regularly alluded to in Deuteronomy (5.15; 15.15; 16.12; 24.18,22). The abusive behaviour of Egypt is referred to at Num. 20.15, 1 Sam. 12.8 (LXX), Neh. 9.9–10 (cf. Exod. 18.11b), and the stay in Egypt was like being in a smelting furnace (Deut. 4.20; 1 Kgs 8.51; Jer. 11.4). Ps. 81.6 speaks of the "burden" on the shoulder and the "basket" in the hands of the Israelites.

And the narrative also describes a spiralling movement of liberation. This is encapsulated in two narratives, in which women play the key roles: Shiphra and Puah, Hebrew mid-wives, refuse to co-operate with state-sponsored oppression (Exod. 1.15–22), and Moses' mother, her daughter, and Pharaoh's daughter consciously subvert Pharaoh's authority (Exod. 2.1–10). In each case, life prevails as the women work with God to bring about deliverance.

God works also through Moses, who had had the experience of being "a *ger* residing in a foreign land", presumably, in his case, in Midian (Exod. 2.22). The Israelites, labouring under slavery, cry out (Exod. 2.23) in sighs and groans like the cry of animals (Meynet 2009). God hears them and calls Moses to bring them out of Egypt. The use of the prophetic call narrative shows that we are intended to see Moses not simply as a social activist, but as a messenger representing God's commitment to Israel's liberation (Exod. 3.10–12). Moses becomes the spokesperson for YHWH's protest and YHWH's resolve to deliver. The plague narratives follow, each with the divine imperative: let my people go! The narrative of the tenth plague is strikingly different – there is the simple announcement of the death of the firstborn of the Egyptians, and the account of the night of passage is starkly brief. Finally, Pharaoh expels the Israelites, and the events at sea, where YHWH's word is spoken and fulfilled, are portrayed as the final act of deliverance from Egypt.

Most scholars today would agree that the stories in Exodus are likely to be based on historical experiences dating from the second half of 2nd millennium, but, given the fact that the only source we have of these events is the Bible, it is impossible to be more precise than that. We have to live with the fact that these are not eyewitness reports and that a historically accurate picture of what happened in Egypt during the Exodus cannot be given (Houtman 1993: 189). The narrative does demonstrate, however, that historical experiences can be written up in such a way as to grip the imagination of the reader while reflecting the faith and experiences of later Israel.

The text has been appropriated and recontextualized over the years in different settings by oppressed and dominated peoples. The story has been a mainstay of Latin American liberation theology; it has inspired Black theology in the US and in Africa. The slaves of the southern plantations expressed their faith and longing in spirituals that continually returned to the theme of Exodus deliverance. Martin Luther King drew inspiration from it. On 17 May 1956, the second anniversary of the decision by the US Supreme Court that stated that segregated schooling was unconstitutional, he preached a sermon on Ex. 14.30, in which he said: "a world-shaking decree by the nine Justices of the United States Supreme Court opened the Red Sea, and the forces of justice are crossing to the other side ... looking back we see the forces of segregation dying on the sea-shore" (Newton 1987: 57–58). The Black deliverance was seen as a mighty act of God. For African Christian theology, too, Exodus has been a dominant Biblical motif since the 1970s. Desmond Tutu, in Panama City in 1989, found in Exod. 3.7–10 assurance of God's acting on behalf of the oppressed (Langston 2006: 69). This has continuing political implications for churches: "taking up the experience of the God of the Exodus today means fighting in his name against all forms of injustice and oppression" (Newton 1987: 130). In the US, for instance, the action of the two mid-wives has set a Biblical precedent for civil disobedience regarding unjust immigration policies. In response to the US government's attempt to seal the southern borders, the Mennonite Central Committee encouraged its congregations to adopt, hire, and otherwise aid immigrants irrespective of their status in law (Langston 2006).

And yet the story of Exodus is profoundly ambiguous. The ambiguity is first of all theological. Here I find Houston's critique of José Miranda persuasive (2008: 204–214). Miranda emphasizes that "whether YHWH acts for Israel or against them he acts against the oppressor and in favour of the oppressed". Careful attention to detail indicates, however, that YHWH's intervention is primarily motivated not so much by response to the "cry" of the oppressed, whoever they happen to be, as by the fact that Israel is "my people" (Exod. 3.10); the text of Exod. 4.22–23 leaves no doubt: "then you shall say to Pharaoh, 'thus says the LORD: Israel is my first-born son. I said to you, "Let my son go that he may worship me". But you refused to let him go; now I will kill your firstborn son'". As Houston points out, the problem arises where YHWH's partisanship for oppressed Israel leads to the oppression of other peoples. This is already implied by the account of the climactic tenth plague, the death of the firstborn in the Land of Egypt where all are affected, from Pharaoh to the maid at the mill (Exod. 11.5) and the prisoner in the dungeon (Exod. 12.29) – although these last characters are more likely to be themselves victims of oppression (Houston 2008: 208). But the question is raised in its most acute form by the brutal ousting of the peoples of the land anticipated in Exod. 23.20–33 and Deut. 7 and narrated in Joshua: "when Joshua 'left no survivor and devoted to destruction everyone who breathed' in the whole land (Josh. 10.40, cf. 11.11,14), according to Miranda because they were oppressors, who, it may be asked, were the oppressed?"

Houston turns to Rolf Knierim's analyses of the various reasons given for this destruction. Exod. 23 and Deut. 7 suggest that the Canaanites are to be destroyed because of their polytheism; but as Knierim indicates (1995: 98), it is not polytheism per se that is the problem so much as the danger that presents itself to Israel's identity and its loyalty to YHWH. The destruction of the Canaanites serves the theology of Israel's exclusive election. And so it seems clear that the action of YHWH in delivering the Israelites from Egypt and bringing them into the Land of Canaan is partial and cannot be founded on a concept of universal justice for the oppressed.

If this is the case, does the story of Exodus in fact *subvert* the contemporary discourse of universal human rights? Since the Spanish conquest of the Americas in the 16th century, European theologians, philosophers, and lawyers have been debating the morality of colonial conquest (Moses 2008). Many explorers including Christopher Columbus saw the newly discovered people as subhuman, animals with no soul, with no right to their lands, who were to be killed without a qualm. Millions were consequently enslaved, died of disease, or perished in campaigns of mass murder. The missionary activist Bartolomé de Las Casas documented the horrific brutality of these genocidal practices (Hinton 2008: 442) and in a series of widely-publicized debates in Valladolid championed the natural rights of the American Indians. In doing so, he was echoing the arguments of his fellow Dominican, Fr de Vitoria, and his findings were the foundation for modern discourse on natural and, later, "human" rights (Fitzmaurice 2008). Twentieth-century jurists studied these arguments carefully. So did Raphael Lemkin, who coined the term "genocide" in 1944 and successfully campaigned for its criminalization in international law. Over a twenty-four-hour period from 9 December to 10 December 1948, the UN General Assembly in Paris voted for two major advances in international law: the Genocide Convention and the Universal Declaration of Human Rights. By 1951, the Genocide Convention had become international law. Although it hasn't yet stopped killers from massacring their victims, as events in Rwanda and Bosnia show, it does point to a new era where human dignity comes before state sovereignty.

It emerges that "even Exodus is not an innocent text" (Tracy 1987). It is not free from danger. The flight from bondage in Egypt may be a paradigm of liberation from the perspective of the Israelites, but it is disastrous for the Canaanite inhabitants of the Promised Land. As recent colonial readings have demonstrated, the oppressed all too easily become in their turn oppressors. Today's Moses all too easily becomes tomorrow's Pharaoh (Langston 2006: 70). In the re-appropriation of the story of Exodus, there is a real possibility that it will be used to justify acts of oppression (Prior 1997). It has happened. One might cite the conquest of the Aztecs by Cortés or the Incas by Pizarro. The struggle for political freedom by Oliver Cromwell has to be set against the brutal fate meted out to Irish Catholics. In 1776, just after the US had gained independence, Thomas Jefferson proposed as emblem of the new republic the children of Israel crossing the Red Sea in transit from slavery to freedom; but White Americans of the revolutionary period gave little thought to the application of Exodus to African American slaves, despite their concurrent appeal to it. We may reflect on the impact of the settlement of New England Puritans on the indigenous peoples of North America, where the massacre of the Pequot tribe was described by the Revd Thomas Shepard of Cambridge, Massachusetts, as a "divine slaughter by the hand of the English" (Newton 1987: 59) and the use of the Exodus paradigm by some South African Reformed theologians to seize the land and treat Black Africans as Canaanites.

Referring to the profound influence of Biblical stories on society, Regina Schwartz suggests that "sacred categories of thought have not just disappeared. They have lingered in the modern world where they are transferred to secular ones" (1997). In secular terms, too, the story of Exodus has continuing political resonance. This is a story about power. For Michael Walzer (1985), Exodus refers to a worldly movement within time and space; the Biblical designation of the Israelites in Egypt as the poor and the oppressed, intertwining economic and political elements, has entered the literature of the Western revolutionary tradition. Exodus politics feature within the possibilities of history with the end in view, liberation, being modestly defined. As he himself recognizes, the drawback of this inherently attractive presentation is that he pays little attention to the brutalities of conquest in the Biblical account. Edward Said responds vigorously to Walzer with a "Canaanite" critique (1986). Against the fact that "for the people, solidarity with the oppressed is a moral obligation", he sets "the people's candidly stated need to defeat counterrevolution – that is, worshippers of the Golden Calf and, in the Promised Land, the unfortunate native inhabitants who by definition are not members of the Chosen People". The Canaanites are "explicitly excluded from the world of moral concern" – they are to be exterminated.

Faced with Walzer's "implicit but always unexamined appeal to the concreteness and intimacy of shared ethnic and familial bonds", Said appeals to the strength of the Canaanite position – "being defeated and 'outside', you can perhaps more easily feel compassion, more easily call injustice injustice, more easily speak directly and plainly of all oppression, and with less difficulty try to understand ... history and equality". Does this mean that, as Said puts it, "Exodus is 'a tragic book' in that it teaches that you cannot both 'belong' and concern yourself with Canaanites who do not belong" (1986: 106)?

It is fair to assume that where the oppressed do not consider the possibility of becoming in their turn oppressors the Exodus narrative ceases to liberate – it becomes a tool of bondage (Langston 2006). At this point, one of the most difficult issues to confront is the lingering perception by themselves and others that these oppressors are victims struggling against adversity, rather than aggressors inflicting adversity on others. The point may be illustrated by reference to Australia, a settler society whose history of invasion and dispossession of indigenous peoples is relatively recent and in some respects still continuing. The possessive logic of White sovereignty operates to discriminate in favour of itself, ensuring it protects and maintains its interest by the continuing denial and exclusion of indigenous sovereignty. This logic is evident in the High

Court's Yorta Yorta decision (Yorta Yorta 2002). The Yorta Yorta aboriginal community had lodged an application for native title in respect of the land and waters of North Victoria and Southern New South Wales, traditional Yorta Yorta territory. The Federal Court dismissed their plea for entitlement despite the fact that the extensive archival and field research they assembled to substantiate their claim occupied fifteen metres of shelf space in the Judge's chambers (Moreton-Robinson 2004). Their appeal was effectively dismissed by the High Court. In their findings, the judges effectively represented the Yorta Yorta as a people without any proprietary rights in land.

Ann Curthoys points to the contest between positive and negative versions of the past, according to which the British colonization of Australia is seen either as a worthy enterprise involving the struggle of brave men to redeem the nation or a "profoundly discomforting story of invasion, colonisation, dispossession, exploitation, institutionalisation and attempted genocide" (1999: 1). While this "black armband" view of history is growing in prominence, it is angrily rejected by those who memorialize the sufferings of the settlers in "white blindfold history", according to which White settler suffering confers a right of ownership of the land. A widespread fear by the settlers of loss of land in conjunction with a narrative of White victimhood finds it hard to recognize what they have done to others. As Curthoys indicates, these competing victim narratives make sense to those who tell and receive them. The distinction between history and fiction means very little. While the conflict is not easily resolved, "the emphasis in white Australian popular historical mythology on the settler as victim works against substantial acknowledgment and understanding of a colonial past, and informs and inflames white racial discourse" (Curthoys 1999: 4).

In this inverted narrative of victimhood, I suggest we may discern a process at work which is influential today in the public perception of refugees in the UK and elsewhere. On the one hand, there is a discernible fear of "loss of the land", fear on the part of settled residents that they are being overwhelmed by immigrants; there is fear that these will take over their jobs; plunder the welfare system to their own advantage; and lead to an increase in crime. However irrational these fears may be, they are fuelled unscrupulously by the popular media and by politicians, especially those on the extreme right. Despite their special claim to protection, refugees and asylum-seekers are demonized along with the rest and, because of their history of persecution, arguably suffer more. Citizens and politicians alike are blinded by this inverted narrative of victimhood to the brutality of their public policies, the inhumanity of the ways in which they are implemented, and the unimaginable suffering their decisions have caused and are causing to those who have already had more than their share of ill-treatment.

While the Exodus narrative has been a source of comfort for oppressed peoples, while the account it gives of the mighty acts of a liberating God has strengthened their faith and inspired them with fortitude in their affliction, it remains a profoundly ambiguous text. The partiality of God towards his people brings into question the concept of universal justice. Those who have been oppressed all too easily become oppressors: although solidarity with the oppressed, for the Israelites, is a moral obligation, the Canaanites are nevertheless exterminated. Finally, the oppressors understand themselves as victims. Exodus has not in itself the resources to deal with the theological and political ambiguities which it exemplifies.

Exile

The Bible has been described as "the great metanarrative of diaspora" (Cuéllar 2008: 1). Much of the Old Testament relates to the crisis of exile, the pain and suffering of forced migration, and the consequent challenges of resettlement. But what exactly is meant by "the Exile"? It is "a gloriously slippery term" (Davies 1998: 128), and there have been dramatic shifts in scholarly opinion. Is this a chronological benchmark referring to the fall of Jerusalem in 587 BCE and the associated forced displacement of prisoners? Or does the term admit also the years spent by the Judaean diaspora in Babylonia? Does the use of the term privilege those who were deported to Babylon over those who remained in the land or who sought refuge elsewhere? Or is "the Exile" a "mythopoetic construction"? I do not propose to enter into the detail of these debates except to note that, for most scholars today, the reality of the forced migrations of Judaeans to Babylonia in the 6th century BCE is not in doubt. From the Biblical accounts, supplemented by archaeological and documentary data, the picture that emerges is of waves of people who are forced during this period to leave their homes in Judah. It is clear too that in historical terms the exilic period cannot be demarcated: there is no obvious beginning – witness the many deportations associated with the Babylonian invasions (2 Kgs 24–25) and the earlier Assyrian ones (2 Kgs 17); nor could it be said to end with the Persian conquest of Babylon. Given the remaining diaspora settlements not only in Babylonia, but also in Egypt, Pathros, Ethiopia, Elam, Hamath, and coastlands (Isa 11.11), and the long-standing academic debates over the extent of a "return" to Judah, the exilic period is open-ended.

It is also far from homogeneous. To speak of the exilic period is to speak of different contexts involving the different life experiences of different generations. As in Babylonia forced migration turned into diaspora, there were at least three generations of migrants who are likely to have had a significantly distinct generational consciousness and perspective (Ahn 2011). There was also a remnant community in Judah and refugee settlement in Egypt. New insights from sociology, anthropology, and psychology into refugees and other displaced groups lead scholars, following Daniel Smith-Christopher, to see the Exile not as an event, but as a phenomenon with far-reaching consequences. It may be seen "as a cultural tradition that is repeatedly constructed, reinterpreted, and remembered" (Kelle 2011: 21) as today millions of people continue to be torn from their homes. It expresses the experience of bereavement and loss of identity and defines new relationships with state powers and places called "home" (Davidson 2013: 178).

There is no sustained Biblical account of the experiences of those who were forcibly deported more than a thousand miles away from their homes to Babylon and who made their homes there. Censorship of documents for ideological or political reasons is always possible, and we have to take into account the difficulty or unwillingness of those who have suffered trauma to write or even think about the experiences they have undergone (Albertz 2012; 2003: 1). As individuals, as a people, as the people of God, those who survived the events of 598 and 587 BCE had over time and in different contexts to negotiate a new sense of identity and find fresh meaning in life. This process can be traced throughout the Old Testament. Between and within the texts, there is a cacophony of voices, often conflicting with one another, expressing trauma, lament, ambivalence, and courage, as well as a searching in situations of uncertainty for personal, religious, and political identity. Many of these are suggestive in situations of displacement today.

History and narrative

Historical narratives are never a simple matter of recapitulation of fact: events that are so traumatic as to defy description can be made coherent, as stories organize meaning from the bits and pieces that are remembered. The past becomes memory as these bits of it cohere. It becomes history as these are recorded. There is a narrow distinction between "what actually happened" and imagining incidents: ideological considerations will inevitably shape the way the story is told. Some Jews depicted events of the 6th century BCE as a fracture in time and space that separated the past from the present, a radical discontinuity, an emptiness. For others, however, life continued amid the ruins and with it a sense of coherent purposeful history. As the stories in each case evolved and came to be accepted as true, they confirmed these two sets of attitudes, assimilating what was compatible with these and rejecting what was not.

This is evident in the contrasting emphases of 2 Kgs 24–25, with its élite moral horizons and bleak focus on national politics, and Jer. 39–43, with a more sanguine, people-focused perspective on the same period.

Following 2 Kings, the first displacement, in 598/597 BCE, took place when Judah was already a vassal province of Babylon. King Jehoiakim rebelled against Nebuchadnezzar, confident that he would have support from Egypt; but this was not forthcoming (24.7). The king died, his son Jehoiachin decided to give up the throne, and the Babylonians quelled the rebellion. The king, the royal family, thousands of "men of valour", and a tranche of administrators and skilled artisans – guardians of the cultural, religious, and political identity of Judah and a formidable brain drain – were taken by force to Babylon (2 Kgs 24.4–16). Zedekiah was appointed King of Judah. In around 589 BCE, he too rebelled in an attempt at economic and political independence

(2 Kgs 24.20), and Nebuchadnezzar laid siege to Jerusalem. The siege lasted for two to three years and was accompanied by a severe famine (2 Kgs 25.3; cf. Deut. 28.48–57), but the narrator appears to be more interested in the effects of the fall of the city on the monarchy and the temple than in the suffering of the people. As the Babylonian army entered through a breach in the wall, Zedekiah and his army fled towards the Arabah only to be captured on the Plains of Jericho (2 Kgs 25.7).

The tragic dénouement is told in 2 Kgs 25.7–12: Jerusalem and its temple were razed; the temple vessels were smashed to pieces for monetary advantage; and the writer lingers lovingly over the beauty of their craftsmanship (2 Kgs 25.13–17). The destruction of the temple vessels may be seen as further illustration of the nation's annihilation. In Jeremiah, however, there is no mention of the burning of the temple (39.8; cf. 52.12) and the temple vessels are described as being deported intact (27–28; cf. 2 Chron. 36.7; Ezra 1.7–11; 1 Esdras 1.54). These accounts stress a continuity between the first and second temple periods (Wright 2011: 119) and leave the reader with the hope of restoration.

2 Kings continues to describe how Zedekiah was blinded after witnessing the execution of his sons, and how the prisoners of war were brought to Riblah, where they were sentenced and brutally executed (25.18–21). The writer states grimly: "so Judah went into exile out of its land". It didn't, of course. Jeremiah instances how the Captain of the Guard left "some of the poor people who owned nothing" and gave them confiscated fields and vineyards (Jer. 39.10), an endowment of land that is not necessarily to be inferred from 2 Kgs 25.12. For 2 Kings, the "poorest people in the land" were of no account, nor, would it appear, was Jeremiah or the group associated with Gedaliah when he was appointed Governor of Judah (cf. Jer. 40.8–12; 41.10). Jeremiah portrays Gedaliah as a good man who functioned as mediator between the community and Babylon to the extent that Judaean refugees who had fled to Moab, Amon, Edom, and other lands were induced to return to Mizpah (Jer. 40.11; cf. Jer. 43.5), where they "gathered wine and summer fruits in great abundance" (Jer. 40.12). For 2 Kings, however, the appointment of Gedaliah is a historical footnote; following his murder, "all the people" fled to Egypt for fear of reprisals (2 Kgs 25.26). Although again this is rhetorical exaggeration, there are unmistakable implications that, for 2 Kings, the Exodus is being reversed. The cumulative impression is of resounding defeat. No mention is made of a third displacement to Babylonia, recorded in Jer. 52.30, which may indicate retaliation following the assassination.

2 Kings concludes with a note on the release of Jehoiachin from prison, with dining rights at the king's table and a daily allowance for the rest of his life. Although this has been seen as historical revisionism on the part of an editor (Wright 2011: 126), excavations in Babylon have revealed lists of names of prisoners who were allocated food rations, Jehoiachin amongst them. He and his entourage were maintained prisoners at court. There is in these texts no indication of amnesty as in 2 Kgs 25.27–30 though as Bob Becking indicates,

this is not improbable (2011: 158–159). However, the fact remains that for 2 Kings, it is in Babylon, not Judah, that history continues and that Jehoiachin, scion of the royal line of David, lives out his life there as an annuitant. In this grimly unadorned picture of defeat and discontinuity, the authors of 2 Kings testify to the annihilation by YHWH through the agency of the Babylonians of all that gave meaning to their lives and that gave identity to their nation – the land, the temple, the king. For them, this was a traumatic historical experience and a horrifying interruption of God's history with Israel. In Jeremiah, however, there are glimpses of assurance and optimism. Exile in Babylon is seen as part of God's will for good, not harm (Jer. 29.11).

The story of these events is told from different perspectives and in terms of what are in some sense alternative values. They are different versions of the same reality. History is, as Samuel Hynes reminds us of the First World War, not simply there to be told; it has to be remade, to be comprehended, imagined, understood (1992: 431). Historical accounts may be intentionally biased in favour of an ideological agenda, so we need to exercise responsibility in the way we engage with them: there is an ethical dimension to the way the past is represented.

The agenda may be cultural. Andrew Demshuk's important work on the politics of memory (2012) describes how, in the wake of Nazi atrocities, around 12 million ethnic Germans fled or were expelled from an area of central and eastern Europe where their ancestors had lived for centuries; more than 3 million of them came from Silesia. In August 1945, at the Potsdam Conference, part of Eastern Prussia went to the USSR. And it was also decided to cede a quarter of Germany's territory in 1937, including Silesia, to Poland in compensation for the territory lost by Poland to the USSR. These displaced people, aware as time went by that memory of Silesia would die with them, sought to systematize and document what Demshuk calls "the heimat (homeland) of memory", turning it into "cultural memory" (Assmann 2011).

But this record is problematic. Drawing on pre-Nazi roots, it displays racist bigotry about supposed Polish "backwardness" (Demshuk 2012: 22). In the realization that their homeland could no longer in reality be as they remembered it in their imagination – but ruined, decayed, and tainted – they claimed a monopoly on victimhood and failed to mourn or even recognize crimes that had been perpetrated by Germans on peoples of the East, to the point of reinventing the Nazi past as a valiant defence by German victims against Polish aggression (Demshuk 2012: 30).

Historical narrative can also be biased towards a political agenda. A classic example from relatively recent history is the accounting by the Australian government of the "children overboard" incident and subsequent events. The public inquiry elicited these facts: on 6 October 2001, *HMAS Adelaide* intercepted Suspected Illegal Entry Vessel (SIEV) 4, a "leaky boat" heading for Christmas Island with 223 passengers and crew. These were told to "go home" to Indonesia. They refused. The *Adelaide* fired twenty-three rounds of ammunition across the bow. Around a dozen men jumped overboard; on deck, one man, who did not jump overboard, held up a child in his arms. On 8 October, the SIEV 4 began to sink rapidly under tow, and refugees, many of them children, were rescued from the sea by crew members of the *Adelaide*.

The Howard government, on the eve of the Australian federal election, used a grainy video and photographs of children being rescued from the sea to misrepresent what had happened, with the Prime Minister claiming publicly that children had been thrown overboard by the refugees. The state drew legitimacy from the way the story was told. There was a public furore, asylum-seekers were demonized, and the Howard government was re-elected. However, a subsequent inquiry by the Australian Senate Select Committee showed the extent to which voters had been deliberately misled: no children had been thrown overboard, and the government was fully aware of this at the time (Maritime Incident Committee Report 2002).

Memory overwhelmed: Lamentations

The tragic impact of the fall of Jerusalem on those who remained in Judah is embodied in the Book of Lamentations. The testimony has to be transmitted and heard. Yet, how to find words to articulate such experiences (Garber 2011: 309–321)? In her discussion of texts that testify to traumatic events, Shoshana Felman suggests that these are "composed of bits and pieces of a memory that has been overwhelmed by occurrences that have not yet settled into understanding or remembrance ... events in excess of our frames of reference" (Felman & Laub 1991: 5). An attempt may yet be made to articulate such experiences through poetry. Even those who dismiss Lamentations as a hyperbolic literary fabrication recognize that its value as poetry is undeniable; undeniable too are the formal features it shares with traditional laments in the Ancient Near East. The acrostic structure, where the verses follow the letters of the Hebrew alphabet, "imposes a familiar order on the swirling chaos of the world. It implies that suffering is so enormous, so total, that it spreads from a to z, aleph to taw. There are no letters left for suffering" (Lee & Mandolfo 2008: 29). But we must also recognize that the images of conquest, displacement, rape, starvation, and cannibalism evoke the abject horror of many historically attested examples of siege warfare (Kern 1999: 62–85). To read these images in context "is once again to recover Lamentations as a measure of the psychological and spiritual crisis of the exile" (Smith-Christopher 2002: 104).

This is an intense and dramatic work with a range of emotions and character. Through the voices of Daughter Zion, Speaker, *geber*, and Community, it operates dialogically. Dialogue is ongoing; always deeply conditioned by its past, it cannot be restricted to the present; it emphasizes the relational and calls into question any easy identification of cause and effect (Olick 2007: 11). In the present case, it allows for the expression of rending grief, sympathy, powerlessness, anger, and piety. No one voice dominates; God never speaks. The experience of disaster is articulated in the language of lament, highlighting spaces between the worlds of dominion, identity, and ideology, blurring distinctions between fact, fictional narrative, and memory. When combined with motifs from the mourning dirge (Westermann 1994), Lamentations gives voice to timeless pain and suffering. It is able to speak into and out of the experiences of people in the midst of crisis.

In this, the fact that Zion is portrayed as a woman has a particular edge. Paul Kern, in his classic work on ancient siege warfare, notes how, in the Greek tragic poets, women and children "threatened the notion of war as a contest between warriors, undermined the conventional standards of honour and prowess that governed ancient warfare, and paradoxically made war less restrained by creating a morally chaotic city landscape in which not only the walls collapsed but deeply rooted social and moral distinctions as well" (1999: 4). The same might be said of Lamentations. Through the work of Carleen Mandolfo in particular, "an alternative, woman-centred perspective highlights the painful present, the experience of suffering, and with it, the concomitant feelings of shock, betrayal, anger, sadness, and so on" (Middlemas 2012b: 41). Mandolfo sees Daughter Zion, personification of the city, as an unfaithful wife (Mandolfo 2007). But this is to privilege an understanding common to the prophetic literature for which there is no evidence in Lamentations. It obscures other layers of meaning: in the first two chapters, Zion is presented as a violated daughter, forsaken widow, and bereaved mother, the very embodiment of suffering humanity. Her anguish is that of the ruined city and her voice that of all women who are victims of war. The Speaker simply and gently evokes her plight (Lam. 1.1–2). Daughter Zion has tears on her cheeks from weeping all night long. She has no-one to help her; all those who love her have turned against her. The phrase "there is no comforter for her", with variations, is a leitmotif of chapter one (Lam. 1.2, 7, 9, 16, 17, 21; cf. Ps. 69.20). Judah, also personified as a woman, has "gone into exile with suffering and hard servitude"; she may escape, flitting as a refugee from one nation to another, but "finds no resting-place" (Lam. 1.3; cf. Deut. 28.64ff.); she is constantly run to ground (Lam. 1.3). The Speaker accepts, but without comment, that Zion's sufferings are the consequence of sin (Lam. 1.5). Then Daughter Zion bursts in and speaks for herself. Naked, bare, exposed, with no-one to comfort her, she cries to YHWH, the author of her affliction (Lam. 1.9c), but there is no response. Now, her anguish is intensified. The Speaker responds, moved by her misery and grief. Images of rape, hinted at earlier (Lam. 1.8–9), are intensified (Lam. 1.10) with associated feelings of humiliation and shame (Lam. 1.8; 2.1, 15). Again Zion calls out, begging YHWH to see how worthless she has become and imploring those who "pass by" to see the suffering that is before their eyes (Lam. 1.12).

There is, however, a difference between having a voice and being heard – genuinely listening to her voice involves moral and ethical engagement: "is it nothing to you, you who pass by?" The appeal hangs in suspense for all time:

it is addressed to us, our governments, the governments of the world. It is the cry of those women and children, many of them refugees, with babies strapped to their backs, abandoned by people smugglers to die in the Sahara Desert; it is the cry of the refugee in a leaky boat holding up in his arms a dead baby as he pleads for help from a passing ship; it is the abject cry of the dying refugee, destitute in London, whose baby is starving to death at her breast.

The depiction of Daughter Zion in Lamentations has ethical and political resonance. She may be read, as Meverden helpfully points out (Meverden 2011: 395–407), in Agamben's terms as a "bare life figure". She stands both guilty and abject, her death warrants no recompense. She suffers under the hegemony of a sovereign power.

There are atrocity stories: babies and children are starving to death (Lam. 2.12,20; 4.4); mothers are eating their own children (Lam. 2.20; 4.10). There is a general, desperate search for food. Zion bemoans her dying inhabitants as a mother grieves over her children. Her voice is subdued. Humiliated, she endures the "aha!" moment, the triumphant derision, the verbal abuse, the gloating of enemies that is often a precursor to further reprisals (Lam. 2.15–16). The Speaker is clearly moved by Zion's plight, but how can he comfort her (Lam. 2.13)? He urges her to cry to YHWH, day and night, pleading for the lives of her children (Lam. 2.18–19). And he reinforces her prayer, in gut-wrenching agony, tears streaming down his face (Lam. 2.11). She is crushed by the might of Babylon, but her suffering is seen as initiated by YHWH, and in the eyes of both, YHWH's punishment is outrageously disproportionate (Lam. 2.20–22).

Her cries of despair resonate with those of contemporary bare-life figures, the displaced person, the refugee, suffering from "abject treatment" by a sovereign power (Meverden 2011: 406). Those who have fled war zones may experience further abject treatment at the hands of the state as they seek asylum. Enhanced vigilance in the fear of terrorist attack has led, in many countries, to the implementation of emergency measures. These, in Agamben's terms, reveal state sovereignty: "the state of exception is usefully deployed in reaction to precarious migrants and others who are seen as in some way suspect or polluting by the majority nation" (Tazreiter 2012: 36). In the case of the asylum-seeker, such measures include administrative detention, forced deportation, and a series of restrictions on health care, work, legal advice and subsistence. Many are destitute. Even when faced with evidence that such suffering is perpetuated by inhumane government measures, many people in the West react with "righteous coldness" as if it does not finally matter.

To limit one's analysis of Lamentations with Mandolfo to the first two chapters is to pre-empt a reading of the book as a whole (Conway 2012: 102). The book in its final form is meant to be read as a whole and would not be complete without the remaining voices. In chapter three, another voice takes over, the *geber*. His precise identity is unclear, but the term is typically used of a warrior, a strong man who fights to defend his people, perhaps a king, perhaps a judge. He stands in the tradition of piety of the Psalms (Westermann 1994: 193).

Following his opening lament (Lam. 3.1–21), the *geber* affirms the goodness and compassion of YHWH, who "does not willingly afflict or grieve anyone" (Lam. 3.33). There follows a didactic interlude. Confronted with abject misery, he argues in similar terms to Job's friends: the God who chastizes also heals; God does not pervert justice. So has God been acting against his compassionate nature? The *geber*'s response to this is to summon his fellow sufferers to confess their sins, repent, and plead for forgiveness (Lam. 3.40–47). One day, God will respond (Lam. 3.57). In the meantime, all complaints should be silenced (Lam. 3.39). The *geber* offers himself as a viable spiritual model for the suffering people. But this glib model of submissive piety is framed and challenged by other voices that provide rhetorical boundaries (Balentine 2011: 356). Explanations like his, which fail to account theologically for the full horror of human suffering, are implicitly found wanting.

In chapter four, the description of misery continues in a direct complaint brought by the Community, contrasting the former state of affairs with the present: heroes are fallen; starving mothers are unable to suckle their babies; women are eating their own children; and priests and elders are despised. The fate of king and court is presented as if it were the fate of another group of the city's inhabitants. At the end of the litany of sufferings voiced by Zion, Speaker, *geber*, and the Community, the lament in chapter five enables the Community to express its complaint in the public sphere. Now the complaint component moves beyond the conventional boundaries of the lament genre – its language is political; it voices outrage (Williamson 2008: 68). The Community has suffered greatly; it has been humiliated and degraded. Fatherless children and widows are turned out of their homes (Lam. 5.2–3) and are starving. Their cherished customs have come to an end (Lam. 5.14), and hard labour is imposed on the young. Their dancing has turned to mourning (Lam. 5.15); Mount Zion is desolate and infested with jackals (Lam. 5.17). But there is no answer. YHWH, who is seen by Zion, Speaker, *geber*, and Community as the author of their misfortunes, remains silent, and the chapter ends on a note of foreboding (Lam. 5.22) with a communal cry into the emptiness of YHWH's non-response. An unanswered demand for justice (Hobbins 2012: 171), it indicates the way in which trauma savages a community's trust in itself and its future (Carr 2011: 300).

The suffering described is both physical and spiritual. In her own eyes, Daughter Zion is culpable; she feels shame (Lam. 1.19). But to what extent should a violated daughter, a destitute widow, a bereaved mother, be held responsible for her own fate? To maintain with Mandolfo (2007: 18) that Zion is innocent is to undermine her integrity. However inappropriately, she does not dispute her fault. And she sees siege warfare by the Babylonian Empire as divine judgement. But in acknowledging the force of Zion's sense of shame and guilt, we acknowledge too that the personal story is part of the larger story. Zion's voice fades into the background as the *geber* and Community articulate their particular sense of guilt and responsibility for the present predicament. The struggle of traumatized individuals and communities with feelings of shame and guilt is virtually universal (Smith 1989; Smith-Christopher 2002). Robert J. Lifton maintains that "no survival experience ... can occur without severe guilt" (1968: 489). His study of Hiroshima survivors points to "the creation of a 'guilt community' in which self condemnation is 'in the air'" (1968: 494). Where one's own self or one's own culture is held responsible for bringing on the agony one finds oneself in, there is no easy way out (Carr 2011: 299). But there are possibilities for renewal. The process is religious, and the move from shame to guilt to renewal is particularly evident in contexts of religious faith. A cogent example is the experience of those refugee women, Buddhists from Cambodia, who in the late 1970s questioned whether their own culture was to blame for the horrors of the Khmer Rouge genocide (Muecke 1995: 40). Does Cambodian culture have a bad karma? If so, have they not expiated their sin through their terrible suffering? Are they not now free to look to the future? And there is the case of the Tibetan refugees who fled the Chinese invasion of Tibet to make their homes with the Dalai Lama in Dharamsala in northern India in 1959 (Vahali 2009). The voices of those interviewed by Honey Vahali cover events in Tibet at the time of the invasion; the hardships faced by refugees on their arrival in India; the struggle and endurance of the first generation; and the different perspectives of the second generation. Particularly striking is the account given of the "inner world" of the refugees, especially of the guilt of those who felt they had committed treason by abandoning their homeland (Vahali 2009: 256). Smith-Christopher draws on his field studies amongst Cree Indian Christians in Canada and Aboriginal Australian Christians to suggest that the frequency of the motif "it's all because of our sins" may be one of the ways in which a people in crisis copes with their situation: if one's suffering is seen as one's own fault, due to what one has done and not ultimately attributable to the might of an empire, then there is more hope of future restoration (Smith-Christopher 2002: 81).

Remembrance: Ps. 137

Though there are ongoing discussions about the dating and context of Ps. 137 (Hossfeld & Zenger 2011: 513), there is general agreement that this is a vivid communal lament associated with the experience of deportation and the lives of those who have been displaced to Babylon, both in 596/597 and 586/587 BCE. The anguish of those displaced in 596/597 BCE is intensified by the devastating experiences of those who arrived ten years later after the fall of Jerusalem. In vv. 1–4, there is the grief of those who have been uprooted from all that made their lives meaningful. "Remembering Zion" was a way of holding fast to their homeland, to YHWH, and also of affirming their identity in alien surroundings. Those who in former times were the political, social, and religious leaders of Judah were reduced to corvée labour as diggers of irrigation canals (Ahn 2011: 88). Their captors asked for songs. They were humiliated. How could they sing YHWH's praises as entertainment, there, in a foreign land? In vv. 5–6, the perspective shifts from Zion to Jerusalem, the speaker is profoundly affected by the remembrance; he is determined never to forget the city. Then, in vv. 7–9, in a heightened burst of pain intensified by powerlessness, YHWH is called to remember the fall of Jerusalem and retaliate against Edom and Babylon accordingly.

While this text has its own world and its own history, there are important resonances with the situation of many refugees today. With Smith-Christopher, "a dialogue with social-scientific approaches is crucial to the continued clarification and enrichment of our historical and textual understanding" (Smith-Christopher 2012: 155). The theme of remembrance is key.

First, the nostalgic weeping of the deportees (Ps. 137.1–4) and the determination never to forget their homeland (Ps. 137.5–6) is typical of first-generation diaspora populations. It may be understood as an attempt by survivors of massive chaos to cling on to meaning and identity, an act of defiance, an attempt to keep alive a world that might otherwise vanish from memory. The phenomenon is well documented, and I am indebted in what follows to Demshuk's analysis of those millions of people who were uprooted from their homes in Silesia following the Second World War (Demshuk 2012). They held in their consciousness two images of *heimat* ("homeland"). First, they continued to derive solace from the *heimat* of memory, an idealized realm preserved in their imagination. At the same time, they were all too aware that their *heimat* was transformed, destroyed, part of a foreign land. The two images of *heimat* were incompatible, and the refugees gradually came to realize that they could never return to the Silesia they had known. The trauma they shared shaped the collective nostalgia "which only started to take shape when the world they longed for was already gone and could not be retrieved as they remembered it" (Demshuk 2012: 16).

This corresponds to the idea of "collective memory" described by Maurice Halbwachs: a product of individual memories shaped collectively through membership of a social group, where memory is seen as "an active process of construction and reconstruction in time" (Olick 2007: 10). In this sense, memory is not an agency of storage but the life-blood of the group. But, at the same time, it is also the group's cultural inheritance (Olick 2007: 6). And so, as Jan Assmann observes, "because every group strives for durability, it tends to block out change as far as possible" (Assmann 2011: 26). Can these two impulses be reconciled? What are the implications for diaspora groups?

Although the Silesian Germans knew they could never replace the *heimat* of origin, they did fashion a new *heimat* in the land of settlement by reproducing practices that tied them to the past they remembered. They sought to reconstruct intimate *lieux de mémoire* in the West – costumes, festivals, anniversaries (cf. Nora 1989: 12). These helped first-generation exiles to feel "at home". However, as we see from Mohammed Chaichian's study of first-generation refugees from Iran living in America, the *lieux de mémoire* are not sufficient to achieve integration. These refugees were torn between living in an increasingly idealized and unattainable cultural past and a society where their "Iranianness" was tolerated but neither appreciated nor promoted (Chaichian 1997).

Recent studies of diaspora refugee communities in Australia show how there can be a creative tension between the cultivation of remembered ties with a former home and public questions of conformity (Hayes & Mason 2012). There is a contrast in this respect between refugees from Nazism after the second world war who had completely severed all ties with home and became committed Australians, and more recent arrivals seeking protection. The Vietnamese boat people still retain links with their country of birth to which they feel they belong and this feeling is transmitted to the next generation. Chinese immigrants reinforce emotional links with home through watching satellite television programmes. This "in-between living", it is thought, dilutes a sense of belonging to Australia. In the 1970s and 1980s there was a growing consensus that in order to assimilate, refugees needed to "forget", to sever all links with the past; and there were concerted attempts to prevent the growth of alienated ghettoized refugee populations (Hayes & Mason 2012: 2). In particular, as Robert Mason indicates in his study of Australia's Salvadoran community, there was unwillingness to condone refugees bringing past political experiences or disputes to their new homes (2012: 96). The 20,000 or so Salvadoran refugees living in Australia in 2006 were obliged to regard Australia as their new and only home. The suggestion of a "successful" settlement belied the "traumas of unbelonging" identified by L. Vickroy as the "loss of homeland, fragmented or diminished sense of self, sense of homelessness and dislocation, isolation and alienation" (2005: 112). Despite this, he continues "those who identify collectively as political refugees ... possess an identity with strong normative aspects, which can aid in the sustained articulation of their collective traumas across multiple situations". The Salvadorans successfully maintained lasting emotional bonds and a continued sense of solidarity with their homeland over three decades of diaspora life in Australia (Mason 2012: 95).

Second, at Ps. 137.7–8 YHWH is called to "remember" the devastation of Jerusalem; implicitly, he is called to exercise retributive justice (cf. Ps. 79.10,12). Daughter Zion suffered terrible things in the siege of Jerusalem; it is quite likely that Jewish mothers had seen their babies slaughtered by Babylonians. What was to happen in the "paying back" of Daughter Babylon is left to the imagination, but the shocking fate evoked for her babies is clear. Baby-bashing is referred to also in 2 Kgs 8.12, Hos. 13.16, Neh. 3.10, and in the oracle against Babylon in Isa. 13.16. Images of brutality "seem to function in our sources as images reflecting a vision of a world without limits or structure or morality, in which men violated deep-seated taboos" (Kern 1999: 85). Kern continues: "only siege warfare engulfed women and children so commonly that we naturally associate their destruction with it".

But can it ever be morally acceptable to slaughter women and children, the most vulnerable of civilians, with such indiscriminate brutality? To do so is to treat them as something other than human. For Judith Butler,

> if one "feels" for the children or, indeed, if one comes to regard the children as those whose lives are being unjustly and brutally destroyed in an instant, and in grotesque and appalling ways, then that kind of "sentiment" has to be over-ridden by a righteous and cold military rationality. Indeed, it is not only a cold military rationality, but one that prides itself on its ability to see and feel past the vision of massive human suffering in the name of an infinitely expanding rationale of self-defense. We are asked to believe that these children are not really children.
>
> (Butler 2010: xxvii)

It is just such a mindset that enables individuals and governments to see refugee children in impersonal terms, to seize them from their beds in "dawn raids", to hold them, often severely traumatized, in detention centres (Lorek *et al.* 2009). Wherever we fail to conceptualize the child as a person, we cannot understand "this life as a life worth living, worth sheltering, and worth grieving" (Butler 2010). The most sobering example of this in today's world is the case of the children of South Sudan. According to UNICEF, 25,000 or so have been abducted since 1986 by soldiers of the Lord's Resistance Army, and another 40,000 unaccompanied children, "night commuters", walk every night from their homes to towns in search of protection from the threat of abduction. This is in the context of massive displacement due to civil war. Eighty per cent of the 1.4 million people forced to flee the conflict to camps are children and women. The stories told by surviving children are chilling. Human Rights Watch in 1997 reported this statement by a fourteen-year-old:

> I saw quite a number of children killed. Most of them were killed with clubs. They would take five or six of the newly abducted children and make them kill those who had fallen or tried to escape. It was so painful to watch. Twice I had to help. And to do it, it was so bad, it was very bad to have to do.
>
> (Kamya 2011: 237)

The dehumanizing of victims, when combined with a justified need for revenge, can lead us to see the perpetrators of violence themselves as victims. A classic instance of this is the so-called "Vukovar Baby Massacre". Vukovar was a prosperous little town with a mixed community of Croats, Serbs, and others in the east of Croatia near the border with Serbia, and in the War of Independence, its capture was an important objective for the Serbs. After three months of intense bombardment by the Yugoslav People's Army, augmented by Serbian paramilitaries, the siege of Vukovar ended on 18 November 1991. The following day, a Serbian Reuters journalist reported that forty-one Serb babies had been killed in the city. The story was taken up by Serbian television, and a local photographer reported that Croatian soldiers had slaughtered forty-one children aged between five and seven. The next day the Yugoslav People's Army issued a rebuttal, but the damage was done. Thanks to extensive media coverage, Croatians were misrepresented as criminal and genocidal. It emerged at the subsequent War Crimes Tribunals that the fictitious story of slaughtered babies was spread intentionally to inflame Serb nationalists. These concurrently massacred 264 Croatian prisoners of war and civilians taken from Vukovar, and at least 20,000 residents of Vukovar fled as refugees.

With the development of international criminal law, the idea emerged that an emphasis on retributive justice would deter future mass atrocities and reduce the number of refugees. Retributive justice considers punishment, if proportionate, to be the best response to crime. Scaled to the severity of the offending behaviour, it atones for damage already done. It is perceived to enhance international peace and security. But it has not quite worked out like that in practice. This may be illustrated by the conviction and subsequent acquittal of the Croatian leaders Gotovina and Markac, who between July and September 1995 implemented Operation Storm to take control of the Krajina region of Croatia and who created 150,000 refugees. Rosemary Byrne's and Gregor Noll's analysis of the Gotovina judgement shows the limitations of international criminal trials in prosecuting crimes that have given rise to mass refugee displacement. The original intent to foster reconciliation by retribution is shown to be inadequate (Byrne & Noll 2013). And this particular paradigm does not invite judges to address the broader substantive questions as to how deeply divided communities are to live with one another.

A refusal to forget: Ezekiel

Ezekiel is a book of unprecedented visionary power. It speaks to and from a situation of trauma. According to the text, Ezekiel was a priest from Jerusalem; he was amongst those who were displaced in 598/597 BCE, and he exercised a prophetic ministry amongst the deportees in Babylonia about a thousand miles away (Ezek. 1.1–3). He was there amongst the exiles "who lived by the river Chebar" (Ezek. 3.15) ten years later when Jerusalem was sacked. He learned of the start of the siege through divine revelation (Ezek. 24.1), and he was brought the news of the fall of Jerusalem and the death of his wife by a fugitive, possibly a recent deportee (Ezek. 24.15–18; 25–26; cf. 33.21). Although there have been attempts to challenge this context, these do not convince: "we can speak of the 6th century witness of the book and regard that as profoundly influenced in content and style by Ezekiel himself" (Joyce 2007: 4–6).

One of the book's most distinctive features is its dual perspective. Although Ezekiel's ministry is set in exile, a significant amount of the content addresses Jerusalem and its inhabitants. Andrew Mein describes the implications of this:

> The idea that there can be Jerusalemites in two different places at once is crucial for understanding the moral world of Ezekiel and the

> exiles. There are in fact two distinct sets of social circumstances which are relevant to their moral interests and moral formation. The first is the old world of home, with its relative wealth, privilege, and status, the second is the new world of exile. As exiles, therefore, Ezekiel's community could belong to two different realms of moral possibility. The first of these is the moral world of the Jerusalem political élite, the second the more limited moral world of exile in Babylonia. However, because the exiles were themselves drawn from the Jerusalem élite, they can be one and the same people, to whom both sets of circumstances are appropriate.
>
> (2001: 258)

The exiles are now a small dominated minority with no political autonomy. Their scope for action is limited to family, business, and immediate community, and their ethical interests are domesticated (Ezek. 14.1–11; 18.1–32). They seem to have enjoyed a certain amount of freedom in Babylonia: they lived in ethnic enclaves (Ezek. 3.15); they received letters from Judah (Jer. 29); they enjoyed some freedom of association (Ezek. 8.1; 14.1; 20.1); and they probably had work, maintaining the Babylonian canals (Ahn 2011: 84–91). And they show signs of "forgetting"; they are apathetic (Ezek. 3.7–11); they discuss what Ezekiel says with one another; and they come again for more – as if the prophet were there to entertain them like "a singer of love songs" (Ezek. 33.33), a "maker of allegories" (Ezek. 20.49), one who "prophesies for distant times" (Ezek. 12.26). They are engaged with what he says, but puzzled. Why is he "moaning"(Ezek. 21.7)?

Ezekiel makes them "remember" catastrophic events, signs of YHWH's judgement against Jerusalem. They are to experience this judgement as being against themselves. By bodily assimilating YHWH's word of judgement (Ezek. 3.1), Ezekiel aligns himself fully with it (Joyce 2007: 79). "In bitterness", he proclaims "words of lamentation, mourning and woe" (Ezek. 2.10) to his fellow deportees. His responsibility as a "sentinel" is fearsome (Ezek. 3.17). Israel has had every chance and is totally deserving of its fate. In the pronouncement of judgement and in the use of spirit language, Ezekiel is in continuity with the prophetic tradition (Joyce 2007: 36), although he handles that tradition with radical freedom (Joyce 2007: 41).

The "remembering" we have here is not the nostalgic longing for a lost *heimat*, but a fusing of different realities: in the power of Ezekiel's imagination, the past is made present. In part, this is achieved through the prophetic signs. Ezekiel prepares "an exile's baggage" and re-enacts for his hearers their forced departure from Jerusalem in 598/597 BCE. This is not, as Walther Zimmerli points out, an evocation of prisoners of war in fetters, but of those who are forced to leave their homes, taking with them a small bundle of possessions and "covering their heads at the grim anguish of departure" (1979: 270). But this past event is also an event already begun. The current people of Jerusalem (who are not directly present, but who also belong to the House of Israel, to whom Ezekiel's message is addressed) will also depart into exile (Ezek. 12.8); even the prince will carry the exile's baggage on his back (Ezek. 12.12) as he leaves under cover of dark.

The meaning is clear. But in terms of impact, there is a distinction between something the prophet does and something he sees. Through the rhetorical power of the prophetic visions, Ezekiel's fellow exiles are drawn to relive their experiences. And through the sustained imaginative power of evocation, today's readers are also drawn into the horror of events. Given the remarkable degree to which this is achieved, there have been attempts within the field of Ezekiel Studies to psychoanalyze a historical Ezekiel (see, for example, Halperin 1993: 185–216). But as these make little concession to the conventions of prophetic literature, I do not propose to linger over them.

However, just as contemporary disaster studies enable us to distinguish between different types of disasters, so too the field of trauma theory "provides a related means of focusing on the aspects of defeat and disaster involved in the exile that goes beyond the more common sociological and anthropological perspectives" (Kelle 2011: 29). When applied to the exile in Babylon, trauma theory throws into prominence the typical human and psychological issues associated with experiences of forced migration and displacement with a particular focus on PTSD (Smith 1989; Smith-Christopher 2002: 89–94). "Traumatic memory" has long been associated with wars (Winter 2006: 7), but it is only after the Vietnam War that it is described in clinical terms as PTSD. Linked then to combat exposure, atrocities, and the death of comrades, it is now seen to affect not only soldiers but anyone exposed to life-threatening traumatic events, notably refugees. Memories of traumatic events are different than normal memories. In a situation of extreme stress, the brain records sensory "snapshots", perhaps a smell, a shout, a face. These are not marked as being in the past. When something trivial triggers something terrifying, that is buried in memory, an individual may immediately relive an aspect of the experience as if it were happening again. His or her historical remembrance is involuntary; it comes alive in the present. PTSD can lead to waking time flashbacks, to uncontrolled anger and irritation, a numbing of feelings, as well as avoidance and disassociation (Herlihy & Turner 2009).

But should these theories be applied to ancient texts? Smith-Christopher, who first made the link between the Book of Ezekiel and trauma theory, advises discrimination:

> In our attempts to carefully and critically remember that ancient societies are not modern societies, and that we must be careful in making comparisons, we run the equally serious risk of denying the human reality of traumatizing experiences of fellow humans, even if those humans experienced these events over 2,500 years ago. On the other hand, the application of contemporary insights certainly can

> risk a tendency to level out the experiences of all peoples into a kind of generic "trauma experience" that denies the unique histories and experiences of the peoples in question.
>
> (Smith-Christopher 2011: 269)

In the light of the traumatic sociopolitical events of the time, the book of the prophet Ezekiel may then with due caution be read through the lens of trauma. The prophetic idioms gain particular force and resonance from the traumatic experience Ezekiel shares with his hearers. He describes this point in history as "our exile" (Ezek. 33.21; 40.1). Even as he proclaims judgement on the exiles, he identifies with them (Ezek. 3.11; 11.15). The prophetic signs and visions draw on typical personal and communal responses to traumatic stress.

Traumatic memory is typically associated with vivid sensory "flashbacks" (Herlihy *et al.* 2012). Those gathered at Ezekiel's feet are brought to "see" the nightmarish motions of YHWH's death squads (Ezek. 9); they "see" the man who took the fire and "went out" (Ezek. 10.7). They "see" the flashing sword in YHWH's hand, polished for slaughter (Ezek. 21.8–17). They "see", in terms of their own experience, the bodies of Egyptians lying in the open field, ravaged by birds and wild animals, the mountains and valleys strewn with corpses, the land drenched with blood (Ezek. 32.4–6), and they "see" too the mass graves of those denied the dignity of a proper burial (Ezek. 32.22–30). As Ezekiel, horrified, pleads with YHWH to abstain from slaughter (Ezek. 9.7; 11.13), the exiles are brought to relive the grim reality which they have experienced and confront the totality of divine judgement.

Where killing is normalized, those responsible become desensitized to a degree that all lives are considered valueless, including their own (Vikman 2005b: 35). Sexual violence perpetrated by victors against the defeated is a feature of this. A commonplace of ancient warfare (Kern 1999: 81), this remains an atrocious, often lethal experience for its victims today; in current conflicts, there is still "a brutality that has defied the progress of civilisation" (Vikman 2005a: 30). In this light, chapters sixteen and twenty-three of Ezekiel are particularly relevant. Ezekiel, strikingly, does not protest at the brutal treatment of the "whore" Jerusalem, or of the sisters Oholah and Oholibah. There are no tears of sympathy as in the case of the Speaker faced with the plight of Daughter Zion (Lam. 2.11). For the prophet, the time for emotion is past (cf. Ezek. 24.15). In his desire to point out the extent to which Jerusalem is culpable, he adopts the viewpoint of the aggressor. In the cold, grim, sometimes grotesque, accounts there is neither love nor compassion; when combined with violent and sexually explicit invective, these chapters shock. While the language is metaphorical, most agree that at a number of points the metaphor breaks down (Moughtin-Mumby 2008: 163). The women are described as if they were real women, and their punishment is seen as an example for all women (Ezek. 23.45–48; cf. 16.41; 23.10). Motivations and influences have changed little over thousands of years; the same gender-specific behaviour manifests itself in modern conflicts. In two respects, the attitudes portrayed in Ezekiel approximate closely to those identified in Elisabeth Vikman's studies of sexual violence in warfare (2005a, 2005b).

First, the women in Ezekiel are seen as subhuman; stripped of their status as human beings, they are also stripped of their entitlement to humane treatment. They are humiliated (Ezek. 16.37) and abused (Ezek. 16.40). The ability to inflict injury with degradation is crucially aided by dehumanization. When civilians are seen to be a subhuman species, this becomes the moral ground on which atrocities are committed (Vikman 2005b).

Then, the fate of Ezekiel's women is understood as retaliation for crimes committed. Their treatment is justified by the conviction that they are entirely at fault: they deserve punishment. But the anger of the abuser gets out of hand (Ezek. 16.42–43), and the woman suffers brutal public retribution (Ezek. 16.37–41). This features frequently in records of warfare: Vikman points to the behaviour of Japanese troops after the siege of Nanking, when, in the space of two months, an estimated 20,000 Chinese women were raped. Testimonies to the sack of Hengyang (Vikman 2005b: 35) point to the fact that rape was seen as an act of revenge following a stubborn defence, "enforcing the subordination of the woman as part of the city and taking revenge on the resistance she was associated with". The victim is made responsible for the soldiers' hardships and the deaths of their comrades. The presence of peers seems significant – with few exceptions, the violence was perpetrated by two or more soldiers (Vikman 2005b: 34).

Similar accounts could be given of refugee-producing situations in Europe, Africa, the Middle East, and Latin America. Many of those who seek asylum in the West are severely traumatized by such experiences, but this is not always recognized by official authorities. As Stuart Turner makes clear, "to understand the bleak personal world that some refugees are forced to inhabit, it is necessary to consider not only the context from which they have escaped, a context that often includes widespread conflict, state violence and even torture, but also the way in which many have to live in their exile. The continuing experience of persecution in a country of asylum may come as a shock" (Turner 1995: 56). In a world where acts of cruelty are the stark realities of many people's lives, traumatic memory is easily activated:

> A caring and just response might involve official procedures that were not just neutral but positively designed to facilitate recovery. It would require an understanding of the overwhelming pressures that make some people risk everything in flight. This process would inevitably need to include work on the reestablishment of trust relationships, between individuals, and between the individual and the state. In the context of a perceived just world, continued victimization and marginalization stand to have important consequences for people already sensitized by prior experience.
>
> (Turner 1995: 62)

In these Biblical evocations of forced displacement, there are many resonances with the plight of refugees today, traumatized by their experiences and lamenting their loss of home. But what happens when those who have found a new home in exile are "resettled" in the country from which they or their forebears originated? We find one possible illustration of this in the Books of Ezra and Nehemiah.

6

A STAKE IN THE PLACE

Ezra-Nehemiah: history and ideology

The story goes something like this. A "remnant of the people" returns to Jerusalem, under YHWH's prompting, after the Persian conquest of Babylon in 539 BCE. They are seen as legitimate heirs to Israel's tradition, though it is likely that most of them had never lived in Judah before, and several have non-Jewish names. These are far from being destitute refugees. Under the auspices of King Cyrus, they set off for Jerusalem with their servants and their animals, laden with bullion, temple offerings, and accoutrements (Ezra 1.5–2.67). Led by Sheshbazzar, a prominent member of the House of Judah (Ezra 1.8), and encouraged by the prophets Haggai and Zechariah, they overcome various vicissitudes to rebuild the temple, which was eventually completed, according to Ezra 6.15, in the sixth year of the reign of Darius (515 BCE). Around eighty years after this first voyage, a sizeable caravan of priests, royalty, laity – possibly around 5,000 people (Williamson 1985: 110) – journeys to Judah (Ezra 7.1). They are led by Ezra, priest and scribe, whose aim is to re-awaken the people's allegiance to the Law of Moses (Ezra 7.25). Back in Susa, thirteen years later, Nehemiah, cupbearer to King Artaxerxes, hears by accident that the walls of Jerusalem are in ruins (Neh. 1.3). Armed with a royal safe-conduct and supplied with timber from the king's forest, Nehemiah sets off for Jerusalem with his bodyguard. There, he reconstructs the city, repairs its walls, and establishes structures of government. And the narrative foregrounds the ejection of "foreigners" from the community.

The story is well told. Ezra's account of the rebuilding of the temple has been described as "a ripping yarn" (Grabbe 1998b: 17). Ezra and Nehemiah speak for a large part of the narrative in the first person, which gives an impression of immediacy. Although many have pointed to the unclear chronology and the uncertain provenance of the various official documents and decrees which lace the chapters of the book (Grabbe 1998b: 19), Nehemiah's "memoir" (Neh. 1.1–7.5; parts of 12.27–43; 13.4–31) is short and vivid and almost certainly written close to events (Williamson 1985: xxiv). But can we accept his one-sided perspective on the situation as the last word on the subject? His account is highly prejudiced – Nehemiah is "a liar who cannot be confidently believed about anything" (Clines 1990: 17).

What form does this mendacity take? There is more here than a simple account of events. The narrative is drenched in ideology: there is an exaggerated sense of election by race. Ezra-Nehemiah recognizes those who "return" from Babylon as "the remnant" (Ezra 9.13–15), the "holy seed" (Ezra 9.1–2; Neh. 9.2), the embodiment of the true Israel of the Exodus, wilderness, and conquest traditions – to the exclusion of all others (Ezra 2.70; 3.1; 6.16, 19–22; 9.1; Neh. 7.7; 9.2). In the interests of legitimacy and racial purity, they are given genealogies and counted out in lists (Ezra 2.1–60; 8.2–14; Neh. 7.6–72) whose primary function is to establish continuity with pre-exilic Israel (cf. 1 Chron. 1–9). But Ezra goes further than the chronicler: those who cannot prove their descent are excluded from the community (Ezra 2.59–63). Only those of proven pedigree, heirs of Israel, have claim on YHWH, the temple, and the land of Judah. Seamlessly, it appears, all these repatriates "returned to Jerusalem and Judah, all to their own towns" (Ezra 2.1).

The ideology of repatriation

Like most propaganda, this account presents facts selectively. For a start, it ignores the majority of those whom the Babylonians had displaced from Judah and their descendants. From archaeological evidence, the number of "returnees or new immigrants" appears to have been relatively small (Moore & Kelle 2011: 456–457). There was no dramatic decrease of Judaean names in Babylonia at the beginning of the Persian period (Pearce 2012), and it appears that the return of Babylonian Jews to their country of origin was a gradual process over time (Barstad 2003; Lipschits 2003). Not all may have wished to uproot themselves: descendants of the first-generation émigrés are likely to have had fairly settled lives. An important essay by W. Lee Humphreys inaugurates the view that Dan. 1–6 and Esther, for example, set out "a life-style for Diaspora". He suggests that "in certain circles at least the possibility of a creative and rewarding interaction with the foreign environment was present and could work for the good of the Jew" (Humphreys 1973: 213), and he argues that the stories show how "one could, as a Jew, overcome adversity and find a life both rewarding and creative within the pagan setting" (1973: 223). Jer. 29 and Ezekiel point to a subject population that maintained communal identity, where family life was possible, and a degree of self-government. Second or third generation descendants of the original deportees may have married local women and raised children (Wilson 2012: 134). These inferences are supported by non-Biblical documentary evidence. The Murashu Documents, lists of the business dealings of Judaeans deep into the Persian period, show that Judaeans were employed in small-scale agriculture, and as low-level officials, clustered in places like "al-Yahudu" ("Judahville") in the Nippur region (Pearce 2012: 270). With improved conditions for agriculture following a period of global warming, some may have preferred to stay where they were rather than return to uncertain circumstances in the "land" (Becking 2012: 59). Ezra attaches no blame to those who chose to go to Jerusalem later; the blessing of divine providence was not exhausted by the first group who had returned. But there appears to be no place in the book's ideological scheme of things for those who chose to remain in Babylonia.

Nor is there mention of the diaspora communities in Egypt, formed over the years of waves of refugees from Samaria and Judah. Jer. 44 opens with a sermon addressed to the fugitive communities of Jews at Migdol and Tahpanhes, on the delta, Memphis, half-way south, and Pathros, the south region of the first Nile cataract, whose capital was Elephantine. These communities reflect a period when the Jews were well settled, not in the immediate aftermath of the events of 587/582 BCE (Carroll 1986: 731). Papyri and ostraca in the Elephantine Archive conjure up the everyday lives of Jewish soldiers and stone masons and their families in a cosmopolitan military colony on the turbulent frontier between Egypt and Nubia. They were open to the practices of the Egyptians: they swore by the Egyptian goddess Sati, consort of the ram-headed Khnum (Modrzejewski 1997: 33) as well as by YHWH. Nonetheless, these Egyptian Judaeans might justifiably have seen themselves as inheritors of the ancestral traditions of Israel. They created a magnificent temple, observed the Sabbath, celebrated Passover, and gave their children Hebrew names. Yet the writers of Ezra and Nehemiah are not concerned with them; their focus is on the *golah* (the returned Jewish exiles) and others in Judah.

The ideology of repatriation today

The privileging of the repatriate Judaeans from Babylonia over others and the exaggerated legitimization of these as the true Israel is ideological. There is a discrepancy between ideological construct and social reality. In this, there are analogies with repatriation policy and practice today. Anders Stefansson's survey of refugee returns to Sarajevo illustrates the fact that there are often "discrepancies between the level of theory and the lived experiences of refugees" (2004: 170). This is exemplified by the way official discourse of repatriation is at odds with the findings of refugee studies. In the late 20th century, repatriation increasingly emerged as a key topic in international circles. Decisions were based on political rather than humanitarian considerations: "dominant states in the international system decide from time to time, in the light of their interests, which solution to the global refugee problem should be promoted as the preferred solution" (Chimni 2004: 73). Since the 1990s, when the UNHCR found "voluntary repatriation" to be "the most desirable solution to refugee problems", there has been a move towards "imposed return". This doctrine was first aired in September 1996 by Dennis McNamara, Director of the UNHCR Division of International Protection, who was faced with increasing pressure from host states, often themselves extremely poor, and from northern states unwilling to share the burden of the south at the level of asylum and the sharing of resources (Chimni 2004). The policy is legitimated by what scholars style "repatriation discourse", a line of thinking based on the questionable assumption that all refugees want to go home. International refugee agencies portray refugees as an undifferentiated mass of individuals who have flight or displacement in common, and they depict repatriation in fundamentalist terms as a return to the familiar context of one's former life (Stefansson 2004: 171, 186).

Refugee studies, however, reject the assumption that the refugees' attachment to their country of origin and their desire to return is a given. In many cases, the relationship will have been abruptly severed. In her study of two Iraqi refugee groups in London, Madawi Al-Rasheed shows how these have different attitudes towards repatriation depending on their previous refugee experience and their relationship to their country of origin (Al-Rasheed 1994). The majority group define themselves as Arab and consider themselves to be from the cultural mainstream of Iraq. These are a socioeconomic mix. The first wave of refugees to Britain in the 1950s were mostly professional middle-class and rich landed gentry who sought asylum because of their opposition to the Iraqi political regime. These were joined after the revolutions, *coup d'état*, and purges of the 1960s by others, many of them leading Communists, who had been involved in the political struggle. The number of refugees increased with the Iran–Iraq War in the 1980s and the Gulf War in 1990–1991. These Iraqi Arabs strongly believe that their exile is temporary and identify wholeheartedly with their home country, to which they plan to return when political circumstances permit. The Iraqi Assyrians, however, are a small Christian minority, who originally came to Iraq as refugees from Turkey during the First World War. Enlisted by the British as levies to protect the British military bases in Iraq and suppress Arab revolts, they co-existed uneasily with the Arab majority after Independence. Many fled for their lives following the two Gulf Wars and see their exile in Britain as permanent (Al-Rasheed 1994: 203–209). For them, repatriation is not an option.

The ideology of the fallow land

To what extent was Judah inhabited when the settlers arrived from Babylon? The question has been addressed exhaustively since Hans Barstad wrote *The Myth of the Empty Land* in 1996, with notable contributions from an archaeological perspective (Lipschits 2011; Faust 2011, 2012), and I do not intend to rehearse the arguments here. It is sufficient to point to the ideological link with the myth of return and to suggest that "the myth of the empty land is a myth for those in exile, and it is a myth of return, which promises that the land will be given back to them at the end of exile, since the land is either empty or inhabited by the 'wrong' kind of people" (Hägglund 2008: 165). Some texts suggest that those who remained were "the poorest people in the land" (2 Kgs 24.14), "vinedressers and tillers of the soil" (2 Kgs 25.12), while 2 Kgs 25.21

and Jer. 52.27 allege that the land became totally empty (cf. 2 Chron. 36.20–21). It didn't of course, but the allegation is another way of discounting the inhabitants of the land.

The Parable of the Figs, attributed to the prophet Jeremiah, is a particularly crude illustration of the denigration of those who had remained in Judah. The vision asserts that only the descendants of those Judaeans who were forcibly displaced to Babylon in 597 BCE have a legitimate claim to live in Jerusalem and Judah. These are "good figs". A choice delicacy, they will be brought back to the land under the protection of YHWH (Jer. 24.5). All others, including the inhabitants of the land, are "rotten figs" that are unfit for human consumption, worthless, and to be destroyed (Jer. 24.9–10). The force of the parable is to discount the population of Judah, the refugees who had fled to Egypt, and any deportees in Babylonia who had not been deported in 597 BCE. Whatever the cause, only those who were deported with Jehoiachin count. They enjoy YHWH's special care; they will be returned to Judah, where they will be his people and he will be their god. The land will be cleared of its existing inhabitants by "sword, famine, pestilence" and become vacant, ready for the returnees. This functions as a "myth of return" for diaspora Jews.

The myth of return today

What resonance might this have in the lives of a diaspora community today? A study of Israelis living in Toronto, a small minority, shows how myths of return can solve an apparent contradiction between a nationalist ideology and the fact that these Israelis are still living in diaspora (Cohen & Gold 1997). By postponing the total integration of the Israelis into the host society, they construct an Israeli identity which takes on a life of its own: "on a social level, the myth of return ... involves preserving a distinctive language, reproduction of cultural symbols, reinforcement of shared biographies and intensification of 'us versus them' stereotypes. The ethnicization of a group of migrants is essential if the ultimate symbolic objective of the group is to return to the homeland" (Cohen & Gold 1997: 376). These particular migrants readily distinguish themselves from the existing Jewish community in Toronto. Unable to integrate into the existing Jewish community, these Israelis emphasize their otherness with selective modes of exclusion. Most significant of these is language, in this case the use of spoken Hebrew, which distinguishes them from the "Canadian Jews" and ensures that the national culture is preserved (Cohen & Gold 1997: 381): "Hebrew is instrumental in the production of authentic Israelness at impromptu 'sing-alongs'" and other community gatherings. The "Canadian Jews", permeated with Zionism, stigmatize the migrants from Israel as *Yordim* – a derogatory Hebrew term to describe those who "descend" from the land of Israel to the Diaspora (Cohen & Gold 1997: 375). For their part, the Israelis stereotype the "Canadian Jews" as "formal, cold, naïve, beer-drinkers, and couch potatoes" (Cohen & Gold 1997: 389). Such stereotypes serve as boundary-markers, enhancing the sense of superiority of the Israelis.

But what happens when the myth of return becomes reality? There can be a "reverse culture shock" – the repatriates may feel like outsiders, strangers in their home. For Nicholas Van Hear, "the reception of returnees by those who stayed behind can vary as much as reception in a new society, particularly when the period abroad has been long. It is an obvious fact, but it bears noting that both the returnees and the home community will have changed during the absence of the migrants" (Van Hear 1998: 56). Relationships between repatriated refugees and their former home communities can be contentious. As the visions of home and of return nourished in exile engage with the different circumstances of life in the places to which they return, issues of land title, political affiliation, cultural practices, and religious beliefs frequently give rise to conflict (Stefansson 2004: 178).

Refugee studies generally bear this out. Jonathan Bascom's study of the reintegration of returnees to Eritrea (Bascom 2005) reveals a lack of solidarity between those who returned and those who had remained in Eritrea. In particular, there were tensions over the ownership of farmland. Many had expected to return to the village of their birthplace and reclaim their ancestral land; but that was problematic. These findings are reinforced by a study from Sarajevo which focused on refugees who had returned after the Bosnian War (Stefansson 2004). Stefansson points to clear divisions between the returnees and those who had remained at home. Those who returned felt structural discrimination compounded by accusations of having betrayed Sarajevo by fleeing abroad; they found that those who stayed behind took no interest in hearing about their experience of being refugees, but merely wanted to preach about their own suffering during the war. Tensions were exacerbated by the fact that some returnees felt superior because of their experience in Western countries.

Ezra-Nehemiah: ideology and politics

The peoples of the land

How did those who did return to Judah relate to the "peoples of the land"? For Ezra-Nehemiah, these are clearly to be kept apart, but details are murky (Ezra 9.2,11). Who are these "people"? Their identity is by no means obvious (Rom-Shiloni 2011: 134–135).

In Ezra 1–6, there is obvious hostility between the "people of Judah" and the "peoples of the land". Described as "the adversaries of Judah and Benjamin" (Ezra 4.1), these "adversaries" are said to be of foreign origin, descendants of multi-ethnic deportees from Assyria (2 Kgs 17.24–28). They may have farmed the land for decades within Judah or in neighbouring territories, but the possibility that true Jews may be amongst them is too remote for the writers of Ezra-Nehemiah to contemplate. When they offer to help with the rebuilding of the temple on the grounds that they worship the same god (Ezra 4.1–3), the offer is spurned "by the heads of families in Israel" with the rebuff: "we alone will build to the LORD, the God of Israel". And so "the repatriates separate themselves from this mongrel 'other' population by advocating their own genuine and distinctive status; in religion, culture, national history, and politics, the repatriates are ... 'the [true] Judeans (Jews)'" (Rom-Shiloni 2011: 136).

Then, second, there are those who are characterized anachronistically as Israel's ancient enemies: Canaanites, Hittites, Perizzites, Jebusites, Ammonites, Moabites, and Egyptians (Ezra 9.1). Most of these had long ago assimilated or ceased to exist. But in ideological terms, they are foreigners par excellence, people with whom relationships are forbidden by the Torah (Deut. 7.1–4; Exod. 23.23–24; 34.11; Lev. 18.1–5).

And third, Neh. 9.2 opposes in broad-brush terms "those of Israelite descent" to "all foreigners" without distinction; the use of the Hebrew word "seed" (cf. Ezra 9.2) points here to an exclusively racial understanding of "Israel" (Williamson 1985: 311). The repatriates swear on oath to cut themselves off from the "peoples of the land", reinforcing the oath by entering into "a curse" (Neh. 10.28–30).

The bottom line in each of these cases is that the *golah*, the returned Judaean exiles, are to have no relationships with the "peoples of the land", who are designated as "foreign". There is a distinction to be drawn here between Ezra and the Nehemiah memoir. For Ezra, only the "sons of the *golah*" are "Israel" (Ezra 3.8; 4.1–3; 6.16, 21; 9.1–2). These are to have no relations with any others – whether inhabitants of Judah or neighbouring lands. The Nehemiah memoir, however, doesn't refer to the *golah* as the ideal Israel. At least once, Nehemiah identifies Judaeans as "sons of Israel" (Neh. 2.10); he is a Judaean nationalist (Houston 2004). As Governor of Judah, he singles out for criticism chiefly his political opponents: Sanballat the Horonite, Tobiah the Ammonite, and Geshem the Arab (Neh. 2.10, 19; 4.1; 6.1–9, 12–19; 13.1–9). Their designations are contemptuous. Sanballat, according to the Elephantine Papyri, was Governor of Samaria, though Nehemiah never credits him with the title (Williamson 1985: 182). Instead, he regularly describes him dismissively as "the Horonite"; we are probably meant to understand that Sanballat came from Beth-Horon, a few miles north of Jerusalem (Williamson 1985: 182). While he can scarcely be judged to be a non-Israelite, in a Judaean perspective he is "foreign". Tobiah appears to be a younger colleague of Sanballat, possibly appointed to temporary authority in Judah pending the appointment of the next governor (Williamson 1985: 184; cf. Neh. 6.17–19). His name, with the ending "-iah", is unmistakably Israelite, yet Nehemiah fails to recognize his Israelite ethnicity, and the designation "Ammonite" is meant pejoritatively (cf. Deut. 23.3–4). Geshem, belittled as "the Arab", appears from archaeological inscriptions to have been a ruler of considerable power and influence (Williamson 1985: 192). Whether or not the alliance is serious in its aim to fight against Jerusalem (Neh. 4.7–8) is debatable (Williamson 1985: 225), but it is clear that Neh. 4 associates their "foreignness" with discreditable character: non-Judaean "regional dignitaries are represented as thieves and cut-throats" (Grabbe 1998b: 162), and they are denied any civic, legal, or cultic rights in the Jerusalem community (Neh. 2.20b; Williamson 1985: 192). They have no stake in the nation.

The exclusion of foreigners

Can the exclusion of foreigners be justified in legal terms? In Neh. 13.1–3, the people hear a short extract from the Book of Moses and overinterpret what they hear. The quotation of Deut. 23.1–9 is selective. In Deuteronomy, the admission or exclusion of "foreigners" from the "assembly of YHWH" is largely contingent on ethical factors (cf. Gen. 12.3). Ammonites and Moabites are to be permanently excluded from the assembly because they had failed to supply the Israelites with food and water on their flight from Egypt. Edomites and Egyptians, on the other hand, have a real prospect of incorporation – in the case of Edom because of its kinship with Israel, and in the case of Egypt on ethical grounds: Egypt showed hospitality to Israel in the time of Joseph (Gen. 46–50; Houten 1991: 101), and this is in conformity with Israel's own mandate to show kindness to the sojourner (Deut. 14.29). Nehemiah, however, air-brushes Egypt out of the picture, and Deuteronomy's positive ethical impulse is stifled. Against the thrust of Deut. 23.1–9, the people generalize the ban on Ammonites and Moabites to exclude "all those of foreign descent".

For Nehemiah, the very presence of foreigners is defiling. This is underscored by Neh. 13.4–9, where the first person narrative gives an impression of immediacy. Nehemiah had been away from Jerusalem "for some time" (Neh. 13.6) – long enough for the priest Eliashib to prepare a large storeroom in the temple for his relative Tobiah, who had influential connections in Jerusalem (Neh. 6.17–19). Tobiah, allegedly "an Ammonite" (Neh. 2.10,19), a "foreigner" par excellence (Neh. 13.1), has "no right in Jerusalem" (Neh. 2.20). On discovering what Eliashib has done, Nehemiah in fury throws out all of Tobiah's furniture. Then he orders that all the chambers in the temple be purified. Not just Tobiah's room, but all the rooms in the vicinity of the polluted chamber have to be decontaminated.

It is instructive to compare this passage with Ezek. 44.6–16, which is likewise concerned with the profanation of the sanctuary by foreigners. Ezekiel has priestly concerns (cf. Lev. 22.25) about foreigners who have been admitted to the sanctuary and allowed to serve in the temple. For him, this is an abomination. These people are uncircumcised; they lack "the great confessional sign of genuine descent from Abraham" (Zimmerli 1983: 454); there is a sense of ritual unfitness. Hence the need to exclude them. But in Nehemiah's account, there is no mention of circumcision and Tobiah is a lodger, not a temple servant. The reason for his exclusion is his status as a "foreigner". The implications are that foreigners carry within themselves the bacillus of impurity. And the expulsion of Tobiah is not a dispassionate act. Nehemiah's rage in throwing out all of his household furniture is excessive, and we may assume with some degree of certainty that it is fuelled by personal vindictiveness towards one of his chief opponents, the leading representative of the native Jews (Neh. 2.10, 19; 6.19). Was Nehemiah's fury energized by the awareness that in his absence Tobiah might have set up a power base in the Jerusalem temple? The smug air of religious rectitude rings hollow (Neh. 13.14).

The divorcing of foreign wives

Both Ezra and Nehemiah single out for particular attention one special category of "foreigners" – those who are referred to generically as "foreign wives". Chapters nine and ten of Ezra have been described as "amongst the least attractive parts of Ezra-Nehemiah, if not of the whole Old Testament" (Williamson 1985: 159); they are "xenophobic" (Smith-Christopher 1994: 256; Grabbe 1998a). David Clines is "appalled by the personal misery brought into so many families by the compulsory divorce of foreign wives [and] ... outraged at Ezra's insistence on racial purity" (Clines 1984: 116). It is reported to Ezra that all the people, including the priests and Levites, have been intermarrying with women alleged to be members of ethnic groups mostly long ago extinct, Israel's archaic enemies, and lambasted as unclean. The implications are pejorative: the choice of a non-Israelite spouse is deviant.

The leaders of the community have been foremost in "taking some of their daughters as wives for themselves and their sons", faithlessly mixing the "holy seed" with the "peoples of the land" (Ezra 9.2) and contaminating the purity of the gene pool. Implicit here is an appeal to the Holiness Code, in particular to Lev. 19.19, which forbids the mixing of unlike animals, crops, and materials. In prohibiting "mixed" marriage, does the community see itself as racially distinct from others? Those who have offended are named and shamed (Ezra 10.18–44) by a committee formed for that purpose. The guilty priests pledge to send away their wives and offer a ram in reparation. The other culprits, with no guilt offering prescribed, also banish their wives and their children. Still stereotyped as "foreign" and maligned implicitly as a cause of sacrilege, however unintended (cf. Lev. 5.17–19), the women are nameless and voiceless. There is no recognition of their humanity, and no provision is made for their needs or those of their children.

In his attempts to coerce men to send away their foreign wives (Ezra 10.3), Ezra goes much further than the provisions of the law. Deut. 7.1–4 prohibits mixed marriages to minimize the risk of Israelites worshipping foreign gods, but does not advocate divorce – and neither does Exod. 34.15–16, which likewise proscribes mixed marriage for fear of apostasy. Ezra uses the formulaic injunction against intermarriage: "do not give your daughter to his son, or take his daughter to your son" (Deut. 7.3), but replaces Deuteronomy's motive clause "for they will turn your son away from following me, that they may serve other gods" (Deut. 7.4) with an injunction against outsiders entering the assembly (Southwood 2011b: 2). This is manipulation of the text for polemical purposes. Ezra is chiefly concerned to monitor the membership of "the assembly" and to maintain Israel's ethnic identity. The "sending away" of foreign wives is, in his eyes, a necessary part of this. By coercing the returnees to dissolve mixed marriages, he misinterprets the law along racist lines (Williamson 1985: 161).

Children who cannot speak Yehudit

If Ezra's measures have already taken place, they have clearly not worked. After his return from Susa, Nehemiah discovers that some Jews had married "women of Ashdod, Ammon, and Moab" (Neh. 13.23). And even more shocking, he sees children who "could not speak the language of Judah" (Neh. 13.24). Nehemiah is outraged to find that half of the children he met were fluent in Ashdodite, but unable to speak Hebrew. Much more is at stake at this point than land tenure (Smith-Christopher 1994: 244). The problem here is "not so much speaking a foreign language as the inability to speak Hebrew" (Blenkinsopp 1988: 363). If we take language to be "the symbol of ethnicity" (Southwood 2011b: 8), this is symptomatic of a deeper problem – the need to preserve ethnic identity. Although, as Katherine Southwood demonstrates, there is no straightforward connection between language and ethnic identity yet in some conditions, "religious and ethnic groups emphasize the centrality of language to the extent that it becomes the primary means of marking off the boundary … between 'us' and 'them'" (Southwood 2011b: 13). Although it is not quite clear what is meant by "Ashdodite", it is quite clear that what is at stake for Nehemiah is the ethnic identity of the Judaeans as symbolized by Hebrew (Southwood 2011b: 15). *Yehudim* is identified with *Yehudit*. The language of Judah is "the symbolic body-guard protecting group identity" (Southwood 2011b: 17). The language of the children will have long-term consequences for the allegiances to Judah of future generations.

The relationship between language and ethnic identity was still a live issue at the beginning of the 20th century, when President Theodore Roosevelt insisted, "we have room for but one language here, and that is the English language, for we intend to see that the crucible turns out people as Americans, and not as dwellers of a polyglot boarding house; and we have room for but one sole loyalty, and that is loyalty to the American people" (Ruiz 2011: 110). These remarks were reflected in US policy most notably in the wake of the Spanish-American war, when Cuba and Puerto Rico became US possessions: the Americanization of the Puerto Rican population included a disparaging of their spoken language: "the English language was the medium, and 'Americanization' was the unmistakable message" (Ruiz 2011: 112). The attempt to avoid linguistic assimilation strengthened a sense of national solidarity.

Enforcement

Nehemiah does not just urge the violators to separate; he reinforces the repudiation with brute force. In Neh. 13.23–25, in a violent outburst of abusive behaviour, he contends with Jews who had married foreign wives, curses them, beats some of them, and pulls out their hair. Although this outburst of rage is consistent with his behaviour in Neh. 13.8, this is scarcely the sort of behaviour one might expect of a governor – one may speculate that he gave vent to his rage in this way as a last resort, in awareness that his policy was failing. The dangers of intermarriage with "foreigners" are still there, even in priestly families (Neh. 13.28). With zeal that goes far beyond Ezra's divorce procedures (Williamson 1985: 399), Nehemiah banishes one of the sons or grandsons of the high priest. This man had offended by marrying the daughter of Sanballat "the Horonite", a non-Judaean and therefore, in Nehemiah's eyes, a "foreign woman". In this, the whole family had "defiled the priesthood" (Neh. 13.29). Although the man is not yet a high priest, there may be reference here to the requirement in Lev. 21.14b–15 that a high priest should marry a "virgin of his own kin", *kin* in this case referring to his patrilinear kinship group (Milgrom 2000: 1879). Ezek. 44.22 offers an interpretation closer to the spirit of Nehemiah, specifying that the high priest should marry "a virgin of the stock of the House of Israel". Although the details of this episode in Nehemiah are sketchy, in the context of the hostile ethnocentricity of chapter thirteen as a whole, we might infer that here too we have overzealous enforcement of the law in racist terms. And so the book comes to its chilling conclusion: "thus I cleansed them from everything foreign" (Neh. 13.30).

Ideology and politics

In Jewish tradition, Ezra and Nehemiah are treated as two strands of an original work and separate from other Biblical books (Williamson 1985: xxi). They reveal a close connection between ideology and politics. This perception is fostered by the fact that the Hebrew word for "assembly", *qahal*, may be understood in religious or civil terms. In some respects, the assembly in Ezra has a religious bearing: YHWH calls not one but many individuals to go to Jerusalem to rebuild the temple (Ezra 1.5), and the group in total is referred to as an "assembly" (Ezra 2.64). But as questions emerge around membership of the assembly, the emphasis becomes one of public law. For Wolfgang Oswald, the status of foreign women and their children is a civil matter (Oswald 2012: 3) and the legislation analogous to that of the Greek legislative assemblies under Pericles (2012: 6). In Ezra 9–10, a public body consisting of "the sons of the *golah*" pronounces that foreign wives and their children are to be expelled, and severe sanctions are imposed on anyone who refuses to comply with the expulsion order (Ezra 10.8). There is a similar political pattern in Neh. 9–10, although without reference to the *golah*.

Oswald pursues the point that the expulsion from an institutional body like those in Ezra 10.8 or Neh. 9–10 "attests that the actors defined themselves politically as an association of persons. A political entity of this type is commonly referred to as a 'citizen state', and membership in the assembly is equivalent to citizenship" (Oswald 2012: 6). The argument is persuasive. Each book reflects the ideological concerns of the editors, and ideology and politics are never far apart. But there is a difference of emphasis between Ezra and Nehemiah. In Ezra, the political identity is sectarian; in the Nehemiah memoir, it is nationalist. For Ezra, the "sons of the *golah*" alone are portrayed as heirs of Israel, a righteous remnant, divinely called. Their sights are on the rebuilding of the Jerusalem temple and the regulation of their restored community lives by the Torah. In Babylonia, where there was no temple, the purity regulations had provided a certain continuity: "Ezekiel's ritualization of ethics extended the symbolic language of the Jerusalem temple beyond the strictly priestly sphere and enabled the institution to remain central to the community's social values and aspirations" (Mein 2001: 261). Their scope for political engagement, however, was circumscribed: that community was a dominated minority; only in the "limited spheres of family, business, and the immediate community" were its members free to make moral or ethical decisions (Mein 2001: 260). This relative passivity in the face of larger political issues may have continued into the new life in the Land. Although they have been given "a stake in (YHWH's) holy place" and a fresh lease of life by "the kings of Persia" to set up the temple, the Jews are still subject to their Persian overlords; they are "slaves" without significant political freedom (Ezra 9.8–9; cf. Neh. 9.36–37). They are, however, provided with "a wall in Judaea and Jerusalem" (Ezra 9.9). The idea of a literal wall around Judaea and Jerusalem is odd. But the Hebrew word used here for "wall" is not the normal word for a city wall; it usually refers to a wall around a vineyard (Num. 22.24; Isa. 5.5; Ps. 80.12; Prov. 24.31; Williamson 1985: 136). And the vineyard is a traditional metaphor for Israel (Hos. 2.8; Isa. 5.5; Ezek. 13.5). So the *golah,* qua Israel, is assured of divine protection through the Persian regime as it rebuilds the temple.

Taken together, the evidence, in the case of Ezra and his community, points to a sectarian identity, where "sect" is defined by Yonder Gillihan as "a particular form of voluntary association whose ideology … is in tension with particular aspects of its society", leading to a certain degree of separation from broader social life (Gillihan 2011: 65). Such separation would protect the sectarians from the "imprints and defilements of apostate Israel". We may in passing distinguish certain features here which we see in a more highly developed form in the Dead Sea Scrolls: the role of the "teacher of righteousness"; the conviction that the Torah contains the essential constitution and laws for Israel; the exclusion of transgressive members from the community (4QD fr. 118b-21; 1QS 1.16–3.12); the emphasis on rules of purity; and, in 1QS, the vitriolic abuse of foreigners and separation from them. As Barton observes drily, "typically sects are bound internally by strong moral standards, but they have nothing to say about the external world, which is a *massa perditionis* and is going to the devil" (Barton 2003: 156).

In Ezra, a sectarian identity is reinforced in racist terms. The book's xenophobia is based on an ideology of election by race, with the implicit assumption that inherited characteristics are passed on genetically. Foreign wives in particular are seen as a biological danger to the purity of the *golah*, whose original inherited traits could only degenerate by "race-mixing" to the point where it lost its distinguishing characteristics and was doomed to extinction. Hence the elimination of domestic non-conformists by a self-purge of the community. Though Ezra is presented as a guardian and teacher of the law, in the divorcing of foreign wives, and the expulsion of them and their children, he goes beyond the Torah.

But is there not a tension between an ideology of sectarianism and an ideology of race? Are the defining features in each case not different? Can these be held together? Here, an instructive parallel may be drawn with studies of the "settler mentality", notably Pamela Clayton's analysis of the traditional settler mentality in Northern Ireland (Clayton 1998). She suggests that "only the term 'racism' adequately implies the viciousness of the stereotype of the inferior group and the peculiar mixture of contempt, hatred and fear that characterises the feelings of members of the dominant (but insecure) group towards the inferior (but threatening) group" (Clayton 1998: 53). The more obdurate among the Protestants "display many features of settler racism and attitudes towards the 'natives'. Settler racism has the added dimension of fear that the settlers will be dispossessed ... Many Protestants see Catholics as the Other, the eternal enemy, always a threat". And Clayton continues: "as a group Catholics are considered both inferior and dangerous. They have been accused of being lazy, dirty, devious, treacherous, violent, over-fecund, irrational ... superstitious ... and in thrall to manipulative leaders ... By contrast, Protestants portray themselves as hard-working and competent, independent in deed and thought, peaceful and law-abiding, but manly and resolute" (Clayton 1998: 54). All these stereotypes, she concludes, mirror those found in other settler colonies.

The Nehemiah memoir foregrounds the Judaeans as "sons of Israel", not the *golah*. The emphasis is nationalist. The city walls which they reconstruct are defensive and protective, but their value is also emblematic; they mark a barrier between citizens and their enemies, a *cordon sanitaire* to keep out aliens and real or imagined contagion (Newey 2011).

Today's barriers are erected against asylum-seekers and refugees. State-skirting palisades are erected to keep them out, like the border fence whereby the US proposes to close off its two-thousand-mile southern border to prevent illegal immigration; or the Via Anelli Wall in Padua, a three-metre-high structure of steel eighty-four metres long, which for one year sought to separate the citizens of Padua from their Arab neighbours, mostly people from Africa seeking asylum in Italy; or the eight-metre-high wall that the UN calls "the separation barrier" and the Israeli authorities "the security fence" – the wall that separates Israel from the West Bank, snaking through and around Bethlehem. All these walls rely on an arbitrary division into citizen and alien, but the attempts of their builders to exclude the Other, the stranger, are not always successful: "there never was a golden age of walled security and hermetic exclusion" (Newey 2011). If walls, actual or metaphorical, are built to deny insecurities with a semblance of strength, are they anything more than "a front in the face of waning sovereignty" (Newey 2011)?

Enemies within

In Nehemiah, enemies within are expelled. If these policies are the equivalent of modern citizenship laws as Oswald suggests (Oswald 2012: 17), they are implemented in ways which are xenophobic and racially prejudiced. This is not a peculiarity of an ancient culture. In Europe today, attitudes have hardened, as society has become increasingly diverse and people fear that "traditional European values" are being relativized. This has "cast doubt on the long story that held us together, with its passage through the Enlightenment to liberal democracy, Europe's unique discovery, which it meant to hand down across the generations" (Harding 2012). With multiculturalism, identity has become an issue.

Following 9/11, politicians and the popular press became increasingly concerned about the "enemy within" and felt at liberty to talk critically about the minorities in their societies. No longer were these seen in terms of their country of origin, be that Bangladesh, Pakistan, Afghanistan, Iran, or Iraq: all were blanketed together as "Muslim". Fears of Muslims became entrenched. Mammad Aidani, in his study of the Iranian refugee diaspora in Australia, instances a woman called "Huri". Though she had respect for her religion, she had never worn Islamic dress and had begun to feel integrated into Australian life when 9/11 turned everything sour:

> I spent most of my life in an Islamic society and was tired of justifying that I was a pious woman to traditionalists … so I would insist not to mention the name Islam very often. And here I'm subject to a different kind of humiliation. I proudly utter that "yes, I'm a Muslim young woman". It's not about faith really; it is my dignity; when it is under pressure it defies the rigid rules … I'm part of that world and I'm part of Iranian culture and I feel so sad that our people here are under so much anxiety because of terrorism … Of course, I'm upset … In my country as a woman I was respected, but here I'm just a person out there, and worse, some-one from the Middle East and a Muslim.
>
> (Aidani 2010: 54)

As Aidani observes, "Huri has been transformed into an ideological subject of September 11, 2001" (2010: 55). Her identity is distorted, and as a person she is stigmatized. Over the following years, Pym Fortuyn and Theo Van Gogh voiced the anti-Islamic sentiments of many beyond the boundaries of Holland, and the rise of far-right extremists with their ideological hatred fuels crimes against minorities all over Europe.

Islamophobia is not something new. It was widespread long before 9/11. But the destruction of the twin towers gave rise to institutional Islamophobia, where Islamophobic discourse was modified into a discourse of anti-terrorism. A well-publicized case illustrates this well (Zaoui 2006). A military coup in Algeria had forced Ahmed Zaoui, a democratically elected politician for the moderate wing of the FIS, *Front Islamique du Salut* (Islamic Front for Salvation), to flee to Europe and then Malaysia. In December 2002, he sought political asylum in New Zealand. The New Zealand authorities were convinced that they had caught an important terrorist suspect. He was imprisoned for the next two years, the first eight months in solitary confinement in a maximum security prison. In the meantime, the Algerian government convicted him on trumped up charges and served him with six life sentences and two death sentences. Only gradually did the New Zealand authorities come to accept that he was in fact a political refugee. But allegedly because he was considered to be "charismatic" (Brown 2012), he was thought to be capable of attracting radical Muslims to New Zealand. He was served with a security risk certificate and kept in custody. In 2004, he was released on bail, and in 2007 the security risk certificate was withdrawn and Zaoui's family was allowed to join him in New Zealand permanently. His story and that of Mohamed Haneef (Haneef 2007) in Australia attracted considerable media interest.

Both Zaoui and Haneef are Muslim, and they were treated by the authorities in a way that could only be described as institutionally Islamophobic (Brown 2012: 155). The cases were intensely politicized. They "highlighted an amalgam in public discourse of Islam, fundamentalism and terrorism". However, Malcolm Brown continues, "the front line is not airport security, but the need for a more sophisticated understanding of Islam and of fundamentalism that recognises the diversity inherent in both phenomena. This can contribute to the security of Muslims, including Muslim migrants, and of their host societies" (2012: 160).

Government attitudes in the West towards migrants generally have hardened. Over recent years, they "have decided to treat migrants from the less developed world as an undifferentiated evil: refugees, economic migrants, drug traffickers, and terrorists are officially categorized as presenting a unified threat, and will all confront a common policy of deterrents" (Hathaway 1993: 723). In times of recession and insolvency, refugees who are already in the country are regularly cast in hostile terms as competitors for rare jobs and a drain on the Exchequer however much their papers are in order and they pay taxes like any other citizen. This suspicion of the Other is reflected in family legislation: "mixed" families where only one of the partners has citizenship have been targeted by harsh rules. Where possible, measures are taken to exclude non-EEA partners of EU citizens and their children. Soon after the attacks on the twin towers,

Denmark passed laws making it hard for citizens to marry partners from outside the EU and impossible if they were under twenty-four. France followed suit, and in 2012 Britain's draconian Immigration Rules were calculated to break up 17,800 such families a year.

Ethical concerns

Given that Ezra-Nehemiah, with its xenophobia and misleading ideology, is in the Bible, what are we to do with it? To disregard it is not a viable option (Snyder 2012: 142). First, we have to recognize that here we probably see reflected an ongoing dialogue around inclusion and exclusion within Jewish society at the time the book was edited, "an exegetical debate centering on identity that was conducted by Jews in the Achaemenid period and has left its traces in the Hebrew Bible" (Schaper 2011: 28). We might recognize the difference between, say, Ezra 10.2–3 and Isa. 56.3, 6–7. Both were composed around the same time and both refer directly or indirectly to the prescriptions of the Torah but in quite different terms. While Ezra 10.3 goes well beyond the Torah in prescribing coercive divorce, Isa. 56.1–8 appears to contravene Deut. 23.2–9 in an expansive vision of conditional inclusiveness. In this, Isaiah is also directly opposed to Ezek. 44.6–9 (cf. Neh. 13.1–3). There is no scope here to discuss this "inner-Biblical exegesis" except to suggest that the interpretations of Isaiah on the one hand and Ezekiel and Ezra on the other are mutually exclusive, although each is based on Deut. 23.2–9 (Schaper 2011: 30) and that underlying social and political factors are almost certainly influential. Circumstances led the editors of Ezra-Nehemiah to an interpretation of Scripture that we find unacceptable.

But is that all we can say? Is there not some means of weighing these up as influences on our behaviour today? We may set the xenophobia of Ezra-Nehemiah against the laws in Exodus, Deuteronomy, and Leviticus that protect the resident alien. The Jewish People kept alive their memory of their ancestors as *gerim*, and this was the basis for the moral understanding that protection should be offered to the alien. Deut. 10.19 invites the reader to love the *ger* in his particularity as a stranger; exile in Babylonia affords a new awareness of the "heart of an alien" (Exod. 22.21; 23.9); and finally, a subset of the Golden Rule, "the alien who resides with you shall be to you as the citizen among you; you shall love the alien as yourself, for you were aliens in the land of Egypt" (Lev. 19.34). Doing wrong to aliens should clearly be ruled out. But this is hard to define and equally hard to enforce; what is at stake is more than a legal code (Barton 1998: 79): "the profundity of much that the Old Testament has to say in the field of ethics is bound up with the fact that it thus allows for the intricacy and untidiness of human life" (Barton 1998: 37). In the narratives, Barton continues, "we can see ethical decision-making and, of course, ethical failure in action". The Bible presents us with complex human beings with a range of attitudes and responses to challenging situations; we recognize our affinity with some of these. Ezra-Nehemiah has its place. But the overall perspective is that there is a community of moral understanding between human beings and God, and that this gives rise to special obligations. In the light of this, aliens are to be treated justly, protected from oppression, and, where they are poor and vulnerable, given succour.

7

JESUS

The perspective that the stranger is to be treated fairly and, when vulnerable, given succour is fundamental to the life and teachings of Jesus and foundational for the life of the church.

The gospels may be read as narrative biographies of Jesus. As Richard Burridge demonstrates, these share the same features as ancient biographies: "they are prose narratives of a medium length ... with only a bare chronological structure of the subject's birth ... and their death; in between, they contain stories, sayings and anecdotes about the person, with a constant focus on their words and deeds" (Burridge 2007: 24).

Each evangelist has his own particular way of describing Jesus' life, death, ministry, and teaching, so some things are included and others omitted; but every passage tells us something about Jesus. The gospels are not just collections of Jesus' ethical teachings; there is a strong link between his words, his deeds, and the rest of his life. Jesus' teaching on major moral issues such as wealth and poverty is rigorous and all-demanding, but it is also earthed in his open pastoral acceptance of the vulnerable and marginalized. He also calls people to follow him, to seek to become both "perfect" and "merciful" as God is perfect and merciful: he is a model for all time of how to live a life that reflects God's character on earth.

Jesus the refugee

Both Matthew and Luke preface their gospels with stories around Jesus' birth, but only Matthew portrays Jesus and his family as refugees (Mt. 2.13–15). We read how Joseph, Mary, and the child Jesus are forced to flee Bethlehem. They are in deadly danger. If they stay in Judaea any longer, the little boy will surely be killed by Herod, the paranoid King of Israel (Mt. 2.13). There is no time to lose. And so, in the middle of the night, Joseph gets up and carries off Mary and Jesus to Egypt. There they find asylum. Meanwhile, the savagery they avoided is unleashed as Herod's forces massacre all boy babies under the age of two. And so they remain in Egypt until their exile comes to an end with Herod's death. Even then, they cannot return to Bethlehem. Judaea is now ruled by Archelaus, by repute the most brutal of Herod's sons (Mt. 2.22); there is still a risk that he would seek to kill Jesus. So Joseph takes his family to Galilee, to a town called Nazareth, where they make their home (Mt. 2.23).

The story is significant, though largely unhistorical (Luz 1990: 145; Brown 1993: 36). Matthew interweaves motifs from Old Testament traditions with considerable skill to create a theological prelude to the ministry of Jesus, reflecting a "developed Christian understanding that Jesus the Messiah relived the history of his own people" (Brown 1993: 29). There are parallels with the patriarchal narratives. Joseph, the legal father of Jesus who three times received guidance in a dream (Mt. 2.13, 19, 22), is reminiscent of Joseph the patriarch, who dreamed dreams, narrowly escaped death, and settled in Egypt (Gen. 37.5, 9, 19–20; 39.2). His father Jacob also received guidance in a dream and went to join Joseph in Egypt (Gen. 46.2–4). There are striking parallels too between Matthew's account of the flight into Egypt and the early life of Moses. The context is similar. A paranoid potentate "who did not know Joseph" (Exod. 1.8) ordered that all Hebrew boy babies should be killed. The infant Moses escaped and was brought up in Egypt. So parallels may be drawn between the Old Testament Joseph, the wicked Pharaoh, and the infant Moses on the one hand, and the New Testament Joseph, wicked King Herod, and the infant Jesus on the other (Brown 1993: 112).

The Exodus narrative patterns the story. Just as a murderous Pharaoh's death enables the adult Moses to set in motion the Exodus to the Promised Land (Exod. 4.19–20), so the death of Herod enables Jesus and his family to return to Israel (Mt. 2.20). And the connection between the two narratives is underlined by the use in Matthew, without grammatical adjustment, of the phrase "for all those who were seeking (the child's) life are dead" (Exod. 4.19).

If Egypt is portrayed as the land of Exodus, then Ramah evokes the Exile (Mt. 2.17–18). In Jeremiah, the voice of Rachel, the mother of Israel, is heard from her tomb, near Bethlehem, weeping for her children "because they are no more" as the children of Israel prepare to leave for Assyria and Babylon (Jer. 31.15). This is a place of mourning, where those who are about to set off on the long march gather in fetters (Jer. 40.1). The evocation of the Exile, already alluded to in Matthew's genealogy (Mt. 1.11, 12, 17), adds another layer of meaning to the flight of Israel's Messiah to Egypt.

In evoking the distraught voice of Rachel, Matthew only quotes one verse, Jer. 31.15, but this is followed in Jeremiah with verses that urge Rachel to cease her hopeless lamenting, for her lost children shall eventually return to their homeland. In the same spirit, Matthew goes on to tell us how Joseph, with divine guidance once more, brings his family back from exile. They return to Israel (Mt. 2.21), but not to Bethlehem – that would still be too dangerous. On they go to the district of Galilee (Mt. 2.22), where they settle in an unremarkable town called Nazareth (Mt. 2.23). On return from exile, the family ends up in the place where Jesus will begin his mission (Mt. 3.13; Mk 1.9).

The story of the flight of refugees spans history. Elsewhere, Matthew and Mark evoke those who are forced to flee in terror to the mountains, without stopping to pack clothes, without even a coat. Woe betide them if it happens to be winter and if they are pregnant or nursing a baby! (Mt. 24.16–21; Mk 13.14–19). Now as then, men, women, and children are forced to flee for their lives, leaving their home and their country for an unknown future; and the story has particularly grim resonance in a world where there are so many homeless, trafficked, abused, and traumatized refugee children. To quote Ched Myers, "here is a story for *our* world, which still teems with refugees, lamenting mothers, and the duplicitous schemes of the powerful. But *this* is the world in which God is with us, into which God has come and yet will come" (Myers & Colwell 2012: 170).

The importance of the depiction of Jesus and his family as refugees should not be underestimated. From a faith perspective, an existential link with the family who are forced to flee for their lives reinforces the belief that Jesus can empathize with refugees in their sufferings, enables endurance, and brings hope.

Jesus does not directly address the situation of the refugee in his teaching. The gospels, however, do provide relevant ethical teaching and practice.

The teaching of Jesus

Good news to the poor

An important marker is laid down in Luke's account of the beginnings of Jesus' public ministry in Nazareth (Lk. 4.14–30). As a pious Jew, well brought up, Jesus attends synagogue regularly. He has begun to "teach in the synagogues" (Lk. 4.15), which involves interpretation of Scripture (cf. Acts 13.15). He is charismatic and popular; news about him has begun to spread (Lk. 4.14–15).

On the day in question, Jesus stands up in his home synagogue and is given to read from the scroll of the prophet Isaiah. He unrolls it to find the passage he is looking for, a passage where the prophet claims divine authority for his announcement of good news to the poor and presents his ministry as crucial to that (Goldingay 2014: 291). When Jesus finishes, he rolls up the scroll, gives it back to the synagogue attendant, and sits down. With the eyes of all present fixed upon him, he begins his exposition with these arresting words: "today this scripture has been fulfilled in your hearing". In the person of Jesus, his hearers are to understand, the prophecy of Isaiah is fulfilled. Jesus is implying not only continuity with the prophet, but also a claim to be his contemporary voice. Jesus, God's anointed one, has come to bring good news, not in general terms to the "poor" as in most English translations of the Bible, but to the *ptochoi*, the destitute, the very "offscourings of the city" (Lk. 4.18; Esler 1998: 172). In Jesus, God's power and justice have become active and perceptible again in history (Bovon 2002: 151). Through his words and later through those of his disciples (Acts 14.3; 20.24,32), the destitute find well-being.

But this is not a message that finds universal acceptance. There is a tension between God's plan and the will of the people; in his hometown, the prophet is unwelcome (cf. Mk 6.3–4) – so much so that his hearers try to lynch him (Lk. 4.29). The reason for their sudden rage is not explained (Bovon 2002: 156). But they may have felt that "Joseph's son" was claiming too much for himself. The verses he read from Isa. 61.1–2 say something about the role of the speaker. For John Goldingay, "the 'I' is that of a prophetic king, or rather of a kingly prophet" (Goldingay 2014: 291). But this may be nuanced further. As Houston points out in a careful analysis of the passage, the "self-proclamation is not ... spoken *in propria persona* by the prophet" (Houston 1987: 45). To proclaim "freedom to captives, amnesty to prisoners" is the prerogative of the person who has the political authority to put it into effect. The combination of Spirit and anointing is associated traditionally with the king (1 Sam. 16.13): kings are anointed, kings are called to defend the cause of the poor, kings are called to deliver the needy (Ps. 72). The proclamation also has features in common with the legislation in Lev. 25 on economic redistribution, and the idea of a special year of grace occurs also in Deut. 15.1. What we have here then is a specific legal function transferred from monarch to Torah. But the anointed one appropriates to himself once more the legal functions of the Torah. In the mouth of Jesus, Houston concludes, "the one who alone has the authority to proclaim the liberation of which it speaks, has now proclaimed it, and as the words are a legal decree bringing that liberation into effect ... it is now a reality". He continues: "kings proclaimed jubilee; the Torah proclaims a regular jubilee; only the Messiah, as God's supreme representative, can proclaim the final jubilee. His proclamation ... calls into existence a new world" (Houston 1987: 47).

For Jesus, this understanding is ultimately a death sentence (Lk. 23.37–38). But for the moment, he passes through the crowd unscathed (Lk. 4.30), continuing to proclaim good news to the poor in word and deed as he goes on his way to Jerusalem.

The Beatitudes

Jesus and his followers alike saw his ministry as a fulfillment of Isa. 61.1–2 (Mt. 11.5; Lk. 7.22). The Sermon on the Plain (Lk. 6.20b–26) echoes the Nazareth manifesto: here, society is divided into *ptochoi* and rich. In the best tradition of the Hellenistic moralists, Luke's beatitudes are inclined towards the *ptochoi*, while the woes castigate the rich. The poor here are destitute, cowering, hungry, weeping, excluded, reviled, and discriminated against with possible legal consequences, not because of bad behaviour but because of who they are; these are followers of the Son of Man (Lk. 6.22). The condition of abject poverty can never be considered a blessing. But for those who depend upon God (Lk. 14.25–33), the Beatitudes are statements of assurance, with disclosure and promise (Betz 1995: 586) – the Kingdom has already come, though hidden, in Jesus: when God rules and his justice is restored, present relations will be reversed and the destitute *ptochoi* will be made rich (cf. Lk. 1.52–53).

Matthew's gospel, probably written around the same time as Luke, is different in emphasis; while Luke writes for a Graeco-Roman audience, Matthew tells the story of Jesus for Jewish-Christian readers. In the Beatitudes in the Sermon on the Mount (Mt. 5.1–12), the implications of Isa 61.1 might also be presupposed. So when Jesus blesses the poor and those who mourn, we are clearly meant to understand that he is the anointed one, the Messiah. There is a sense of solemnity (Mt. 5.1–2). God through Jesus is speaking again to Israel in a fundamental way as he did through Moses on Mt Sinai (Luz 1990: 224). Jesus, seated on a mountain, is presented as the "prophet like Moses" (Deut. 18.15–20). He "fulfills" the law and the prophets (Mt. 5.17–20). He confirms the truth of the Torah. While the new demands of Jesus may exceed in rigour those of the Torah, they do not contradict them. Righteousness is of central importance to both. And righteousness in Matthew applies to life as a whole. The righteous are defined as "poor in spirit". Although Matthew does not juxtapose the rich and the poor as social types, the religious meaning of "poor", implied by the qualification "in spirit", does not exclude the economic meaning. Indeed, the majority of Jesus' hearers experienced economic inequities: "they knew the meaning of need because they were poor in spirit and poor in fact" (Davies & Allison 1988: 443). They may take heart from the fact that although the earth is not currently in the possession of the righteous, this will be corrected by God's justice in the Kingdom.

The Beatitudes are blessings, not requirements; they presuppose God's grace (Davies & Allison 1988: 466). But in the new way of life that is revealed, there is a close relationship between morality and ethics. The Beatitudes affect moral behaviour and require ethical awareness: "as revelation of a principle, the beatitude shows and opens up a way of life implementing that principle. The pronouncement moreover presents the demand that the person receiving the message takes up in the most serious sense the way of life revealed. It requires no less than a radical decision, as it lays claim to the recipient's entire course and conduct of life" (Betz 1995: 96). For both Matthew and Luke, the co-existence of rich and poor is a concrete test of Christian discipleship. Who is poorer than the person who is forced to flee for their life, leaving everything they own behind? Who is more destitute than the asylum-seeker denied leave to remain, refused permission to work, devoid of welfare benefits, unable to return to their country of origin? The Beatitudes have inescapable consequences: "without adequate response the beatitude turns into condemnation" (Betz 1995: 97).

The Rich Man and Lazarus

This parable (Lk. 16.19–31) brings the message of the Beatitudes to life in a particularly vivid way. It would have had all the greater impact on its first hearers because it draws on a story which everyone knew, the Alexandrian Jewish tale of two funerals: that of a rich man and that of a poor man and their respective fortunes in the next world (Jeremias 1966: 145). Luke makes it his own. A rich man dressed in the finest and most expensive of clothing feasts every day on the most luxurious of food. At his gate, there lies a poor man, a *ptochos*, a beggar. His wretchedness is extreme. He is starving and covered with sores. He would, if he could, eat the rich man's leftover scraps; but he is so helpless that he cannot even drive off the dogs from licking his sores. The rich man, implicitly, does not care. Although there is no indication in the text that he is aware of the poor man at his gate, he cannot not plead ignorance of his existence; he later recognizes him and refers to him by name (Caird 1963: 192). In due course, both men die. The poor man, Lazarus, is carried directly by angels to the consolation of "Abraham's bosom"; the rich man – traditionally known as Dives – is racked with torment in Hades. His plea for a sip of water is refused by Abraham in terms which exactly reproduce the first of the beatitudes and woes (Lk. 16.25). While Dives has already had his good things, Lazarus has suffered evil things (Evans 1990: 615). The reversal has now occurred. Nothing can now be altered. Can Dives' five brothers be forewarned? "No", says Abraham, they have sufficient guidance in "Moses and the prophets". If they ignore the united prophetic witness of Scripture, as had Dives, nothing will convince them even if a person (presumably the reference is to Jesus) were to rise from the dead: "the two failures of Dives belong together: because his mind was closed to the revelation of God, his heart was closed to the demands of compassion" (Caird 1963: 192).

Jesus was not a political economist; he did not examine how a breathtakingly unfair society could be reformed by economic, social, and political initiatives. He didn't develop a robust policy programme to build a better country. But he did call people to relate with active compassion to those who were destitute, an attitude which, if taken seriously today, would effect radical change in political policies and the ways in which these are implemented, particularly with regard to refugees. And he backed his stance with reference to the traditional Jewish idea that the poor are entitled to a share in God's gracious dispensation to his covenant people: "God's presence to the poor precedes financial security and is not dependent on it; but if the privileged want to share in the kingdom with the poor, their attitudes and actions must change in ways that will necessarily have far-reaching social effects" (Cahill 2013: 102).

The greatest commandment

In this central exchange (Mt. 22.34–40), Matthew follows Mark (12.28–31) as his source, but he makes changes. In Mark, a curious scribe asks Jesus: "which commandment is the first of all?" Jesus replies not with one, but with two commandments: love God (Deut. 6.5) and love your neighbour (Lev. 19.18). The combination is startling. As J.P. Meier indicates, Mark's text on which Matthew's is based is the only place in Jewish literature where both Torah texts are cited word for word, let alone together (Meier 2009: 500). Unique too is the categorization of the commandments into first and second, and the indication that there is no commandment greater than these (2009: 572). The scribe agrees and is commended by Jesus for his wise reply: he is "not far from the kingdom of God" (Mk 12.34). In Matthew, however, the Pharisees gather together to test Jesus. Their spokesman, a lawyer, attempts to catch him out. Jesus' attitude to the Torah is on the line: "which commandment *in the law*", the lawyer asks, "is the greatest?" (Mt. 22.36). Jesus responds with the same two commandments as in Mark, and then concludes: "on these two commandments hang all the law and the prophets" (Mt. 22.40). The commandment to love is the greatest commandment and the one on which all the rest depends. The pericope, as Burridge demonstrates, "ends not with the commendation of a scribe, but with how the law and prophets depend on love" (Burridge 2007: 211). Far from setting aside the law, Jesus affirms it and gives it a new interpretation. As if to confirm this, the exchange with the lawyer is followed in Matthew by severe condemnation of those who interpret the law in an unloving manner.

The teaching here is in line with the Sermon on the Mount. Both sum up the law and the prophets in terms of the commandment to love. This is not an attitude of affection, but a way of life. It has radical consequences for Jesus' disciples. The "exceeding" righteousness to which they are called includes obedience to God's will as expressed in the six paragraphs known as the Antitheses (Mt. 5.21–48). These warn Jesus' hearers against a nitpicking, legalistic interpretation of the law, but they do not contradict the Torah. They show by practical examples what sort of behaviour Jesus requires and how his requirements intensify the Torah. Significantly, these are framed by reference to practices of love (Mt. 5.21–26; 5.43–48). Loving your neighbour can present a very radical demand; Jesus extends it to loving your enemies (Mt. 5.43–48; Lk. 6.27), and the Golden Rule, "do to others as you would have them do to you, for this is the law and the prophets" (Mt. 7.12; Lk. 6.31), is another way of saying the same thing. The saying is important; it brings to a climax the central core of Jesus' teaching to his disciples in the Sermon on the Mount. But this instruction is not intended for the disciples alone. The Sermon on the Mount is ethics for the people of God and also for the whole world to which it is proclaimed (Mt. 28.19–20). The words of Jesus are to be obeyed (Mt. 28.20). The challenge to interpret Jesus' commandment in everyday life with any adequacy is enormous: obedience to legal norms such as those cited in Mt. 5.21, 27, 31, 33, 38, 43 is in itself insufficient: Jesus demands more. And what that "more" might involve is revealed through the rest of the gospel narrative, the debates and parables. In these, we see how the law is to be fulfilled according to the greatest commandment, to love God and neighbour (Burridge 2007: 212).

What bearing might an ethic of love of God and neighbour have on our attitudes towards refugees today? I quote from Daniel Carroll R.:

> If the life and words of Jesus in some fashion are important and binding on Christians, then other questions follow. Do we, as

> Christians, have as comprehensive an ethic as Jesus had? If not, why not? What areas of life have been left out? Have attitudes towards (the refugee) been integrated into that ethic? Along with what are normally highlighted as Christian duties, such as honesty in the workplace, fidelity in marriage, and good stewardship of money, must also stand compassion toward the outsider.
>
> (Carroll R. 2013: 116)

The Samaritan neighbour

The guiding principle of Jesus' ethics, the double command to love God and neighbour, is tough love. Burridge puts it well:

> The love of God, which can never be "vapid" or "self-indulgent", is breaking into our world here and now to bring about the eschatological restoration of his people under God's gracious reign. Such love, at one and the same time, makes a "radical and strengthening" demand for a total response, while requiring a more "relaxed" and open acceptance of all those who respond to God's call in love.
>
> (Burridge 2007: 55)

The teaching of Jesus pushes back the boundaries of understanding of his followers (Carroll R. 2013: 110). In what he says and does, he challenges them to see those who may be seen as "enemies" in a different light. Samaritans are a case in point (cf. Lk. 17.11–19). Jews at the time of Jesus loathed Samaritans, and the ongoing animosity between the two gave rise from time to time to acts of atrocity on both sides (Carroll R. 2013: 107). The reasons appear to have been partly ethnic, partly doctrinal. The most obvious distinction between Jew and Samaritan was the mutually exclusive claims of the temples at Jerusalem and Gerizim (Freedman 1992). For religious and historical reasons, Samaritans and Jews were enemies. The pericope at Lk. 9.52b–56 singles them out as the first to rebuff Jesus. For Jesus to present a Samaritan in a good light would have been shocking to his fellow Jews. As John the Evangelist puts it bluntly, "Jews do not share things in common with Samaritans" (John 4.9b).

But when Jesus illustrates neighbourly love, he takes a Samaritan as his model. In Luke's version of the test-exchange between Jesus and the lawyer, the lawyer asks of Jesus: "what must I do to inherit eternal life?" (Lk. 10.25). Jesus replies with another question: "what is written in the law?" (Lk. 10.26). And the lawyer responds with the love command, love God and love your neighbour. Jesus agrees. The lawyer, however, has a supplementary question: "who is my neighbour?" (Lk. 10.29).

Then the tables are turned – the lawyer finds himself being tested. He soon learns that keeping the law requires more than merely repeating the double love command. Inheriting eternal life necessitates practical action. Jesus responds to his question with the Parable of the Good Samaritan (Lk. 10.25–37). A man was beaten up by bandits on the Jericho road and left for dead. A priest, then a Levite, saw him and avoided him. No reasons are given. The next traveller to come along is a Samaritan. The Samaritan, the story continues, had compassion on the wounded man, treated his wounds, and brought him to an inn, where he took care of him; when he left, he promised to pay the innkeeper for any additional expenses. And Jesus concludes with a further question to the lawyer: "which of these three, do you think, was a neighbour to the man who fell into the hands of the robbers?" There is a clear reversal in meaning from the previous dialogue. Then, the lawyer was seeking to identify the neighbour whom he might love. Now, the neighbour is portrayed not as an object of pity, but as a person who has become a neighbour to the wounded man. There is, then, a neighbour at both ends of the communication of love: in the love command (Lk. 10.27), the neighbour is the object of pity; in the parable, he is the subject of pity (Lk. 10.36) (Bovon 1996: 99). Jesus' commentary on the Torah does not commit the reader to "having" a neighbour but to "being" a neighbour, most especially to people who have suffered misfortune. The reciprocity implicit in Lev. 19.18 and in the Golden Rule is played out in the parable. It is the outsider, the stranger, who ministers with love to the needs of the wounded man. Again, expectations are reversed. It is neither the priest nor the Levite, the two heartless representatives of the official cult, but a despised Samaritan who understands the situation of need that he sees before him, shows kindness to the mistreated human victim, and takes steps actively to help him.

In the ways we relate to the stranger, are we, present-day members of Jesus' audience, more complicit and less innocent than we think? Do we have a duty to change our stance, to leave behind our comfort zone of self-centredness, insouciance, and arrogance? Might we even have a need for help from the stranger?

Jesus and the Syro-Phoenician woman

> Few admirers of Jesus's compassion, his commendation of love of neighbour, and his inclusive kingdom message can fail to be disturbed by this story.
>
> (Cahill 2013: 110)

Jesus is travelling in the region of Tyre and Sidon, north-west of Galilee and homeland of Israel's historic enemies, the Phoenicians. He wants to remain incognito, but his reputation has gone before him. A nameless woman finds out where he is living and falls at his feet. Her daughter is possessed by a demon; she begs Jesus to heal her (Mk 7.25–26). Jesus rebuffs her harshly (Mk 7.27). He insists that Jews have prime call on his healing powers, which may have been limited (cf. Mk 6.5; 5.30): "let the children become satisfied first, for it is not fair to take the children's food and throw it to the dogs" (*my translation*). The children (Israel) should be fed and their food should not be taken from them and given to the dogs (gentiles). In the literary context of the gospel, the exclusivist thrust of Jesus' statement is undermined by the evangelist's use of the Greek verb *chortasthenai* ("to become satisfied") which is found in Mark otherwise only in 6.42 and 8.4–8, the two feeding miracles which frame this encounter. In the use of this one word, the narrator reminds us of the God of abundance who says that there will be enough and that, if we share together what we have, then five loaves and two fishes will be more than ample. And the woman's adroit response wins the day: using the same metaphor, she counters Jesus: "yes, Lord, but even the dogs under the table eat the crumbs meant for the children" (Mk 7.28). Jesus concedes the point, and the daughter is healed – this is the only healing miracle in Mark which does not involve a face-to-face encounter.

Must we accept that Jesus looks down on this woman because she is a "foreigner"? This would be against the grain of his recorded teaching and actions elsewhere. Is it perhaps possible that what we have here is a challenge to Jesus' perception of his own mission? If at the time he saw this as primarily a reform of Second Temple Judaism, which he wanted to bring closer to the Torah and the prophets, then he might well at first have regarded the woman and her daughter as outside his scope. But through dialogue, he appears to come to understand otherwise. This happens, not as in Matthew's version, because of the woman's "great faith", but because of what she *says*. The word that she speaks is described as *logos* (Mk 7.29), a word usually used to describe the proclamation of the gospel (Mk 1.45; 2.2; 4.33; Jn 1; cf. Snyder 2012: 173). In Mark's narrative, the woman's "word" recalls Jesus' own prior teaching about the inclusive love of God (Mk 7.1–13). The gracious goodness of the God of Jesus is abundant enough to satisfy the needs of Jews and gentiles alike. Then, in addressing him as "Lord", the woman is using the language of the early Christian church. This gentile is already, it seems, a follower, "the apostolic 'foremother' of all gentile Christians" (Schüssler Fiorenza 1983: 138). And so she teaches Jesus the meaning of his messiahship, and Jesus gains a new perspective on the prophecy of Isaiah and a fresh understanding of Israel's traditional "enemies" (Cahill 2013: 112). Now, he understands that his mission includes not only Israel but also "others" like this non-Jewish woman and her daughter. We know from the letters of Paul and Acts that to accept gentiles and Jews on an equal footing may have been unpalatable and contentious to many; the mission to the gentiles did not take hold until a decade after Jesus' death (Acts 11.19–26). Editors of the gospel texts may have felt it necessary to tone down the missionary thrust and affirm the primacy of Israel.

Today, the exchange between Jesus and the gentile woman has political and personal inferences. First, it demonstrates "the divine economy of enough for everyone, which transcends and transforms even our most dearly held individual or group entitlements ... The task of our churches ... is to help citizens who are anxious about preserving the body politic to see that external borders can't protect us. Quite the contrary: risking communion with the 'political bodies' of immigrants might just save us" (Myers & Colwell 2012: 136–137).

Second, the woman is presented as a Greek, of Syro-Phoenician origin (Mk 6.26), an "inside other". Jean-Pierre Ruiz defines these as "foreigners in their own land ... permanent insiders, according to the ethnic and racial norms of the dominant culture" (Ruiz 2011: 48). In gender and ethnicity, the woman and Jesus are outsiders to each other (2011: 46). They converse in Greek, which is in effect a second language for both. Citing Sharon Ringe, Ruiz finds her Latino/a Bible Studies helpful in reflecting

> on the ways in which the Markan text inverts the insider/outsider relationships that would have existed in the first-century CE eastern Mediterranean socioeconomic context. In the world behind the text, it is Jesus who is the outsider and the woman who belongs to the dominant group; in the world of the text, it is Mark's Jesus who is the dominant figure, and the woman who is an anonymous outsider ... Ringe is led to affirm that "Other" is not a unitary category, either of experience or interpretative lens, but rather one that includes "the Other within the Other".
>
> (Ruiz 2011: 48)

This has implications for the relationship of sojourners to a majority culture and the attempt to bridge the gap through mutual learning rather than rejection or forced assimilation.

The Last Judgement

Mt. 25.31–36 is Jesus' last piece of instruction to the disciples – it carries great weight. The time of warnings is past; nothing can be done now to affect the final judgement. Matthew's depiction is poetic and dramatic. The Son of Man is acting as World Judge in the name of the Father; in his role as a shepherd, he is designated "king" (Mt. 25.34; cf. Ezek. 34.17–24). He judges the nations of the world in exalted solemnity. The verdict is pronounced at the outset. The World Judge separates out the righteous from the unloving and the blessed from the accursed. And in two sets of dialogue (Mt. 25.34–40; 41–45), the reasons for the judgement are made plain. The verdict hinges on whether or not his interlocutors have carried out mundane acts of love to those in need. In each case, the sentence is clinched by the solemn phrase "truly I tell you", as surprisingly the World Judge identifies himself with the destitute; included with the hungry, the thirsty, the naked, the sick, and the imprisoned is the stranger (Mt. 25.35, 38, 43–44).

The classic interpretation of this text is that it is designed to motivate churches to acts of mercy (Luz 2005a: 267). Christians are measured by the works of compassion they may or may not have done for fellow Christians in need, especially the disciples (Carroll R. 2013: 113). Matthew has already given an account of their poverty (Mt. 10.9–10), of their dependence on hospitality

(Mt. 10.11–15), and of the dangers they confront as they go out in Jesus' name (Mt. 10.17–23; 28–29). And readers would recall the exhortation at Mt. 10.40–42 to supply their needs. An obvious parallel may be drawn with the frequent references by Paul to the hardships he endured and his commendation of those who gave him hospitality (1 Cor. 16.5–9; Gal. 4.13–14; Rom. 16.1–2; 1 Cor. 16.10–12). As the Son of Man identifies with the poverty and suffering of his needy brothers, they will remember that in his earthly life, Jesus was a homeless stranger (Mt. 8.20) experiencing hunger (Mt. 21.18), and finally torture (Mt. 27.27–31) and judicial murder: "the text lets the church be aware of the foundation that supports it even in judgment but not by keeping it from judgment" (Luz 2005a: 283). Matthew believed that Christians will ultimately be tested by their Lord on the basis of deeds of love to one another.

Others, however, are not persuaded that the imperative is addressed only to Christians (Davies & Allison 1997: 423), and the text has become firmly rooted in the popular imagination as an ethical demand for all humankind. One obvious reading is that the nations are to be judged according to how they have treated Christians in trouble (Mt. 25.40), but the universal meaning which has taken hold over the years is nonetheless true to the gospel story of Jesus. It exemplifies the love command with its several nuances and illustrates the message of the Beatitudes. "The nations", that is, "all humanity" (Davies & Allison 1997: 422), are being judged as to whether they have fed the hungry, given a drink to the thirsty, welcomed the stranger, clothed the naked, healed the sick, and visited those in prison. For Ulrich Luz, this interpretation of the text enables us to discover anew the poor of the world, amongst them strangers, and with that discovery, God himself: "Jesus is the one who gives new eyes that make it possible to see and to experience anew the poor person and God, and the text is the source of a power that makes possible the judgment of the world" (2005a: 284).

Has the judgement on the nations any bearing today on the UK? Or on the US or Australia? Will the World Judge in any way demand an accounting of these countries' policies towards refugees and the ways in which these are implemented?

Christians as strangers and aliens

1 Peter

1 Peter, written in the early days of the Christian church, uses the term "strangers and aliens" to encapsulate Christian identity in a hostile social environment. This letter, "one of the most disputed writings of the New Testament" (Elliott 1981: 22), was sent, allegedly from Babylon (1 Pet. 5.12–13), to harassed Christians dispersed among four or five provinces or regions of Asia Minor (1 Pet. 1.1). They are addressed as "strangers and aliens" (1 Pet. 2.11). This is often taken, in line with Heb. 11.13–16, as a metaphorical way of

depicting Christians as people who are not at home in this world because their homeland is in heaven (Horrell 2008: 51). John Elliott, however, comes to the conclusion on the basis of a study of the relevant terms *paroikos* and *parepidemos* in Graeco-Roman and Jewish literature that these could apply to specific social conditions. The *paroikos* is a resident alien dwelling abroad without civil rights and subject to political and economic exploitation. This suggests "social separation, cultural alienation and a certain degree of personal deprivation" (1981: 25). The *parepidemos*, on the other hand, is a transient stranger with no opportunity to settle permanently where he lives; he is a visitor. Accordingly, the recipients of 1 Peter are a mixture of permanent and temporary strangers and aliens. In times of political upheaval or economic adversity, they would have been targeted as scapegoats with social suspicion, censure, and animosity (Elliott 1981: 69). While they would have found a home in the Christian community, from the point of view of non-Christians, these are outsiders, socially and religiously, and a potential danger to public order (Elliott 1981: 79). They are met with ignorance (1 Pet. 2.15) and maligned (1 Pet. 3.16). They are suspected of wrongdoing (1 Pet. 2.12; 4.14–16) and met with aggressive hostility (1 Pet. 3.13–14; 4.4). This seems to have been the rule rather than the exception. While many commentators are largely unpersuaded by Elliott's arguments, we cannot exclude some literal social reference in 1 Peter; and Elliott draws attention to historical and social realities in a way that enriches our understanding of the text (Jobes 2005: 31).

The author treads a careful path between conformity and resistance. On the one hand, followers of Christ should be people who "do good"; they should never commit the kinds of crimes which others accuse them of (1 Pet. 2.12); when to be labelled "Christian" is a cause of suffering, it should be accepted with pride (1 Pet. 3.14–15). What does he commend as good behaviour? – in general, behaviour that is socially respectable, honouring the emperor, obeying the authority of governors, submitting to masters or husbands, and not going out of one's way to provoke trouble. However, there is a subtext of resistance, a "hidden transcript" in the words of James Scott, who notes that, while the political conduct of subordinate groups is necessarily circumspect, there may yet be a significant difference between what they say openly and in private (Scott 1990: 4). In 1 Pet. 5.13, greetings are brought from the church "in Babylon". For "Babylon", we may surely read "Rome" (Horrell 2008: 85), the centre of imperial power. The use of the name Babylon, with a mention of diaspora (1 Pet. 1.1), immediately recalls the situation of Israel in Babylon, the evil city par excellence, seat of an oppressive imperial power, and source of great suffering. Readers cannot be at home in such a society. Christians, the author insists, are free people, slaves of God alone (1 Pet. 2.16). A crucial distinction is to be made between fearing God and honouring the emperor; God alone is to be worshipped (1 Pet. 2.17). Readers are called to be faithful to their identity as Christians even when that involves suffering. Suffering in the name of Christ is a cause for rejoicing and blessing (1 Pet. 4.13–14). Christians are exhorted to "give an account of the hope that is in [them]" through their deeds (1 Pet. 3.15). They should have "unity of spirit, sympathy, love for one another, a tender heart and a humble mind. [They are not to] repay evil for evil or abuse for abuse; but ... repay with a blessing" (1 Pet. 3.8–9).

These injunctions apply equally to all community members. In particular, the refusal to perpetuate cycles of abuse must include resisting and ending abuse. If Elliott is correct in assuming that the original recipients of the letter were social outcasts, their experience may not be too far removed from that of many refugee Christians today. Where their residence status is uncertain, these too are strangers and aliens in their host country. They endure rejection and discrimination; they are scapegoated. They are accused unjustly; their claim to be Christian is "found to be incredible" by officials and tribunals. In many cases, if their appeal for asylum fails and they are sent back to their country of origin, they fear persecution because of their Christian faith. Under these circumstances, refugee Christians have much to contribute to majority-culture Christians' understanding of Scriptural promises and exhortations (Carroll R. 2013: 119).

Further, as Carroll R. points out:

> If majority-culture Christians do embrace the immigrant – whether documented or undocumented – this stance could mark them in a particular way as foreigners and strangers in that they would be going against the current of a good portion of public opinion. To take that stand on the basis of biblical convictions may lead to opposition from the broader majority culture. According to 1 Peter, to suffer for doing good is a privilege and part of the pilgrimage of faith.
>
> (Carroll R. 2013: 118–119)

Heb. 11.13–16

Sent to an unspecified church by an unspecified author, this outstanding theological letter was clearly written to encourage Christians to remain steadfast under persecution. The analogies with 1 Peter are obvious. Both refer to the faithful as strangers and aliens. But Hebrews develops a soaring theological argument to address directly the central problem encountered by his readers: even at the point of death, they had not yet witnessed the blessing that God was to accomplish through them. But, he argues, had the patriarchs seen the fulfillment of God's promises (Heb. 11.13)? They were far from their country of origin, strangers and aliens on the earth (Heb. 11.13), temporary residents, domiciled without rights in a country not their own (cf. Ps. 39.12). Yet, they had citizenship in a heavenly homeland that God had already prepared for them (Heb. 11.16), and they saw by the eye of faith the distant fulfillment of God's promises. William Lane cites this apt observation from the Epistle of Diognetus, written in the early 2nd century: "(Christians) dwell in their own countries, but only as sojourners; they bear the share of all responsibilities as citizens, and they endure all hardships as strangers. Every foreign country is a homeland to them, and every homeland is foreign … their existence is on earth, but their citizenship is in heaven" (Diogn. 5.5–9; cited in Lane 1991: 360).

Are there insights here that are applicable to Christians today, as they address what it means to be aliens and strangers? I return to Carroll R.: "what all Christians should appreciate is that the more they can grasp about migration and the experience of immigrants, the more they will understand their faith – that is, the truths of such convictions as the reality of having another (heavenly) citizenship and the rejection that can come from being different, as well as the vulnerability that surfaces with needing to be dependent on God". And he concludes soberly: "sadly, it is not uncommon for Christians not to feel like 'strangers in a strange land'; their place of residence has lost its strangeness, and now they join others in wanting to keep strangers out" (Carroll R. 2013: 118).

8

WELCOMING THE STRANGER

Hospitality in the Bible

I saw a stranger yestreen
I put food in the eating place,
drink in the drinking place,
music in the listening place
and in the sacred name of the Triune
he blessed my house, my cattle and my dear ones,
and the lark said in her song,
Often, often, often, goes the Christ in the stranger's guise.
Often, often, often, goes the Christ in the stranger's guise.

Celtic Rune of Hospitality

If narratives in the Old and New Testaments convey the fact, implicitly or explicitly, that the stranger is particularly vulnerable to rejection, there is also the strong inference that this is contrary to the gracious will of God, according to which the stranger is not to be rejected but welcomed, treated justly, and, when needy, given help. This attitude is conveyed by the ethic of hospitality, which pervades both Testaments.

Abraham and his guests

The ethic of hospitality was an important moral category in the Ancient Near East, and the story of Abraham, Sarah, and their three guests encapsulates it neatly (Gen. 18.1–8). Abraham is settling down for a siesta in the heat of the day at the entrance of his tent by the oaks of Mamre. He may well have dozed off. Suddenly, he becomes aware that three men are standing nearby. At least he assumes they are men; but the reader knows otherwise (Gen. 18.1). He rushes to meet them and greets them with warmth and respect. Long-winded and deferential, he addresses the leader of the group, urging them to stop, rest, wash their feet, and have a bite to eat. They all accept. At speed, Abraham then hurries in quick succession to the tent, the herd, and the servant. The "bite to eat" he had proposed turns out to be a lavish feast: yoghurt and bread and meat – not merely a lamb or a goat, but a fine, tender beast from the cattle herd, with a large quantity of bread made of the finest wheat flour (Gen. 18.6–7). The meal is served, and the men eat while Abraham stands discreetly by. Then, the divine identity of the strangers is gradually disclosed.

The principle that hospitality should be offered to the stranger runs through the Bible. Graciousness to those in need is seen as a way of honouring God (Isa. 58.6–7), and strangers are assured of a minimum of protection and provision. There are several variations on the theme in the Old Testament narratives. Laban, for instance, offers his visitors water to wash their feet and food to eat, while their camels have straw and fodder (Gen. 24.31–33); Reuel chastizes his daughters for not inviting Moses, "the Egyptian", to have something to eat (Exod. 2.16–20); a wealthy couple in Shunem make regular provision for Elisha (2 Kgs 4.8–10); and in time of drought, a destitute widow shares with Elijah the last morsel of food she has for herself and her son (1 Kgs 17.8–16). Job instances the fact that he has kept an open door for the traveller and the stranger as evidence of his integrity (Job 31.32). And the extended narrative in the Book of Ruth portrays hospitality to the stranger as a virtue. If graciousness to those in need is an attribute of God, then the same charitable openness will characterize the people of God. The Biblical challenge to be hospitable to the stranger continues to be set before individuals and Christian communities today.

The Levite and his concubine

The Bible does not spare us, however, the fact that in practice, individuals and societies can and do fail to meet the challenge: a person in need of hospitality may be failed by those who can and should offer protection. Cheryl Exum argues that tragic Biblical narratives make one knowledgeable and "honest about reality" (Exum 1992: 8). Readers are engaged in "a multivalent, inexhaustible narrative world" of good and evil. Illuminated by a "tragic vision", they gain "fullness of insight into the human condition" (1992: 9).

A leitmotif of Judg. 17–21 is that, at the time the stories are set, there is no moral leadership in Israel. There was "no king in Israel" (Judg. 17.6a; 18.1a; 19.1a; 21.25a) and "all the people did what was right in their own eyes" (Judg. 17.6b; 21.5b). This is the context for the narrative in Judg. 19, where terror, violence, and pathos colour the account of hospitality abused.

A Levite from Judah, living in Ephraim, "took to himself a concubine" from Bethlehem, probably a second wife (Niditch 2008: 191). She defies her husband, runs away to her father's home, and stays there for four months, possibly in protest against domestic abuse (Niditch 2008: 192). The Levite goes after her, according to the Hebrew text, "to speak to her heart, to bring her back". His father-in-law greets him joyfully, the prelude to five days of convivial hospitality. The woman is not mentioned. "Truly", as Phyllis Trible observes drily, "this version of oriental hospitality is an exercise in male bonding" (Trible 1984: 68). As the host presses the man to stay yet a little longer, tension begins to build.

Finally, the man insists on leaving even though it is late in the day and sets off with his wife and a servant-lad. They cannot complete the journey to Ephraim before nightfall. With vivid irony in the light of the vicious treatment they will receive from their own people, the Levite rejects the lad's proposal that they spend the night in Jebus – this is a "city of foreigners". So they go on until they reach Benjamite territory after sundown. Here, surely, they will find hospitality! So they sit down in the square in Gibeah and wait. But none of the residents takes them in. The sense of irony increases when it emerges that the old man who finally offers them hospitality is a resident alien, a sojourner in Benjamin, likewise from Ephraim. They wash their feet, eat and drink, and their donkeys are provided for. The travellers are, literally, "enjoying themselves to their heart" (Judg. 19.22) when the house is surrounded by an aggressive and violent mob demanding homosexual favours (Judg. 19.22). The old man appeals to them as his "brothers" and reminds them of the tradition of hospitality (Judg. 19.23). But the hospitality does not extend to women. As a sop, the host offers the rabble the women of the house including the concubine. These they may rape if they wish (Judg. 19.24). When the men do not listen, the Levite throws them his concubine to save himself (Judg. 19.25b). After a night of rape and torture, they let her go. She collapses at the door of the house where she had earlier found sanctuary, her hands clinging to the threshold. The next morning, the Levite is set to continue his journey. In two short Hebrew words, he curtly orders the woman to get up. Where are the words that speak tenderly to her heart? He doesn't appear even to notice that she is dead (Judg. 19.27–28). On his return home, the brutality escalates. In a macabre gesture, he butchers her body as if she were a beast and distributes the pieces throughout Israel. Parallels with 1 Sam. 11.7 are obvious; each incident is a ritualized means of calling up allies to arms. The Levite's gesture, however, "simply arouses horror" (Soggin 1987: 282). In life and in death, the woman is treated despicably. And with the Levite's subsequent misrepresentation of events before the assembly inquiry, the narrator brands him in our eyes as a coward and a liar (Judg. 20.5–7). In the light of this, the variant translations of Judg. 19.30 are illuminating. The NRSV reconstructs the verse according to the Greek text of the Septuagint and has the man instruct the messengers with the body parts what they should say to the Israelites; the AV and the RSV (Revised Standard Version), however, following the Hebrew text, omit both messengers and message and attribute the statement to the people at large: "all that saw it said, there was no such deed done nor seen from the day that the children of Israel came up out of the land of Egypt unto this day" (AV). The contrast between the barbarous treatment of the woman who was rejected by those who should have protected her and the gracious liberation of the Israelites from Egypt could scarcely be more pointed. Finally, readers then and now are instructed to "consider it (literally in Hebrew, 'direct your heart to her'), take counsel, and speak out" (Judg. 19.30; 20.7).

This tale of broken hospitality has clear similarities with Gen. 19.1–11; each is a variation on the theme of weary travellers seeking a bed for the night.

In each case, while the townsfolk are predatory and show no respect of persons, a resident alien offers hospitality. In Genesis, Lot, the immigrant, alone shows proper courtesy to the strangers at the gate (Gen. 19.1–2), while the mob jibe at his immigrant status (Gen. 19.9). In Judg. 19.20, the travellers are taken in by an old hill farmer from Ephraim who is living in Gibeah. In Gen. 19 and in Judg. 19, the men are willing to hand over their women to violence and abuse to placate the rabble. The women are regarded as property to be disposed of at will. They have no say in the matter; they have no voice (Niditch 2008: 193). These ancient texts of terror speak all too vividly of the present. Thanks to the skill of the narrator, pointed questions are asked of a society where it is left to resident aliens to provide gracious hospitality to the strangers, where there is no matching generosity of spirit in the townsfolk, only cruelty. And there is an unrelenting lack of generosity towards women. In Judg. 19, a woman who has sought asylum is rejected by those who should protect her, callously driven out to be gang-raped and finally murdered, her last dying act being to seek asylum once again. The reader reacts with outraged anger and protest, giving voice to the cause of the many unnamed women who in their country of origin and in the country where they seek asylum suffer unspeakable abuse and are treated with callous cruelty. As Trible puts it: "the story is alive and all is not well" (Trible 1984: 87).

Advice to the host

If the ethic of hospitality is fundamental to the Old Testament, it is fundamental to the New Testament as well. The Greek word used for "hospitality" is *philoxenia,* literally, "love of stranger", where *xenos* has the dual meaning of "stranger" and "guest". The virtue of hospitality is urged in several epistles (Rom. 12.13; Heb. 13.2; 1 Pet. 4.9) and given a distinctive twist in the life and teaching of Jesus.

In Lk. 14, 12–14, Jesus is attending a Sabbath meal at the house of a leader of the Pharisees. Challengingly, he gives his host some radical advice about his guest-list. When he gives a lunch or dinner party, Jesus suggests, he should not invite his friends or family or wealthy neighbours; these are bound to want to reciprocate the invitation. Instead, he should invite the riff-raff, the disabled, the poor because they are in no position to repay him. This is a significant reminder of the Biblical principle that those who understand themselves to be blessed by God should in their turn share that blessing. As God is gracious, expecting nothing in return, neither should they: "in contrast to Hellenistic practices that associated hospitality with benefit and reciprocity, Christian commitments pressed hospitality outward toward the weakest and those least likely to be able to reciprocate" (Pohl 2006: 91). In this context, for wealthy Christians to invite the destitute and the disabled to their homes must have been regarded as social revolution (Esler 1987: 194). The message is driven home in the parable that follows (Lk. 14.15–24). The giver of a banquet sends out a messenger to summon the guests. Each one makes a feeble excuse. The host in his anger repudiates them and sends for substitute guests: those without any standing in society, the poor, and the broken. This is the ultimate in gracious hospitality.

There is a certain ambiguity in the practice of hospitality. In inviting his family and friends to a meal, was the host not being hospitable? Is Jesus inviting the reader to prioritize different forms of hospitality? Or is he typically pointing to an extreme position in order to make a point? In what follows, I draw on the insights of Jacques Derrida, who outlines helpfully two different types of hospitality, "conditional" and "unconditional", which can be intertwined (Derrida 2000). Conditional hospitality is a clearly defined way of receiving guests according to certain expectations. The host is expected to invite, and the guest to accept. This prevents the unwanted intrusion of a stranger into the home space. The guest is told how long he or she should stay and the terms and conditions of the visit. Despite its cordiality, an invitation is always a gesture of power. Asking questions of guests is also integral to conditional hospitality. Often, guests feel obliged to tell the host about themselves and their experiences, thus rewarding him for offering refuge. All these factors are meant to neutralize the separateness of the nameless stranger and, in the process, domesticate him or her. Unconditional hospitality, on the other hand, has no "rules". There is no formal invitation. The host opens himself to the unknown, not seeking to understand or domesticate the newcomer. He expects the unexpected. When he takes the guest under his roof, he does not know to whom he is giving shelter. Such absolute hospitality is expressed in silence. The newcomer, without an invitation and thus not authorized to impose on a person's hospitality, stays under the same roof illegally, sometimes secretly, as a nameless stranger.

Derrida's account helps the reader understand the ambiguous nature of hospitality in terms of conditionality. But Jesus' insistence on the gracious, overflowing hospitality of God towards the stranger relativizes all forms of human conditionality and jerks readers out of their comfort zones. The way he advocates is risky – loving the stranger can be countercultural; it requires moral courage, which can be a difficult and frightening virtue to cultivate.

The very openness of hospitality implies risk. What, under such circumstances, counts as justifying risk-taking? Is it the careful consideration as to whether or not it might be a "safe" risk? Or is it the wholeheartedness people invest in the outcome, regardless? Does it make a difference if the risk is for the sake of others (Templeton 1990: 68)?

Jesus as guest

On numerous occasions in the gospels, Jesus is seen to receive hospitality. One of the liveliest is the story, unique to Luke, where Jesus, an uninvited guest, is welcomed by Zacchaeus to his home (Lk. 19.1–10). Zacchaeus is presented in very human terms. We can empathize with him. Curious to see the person who is attracting such a crowd of people, he finds that his view is blocked; he is too small. So he runs to climb a tree to get a vantage point. Then he has to climb down with equal speed to act as host to an unexpected guest. For Jesus to stay with Zacchaeus in his home attracts public attention. There is murmuring. Zacchaeus, after all, is a chief tax collector, a very wealthy man, his riches due implicitly to ill-gotten gains. This has to be seen against the background of the basic harshness of peasant subsistence agriculture, where hunger is common (Lk. 11.5–6) and the prayer of Jesus to "give us each day our daily bread" has literal resonance (Lk. 11.3). But when Zacchaeus announces that he will give "half of his possessions" to the poor, far beyond what might conventionally have been expected of almsgiving, and that he will make restitution beyond the requirements of the law (Lev. 6.5; Num. 5.6–7), Jesus responds by proclaiming that "salvation has come to this house". Although, as is often the case with Luke, the point of this is not quite clear, we may deduce from what follows that salvation comes through Jesus' initiative in treating his host as a "son of Abraham", a fellow member of the people of God (Lk. 19.9). Jesus is then able to act as "broker" between Zacchaeus and God (Esler 2003: 455), and Zacchaeus realizes his responsibilities towards the poor.

Jesus as host

The Lord's Supper embodies unconditional hospitality. Jesus is the host. In Mark (14.22–26) and Luke (22.14–20), this meal, the last Jesus shares with his disciples before his crucifixion, is a Passover *seder*. The focus is on the actions and words of Jesus, blessing bread and wine, thanking God. It was conventional in the early church to see the Lord's Supper as part of a new Exodus (Jn 6; 1 Cor. 10.1–4; 15–17; Heb. 9.15–22): as through the ritual meal, participants engage with the departure from Egypt, they come to see that they are once again being redeemed. As they participate in the effects of Jesus' death and resurrection, they participate once more in God's grace and generosity. This is not the place to weigh the numerous interpretations of Jesus' words, but simply to point to the fact that, at the table of the Lord, all are brothers and sisters (1 Cor. 12.12–13; Gal. 3.27–29; Eph. 2.11–22). In this context, questions of status or legality do not arise. All "come together" to eat the Lord's Supper (1 Cor. 11.20). Eating and drinking is a communal act; a bond is formed by the shared eating and drinking – with God and with one another (Dunn 1988: 617). This is brought home emphatically by Paul in his letter to the Christians at Corinth (1 Cor. 11.17–34). He is clearly appalled by their selfish, cliquish behaviour (1 Cor. 11.20–22). They are not really sharing food; they are not "coming together" to eat the Lord's Supper. "Coming together" is a leitmotif of these verses (1 Cor. 11.17, 18, 20, 33, 34). Coming together to eat and drink at the table of the Lord constitutes Christians as "church".

As the Lord's Supper nurtures in the church's life remembrance of Jesus as gracious host, the Christian sees that unconditional hospitality is not an option. It is fundamental to the community of faith: "it is never far removed from its divine connections" (Pohl 1999: 30). God's hospitality is extended even to those who seem very different, the strangers in our midst.

As Christine Pohl suggests, "this intermingling of guest and host roles in the person of Jesus is part of what makes the story of hospitality so compelling for Christians. Jesus welcomes and needs welcome; Jesus requires that followers depend on and provide hospitality. The practice of Christian hospitality is always located within the larger picture of Jesus' sacrificial welcome to all who come to him" (Pohl 1999: 17).

Hospitality in the early church

Although the earliest groups of followers of Christ were Jewish, they were unique in their proclamation that Jesus was the Messiah, the saviour in whom God's reign had already begun. And some time before Paul wrote his first recorded letter to the Thessalonians, these Christian Jews began to welcome gentiles among their number.

They "devoted themselves to the apostles' teaching and fellowship, to the breaking of bread and the prayers" (Acts 2.42); they shared common meals in their homes (Acts 2.46); worshipped Jesus as Lord (Phil. 2.11); and aspired to practices that embodied God's reign. Amongst these was the forming of communities that crossed boundaries of gender, class, ethnicity, tradition (Gal. 3.28), and the practice of hospitality.

Two distinctive principles of hospitality in the early church are recorded. First, the principle is established that material resources exist for the well-being of the community as a whole – enabling communal bonds between the wealthy and the poor and vulnerable (Acts 2.44; 4.32). Luke gives no attention to what such economic arrangements would entail in practical terms, but he does describe individual and communal commitments to redistribute resources amongst the believing poor, the hungry, and the sorrowful, for whom the gospel is good news. Barnabas, the Levite from Cyprus, is upheld as a shining example (Acts 4.36–37; cf. Acts 6.1–6). Christians are exhorted to work towards institutional arrangements congruent with the equality of the people of God (1 Cor. 11.20–22). However, we might also infer that this was, to some extent at least, being honoured in the breach (Acts 2.45). If property was really held in common, would anyone be selling it? The example of Ananias and Saphira illustrates how the practice was open to abuse (Acts 5.1–11). The challenge today, as then, is to find appropriate ways to institutionalize the principle that property exists for the corporate well-being of the people (Ogletree 1985: 133).

The second principle is almsgiving, illustrated by Paul's collection from churches in Galatia, Macedonia, and Achaia for impoverished church members in Jerusalem. The example was set by the Antioch church (Acts 11.29). Paul encourages the Christians at Corinth to put aside a sum of money every day to this end (1 Cor. 16.1–4); but when it transpires that they have been reluctant to comply, Paul eloquently exhorts them to generosity (2 Cor. 8.9). And he instances the eager, self-sacrificial, loving, giving of the Macedonian churches from a situation of extreme poverty. It seems that the Corinthians finally responded positively (Rom. 15.25–27).

Hospitality today

Where provision of care is seen to be a matter for the state, hospitality for the needy is understood primarily as a matter for the social services, with dedicated paid care professionals. But where the state is unable or unwilling to fulfill its responsibilities to provide adequate financial and material care for the poor and alien, where refugees are treated with scant regard for their humanity, the churches find they have an important role to play. As they exercise hospitality, they affirm the value of all human beings in the eyes of God and challenge governments to make their practices towards asylum-seekers and refugees more humane and compassionate.

Their hospitality is exercised partly in charitable action and partly in advocacy. In the US, there is "a developing consensus among a large number of widely diverse Christian leaders that comprehensive immigration reform is a biblically grounded imperative" (Carroll R. 2013: 138). Lutheran congregations "struggle to be faithful to God's love by embracing these new neighbours through ministries grounded in love and justice" (Bouman & Deffenbaugh 2009: 95–116): "first we welcome the stranger, then we work with them to address our broken immigration system" (Bouman & Deffenbaugh 2009: 84). The Roman Catholic Church has taken the lead in campaigning against the humanitarian problems associated with the US border wall, the barrier that has been constructed along seven hundred miles of the Mexican border to stem the number of undocumented immigrants and drug smugglers into the US from Mexico. In the UK, many churches and Christian organizations are doing what they can to support refugees (Snyder 2011: 570–573; 2012: 215–217). Christian volunteers attend hearings, UK MPs' advice sessions, and removal centres; they provide day-to-day practical advice and emotional support. Others become involved in public debate, while many act together, often in conjunction with NGOs, to challenge harsh and cruelly implemented government policies. In Australia, Erin Wilson outlines the ways in which "Faith-Based Organizations have used concepts and practices consistent with faith-based hospitality to challenge public discourses, provide services to asylum seekers that ameliorate the harsh effects of government immigration policies and eventually contribute to changes in those policies" (2011).

Philanthropy

Motivated by philanthropy, many individuals and groups respond generously to particular need; churches and secular NGOs do what they can to alleviate the immediate effects of poverty on their doorstep; individuals and governments donate generously to charitable appeals to help millions of refugees worldwide. Food, shelter, medical aid, and supplies of drinking water are undeniable emergency needs; the delivery of these with considerable professional competence by international agencies has saved thousands if not millions of lives.

But, in the light of the gospel ethic, we must still ask: is philanthropy enough? Can it sometimes even undermine human dignity? Barbara Harrell-Bond was one of the first to explore the relationship between refugees and those who help them: "all human beings are dependent on others to a greater or lesser extent; the issue is not being 'helped' *per se*, but the relative powerlessness of the recipient vis-à-vis the helper" (1999: 139). Although her research is focused primarily on refugee camps, her conclusions are applicable wherever refugees are dependent on others for the necessities of life (Harrell-Bond 1999; 2002). In the majority of camps, refugees are dependent on outside help – but, she notes, problems arise with the kind of help they receive and the way help is provided. The bundles of used clothes, for instance, are often inappropriate, for men in particular. Harrell-Bond instances the surplus of nylon quilted women's dressing-gowns donated to refugees in South Sudan; these were, in her experience, the only garment available for Ugandan men to wear if they wished to keep warm. Donations of food are often so unfamiliar that recipients do not know how to cook it. Refugees sometimes wonder whether donors respect them enough, whether they consider them as fellow human beings (Harrell-Bond 1999: 142). Assistance programmes depersonalize, as people are identified by numbers: their dignity is further undermined by the regimental distribution methods that are seen to be necessary by camp authorities. Abuse of power by officials is always a possibility. Measures designed for short-term efficiency are unsuitable for situations where the camps are the main living environment for years and, for some, for more than one generation.

Harrell-Bond argues that until refugees have access to effective legal remedies, humanitarian assistance will continue to be inhumanely delivered. What is needed, she suggests, is a "rights-based humanitarianism" that goes beyond "private charity or governmental largess". And she continues: "this approach is not about discretionary assistance when the mood for benevolence takes us. It is about defending, advocating, and securing the enjoyment of human rights. It also implies a shift from seeing beneficiaries of humanitarian aid as 'victims' to be pitied to survivors of adversity – who often demonstrate unimaginable strength and dignity in the most adverse circumstances" (Harrell-Bond 2002: 52).

Are there ways in which religious faith, nurtured on the Bible, can assist in addressing these issues? Can it permit an engagement in humanitarian policy-making that is true to Biblical principles? Historically, religious commitments shaped the understanding of humanitarianism. They were central to the formulation of the Universal Declaration of Human Rights. However, as humanitarian principles became codified in law, the discourse of humanitarianism became separated from that of faith. As Alastair and Joey Ager suggest, this has brought problems (Ager & Ager 2011: 459). As religious belief was marginalized, the ideological agenda of liberal materialism came to dominate. And yet, "religious narratives and institutions, whilst at the margins of international humanitarianism ... are at the core of the experience of the vast majority of communities facing crisis and, perhaps as crucially, of the majority of national humanitarian agency staff" (2011: 465). A religious faith that is grounded in the Bible can clarify core humanitarian values; it can support a human rights framework that is able to define and protect human dignity; and it can find appropriate ways to address religious experience and well-being. "In short", Ager & Ager conclude, "if secularism cannot intellectually sustain a robust defence for the foundation of human rights, can religion (once more) be effectively mobilized to protect it?" (2011: 467).

Dependency

Snyder (2007) raises the significant question: is an approach based solely on "doing our duty" to the vulnerable adequate? Is there not a risk of succour being seen as one-way traffic, reinforcing stereotypes of vulnerability and weakness rather than resilience? How to struggle with rather than struggle for? Where there is a mutual exercise of responsibility and a mutual recognition of human dignity, refugees will come to participate in their own welfare provision. Referring to the UK, she writes:

> People seeking sanctuary also help to settle one another, through informal friendship networks and as participants in projects and activities. Some asylum seekers become de-facto members of the historic mainstream denominational churches they attend – rather than simply recipients of their services – and act with established community Christians as volunteers in projects or to challenge policy. Others choose to form or join new churches, mosques, temples and gurdwaras connected with their country, region or language of origin, and research has shown that these faith communities can contribute significantly to the ability of individuals to settle and succeed in a new country.
>
> (Snyder 2011: 568)

And yet the question remains: how can one supply essential aid without incorporating refugees as dependent beneficiaries (Zetter 1999: 74)? The question applies to individuals; it applies also to the camps. The challenge would be hard enough if it were simply a matter of logistics. But, as Roger Zetter notes, "the interests of all the actors (except refugees) are best served by containing and controlling refugees – political, diplomatic, logistical, security, media profile – in short, by sustaining dependency" (1999: 74). Refugees gradually cease to be seen as people with problems – they become the problem. According to the agencies, the best way of making refugee populations self-sufficient is to "manage" them in camps, but the results have been disappointing, and responsibility for this is frequently attributed to refugees themselves (Harrell-Bond 1999: 148). It is held that during the time they are given outside assistance, they adopt attitudes which impede their progress to self-sufficiency. To blame refugees for adjusting to the social structure of the camps is surely unfair, but the idea has emerged amongst humanitarians that "the more you give, the more dependent people become". If all this would seem to indicate a need for more appropriate international assistance, then one has also to take account of the fact that substantial numbers of refugees survive through their own strategies and resourcefulness. Survivors of adversity, they often demonstrate unimaginable strength and dignity in the most adverse circumstances. Harrell-Bond cites tented camps in the Sahara Desert where refugees live in extremely unfavourable conditions (1999: 156). Although they depend for survival entirely on aid supplied by the Saharawi Red Crescent, they prefer to dispense with the help of humanitarian agencies and "actively used their time in exile to build a twentieth-century democratic nation". This applies as much to the context of a developed country as it does to the developing world. Following the expulsion of Asians from Uganda by President Amin in 1972, an important study by V. Robinson of East African Asians in the UK found that, despite extensive racial exclusionism in the UK at the time and a deep economic recession, these acquired better formal qualifications than their Indian or White British counterparts, were overrepresented in self-employment, and had transformed their socioeconomic profile more rapidly than the other two groups (1993).

Is there not a danger that a continuing focus on the need of refugees pathologizes their experience, fixing them in a discourse of vulnerability? This also undermines their humanity. Loving one's neighbour has to involve an appreciation of the resilience of many refugees and the considerable resources they display in responding to the challenges faced in forced migration.

A place for living together humanly

The French philosopher Yves Cattin evokes hospitality in these terms: it

> makes the one who approaches me my neighbour, even if he or she comes from the ends of the earth. Hospitality sets in motion processes of reciprocal knowledge and recognition ... it allows others to exist, in opening up a place for them where they can show who they are. Then ... respect becomes the communion of our similarities; it becomes the invention, beyond the recognition and surmounting of our differences, of a place for living together humanly.
>
> (Cattin 1999: 12)

We have already seen (p. 79) how the provision of "cities of refuge" (Exod. 21.12–14; Num. 35.11–15; Deut. 4.41–43; 19.1–13; Josh. 20.1–3) enabled fugitives to take refuge in any one of six designated cities on either side of the Jordan. These safe havens for Israelites and aliens alike permitted due process and ensured that those accused of homicide were kept safe from private vengeance. In due course, the concept was adopted by the church, and for upwards of 1,000 years cathedrals, churches, and monasteries were seen as asylum sanctuaries where fugitives and outlaws could ask for protection. The sanctuary was inviolate. Not until 1989 did the state intervene, when UK police removed a Sri Lankan refugee, Viraj Mendis, from the Church of the Ascension, Manchester, where he had been given protection for the previous three years. In his insightful exploration of ancient and modern histories of sanctuary, Philip Marfleet shows how the duty to protect the refugee shifted over time from church to state (Marfleet 2011). In the UK, the church privilege was abolished by James I in 1623. No longer was sanctuary linked to sites where protection was an expression of saintly or God-given authority. But an influx of persecuted Huguenots in the reign of Charles II raised the matter of sanctuary once again. This is significant for two reasons. First, when the king offered them asylum in 1681, the nation-state as a whole was judged to be the place of sanctuary, not just religious sites (Marfleet 2011: 440). And this may also have been the first occasion when a state formally offered protection to people who were associated with another state – the first time when refugees were recognized as a category of persons requiring protection. This anticipated developments across Western Europe, and today the territory of the nation-state still defines the boundaries of asylum. Refugees and asylum-seekers are completely dependent on the will of the sovereign state. Since 9/11, the interests of national security have dwarfed humanitarian concerns, making it likely that a number of those who apply for asylum are not receiving the protection they need. The very concept of asylum has become vilified and criminalized through notions of bogus asylum claims and terror threats.

The ideal of refugee protection, however, continues outside the formal arrangements of the state and inspires protest often in defiance of the law, where that is perceived to violate the norms of humanity. This was typified in Europe by organized efforts to give sanctuary to Jews during the Second World War and in the US by the 19th-century Underground Railroad: an extensive network of safe houses to protect escaped slaves fleeing from the southern to the northern states, Canada, and Mexico. In the same model came W. Sloane Coffin's call in 1966 for "sanctuaries for Draft resisters" and, recently, the concerted movement to assist refugees from Central America. Churches were hugely active in the movement and "sanctuary communities" confronted the US state when its immigration policies violated norms of humanity. In 1982, some churches defied the state by declaring their churches to be "a 'sanctuary' for undocumented refugees" (Marfleet 2011: 451). Although these churches ran the risk of prosecution, this "modern railroad" soon spread with homes and churches made available to migrants in most states to the consternation of state and federal officials (Bouman & Deffenbaugh 2009: 91–93). Christian communities stand together in solidarity to protect the weak and vulnerable, and confront oppression as they stand by the poor.

In the UK there has been a steady growth of Cities of Sanctuary. This is essentially a movement for cultural change. The vision of cities seeking to inspire individuals and organizations to promote an ethos of welcome for people seeking sanctuary led to the declaration of Sheffield in September 2007 as the UK's first "City of Sanctuary". This initiative spread to a network of towns and cities across the UK, and further groups are being developed. These differ from one another according to local context: "while the general orientation of the movement remains the same ... there is considerable freedom for local groups to define and claim ownership over their own sense of sanctuary" (Darling 2008). "Streams of sanctuary", theme-based networks of groups from different sectors, Arts, Faiths, Health, Maternity, Schools, make a public commitment to welcome and include refugees and people seeking asylum in their usual activities. Through events and activities, relationships are fostered between asylum-seekers and local people. And so "City of Sanctuary seeks to influence the political debate on sanctuary indirectly through cultural change" (Core Principles 2008); it does not engage directly in political lobbying or anti-deportation campaigns.

Admirable as the vision of changing public culture may be, some questions remain. Is the notion of "protected space" sufficient? First, how does the local organization ensure that local politicians are sufficiently committed to the fact that they serve a City of Sanctuary for local councils to remain accountable to that ethos? Second, when faced with the destructive effects of government policies on local individuals and families, is there not also an imperative to challenge asylum policy and practice when it is seen to be unjust or inhumane? Are provision and protection complete without advocacy? Third, in the Biblical cities of refuge, the protection afforded would seem to have little to do with the problems of the hard-pressed stranger as we know them and everything to do with the provisional protection of the homicide from the avenger of blood (Crüsemann 2003: 225–234). Might an overreading of the Biblical references buy into an understanding of refugees that is tainted by association with homicide, thereby enhancing a political discourse of "threat" and "illegality"? Is this not reinforced by the fact that those who have committed no offence other than to desire asylum are deprived of their liberty, in the UK and in Australia at least, for indefinite lengths of time?

Cities of Sanctuary has to be seen as "part of that wider context of movements and organizations which challenge current asylum policies" (Darling 2008). It values and owns an ethos of hospitality to refugees and those who are seeking asylum; it reclaims sanctuary as a virtue: "contemporary sanctuary activists draw on ancient traditions: they also engage with a continuous history of protection which suggests that empathy and solidarity are indeed integral to all forms of social organization" (Marfleet 2011: 452).

Today, however, hospitable attitudes towards the stranger cannot be assumed – within or without the church. Snyder cites English (UK) churches that were found by refugees to be "not so friendly" and some members of congregations who "had reservations about welcoming those seeking sanctuary on the grounds that they could be doing something illegal" (2011: 575). Many are simply reflecting a more general hardening of heart since the attacks on the twin towers in New York on 9/11 and the terrorist attacks in London in July 2005, since when asylum-seeking and immigration have been linked to terrorism and national security. Attitudes to the stranger changed: "in the ripple effects of September 11, 2001, something ugly has emerged, slouching from Ground Zero: a hardening of the heart toward the immigrant stranger among us" (Bouman & Deffenbaugh 2009: 2). In the face of this, the church's distinctive calling has to be affirmed (Bretherton 2010: 211). For the Christian advocacy of hospitality is firmly grounded in Biblical testimony to the gracious hospitality that weak, vulnerable human beings have received from God. As Christians are continually roused to remember this, they in their turn will be generous in the hospitality they show to the poor, the marginalized, the refugee. This inevitably leads to a greater awareness of social practices that are inhospitable. Where these result from political policies, Christians are challenged to call these into question.

9

CONCLUSION

God through Moses exhorts his people to love the stranger as themselves (Lev. 19.34). All other narratives are judged by that – whether in the Bible or the narratives of today. Though these are often found wanting, the overarching perspective of the Bible is that there is a community of moral understanding between human beings and God, an understanding that because God loves and protects the stranger, so should we.

There is a close similarity between the ethical norms of the Old and New Testaments. Both aspire to divine attributes in society; both exhort readers to act justly and with compassion. Good behaviour to the poor and marginalized is central. Concern for the well-being of the sojourner in particular is manifest in Old Testament law, and the reason also is made clear: Israel is called to love the sojourner because God does (Deut. 10.17–19; cf. Ps. 146.7–9). The exhortation to "love your neighbour as yourself" (Lev. 19.18; cf. Mt. 22.34–40) was extended to the sojourner because of the experience of the Israelites under Pharaoh (Lev. 19.34). They knew, after all, what it felt like to be an oppressed minority. They were given to understand that the neighbour to be loved was not just a fellow Israelite, but that it included persons outside the circle of fellow countrymen, strangers in their midst. And God reminds them that when he saved them from horrible experiences as immigrants, this revealed something about his person: God loves the helpless and powerless, including sojourners. And to ignore the cry of such people is a sin (Deut. 24.14–15).

Along with other people at risk, the widow, the fatherless child, and the poor, the sojourner is in a potentially precarious situation. But in the Torah, he is provided for at different levels, and all are involved, from the individual to society as a whole: in families, he shares in the Sabbath rest and is included in festival celebrations. In the community, he benefits from gleaning, he receives his share of tithes, and, at legal gatherings, he may expect a fair hearing.

In the gospels, these ethical norms are interpreted in the life and teaching of Jesus. Matthew depicts Jesus expounding the Torah on the mountain, like Moses (Mt. 5–7), debating with teachers of the law and teaching in parables. The climax of his teaching is his answer to the lawyer's question as to the greatest commandment and an unequivocal denunciation of those who fail to fulfill the law or who interpret the love commandment in an unloving manner (Mt. 22.34–40; 23; 25.31–46). The double command to love God and one's neighbour, even one's enemy, is the driving force behind Jesus' attitude to the law.

There is a rich interplay between the "world in front of the text", in Ricoeur's terms (p. 3), and the world of today. Through the exercise of ethical imagination, we are able to see and name inhumanity and injustice for what they are. We will see how refugees bear the cost of war and its beastliness, and how they are sometimes forced to flee malevolent and barbarous social prejudice. We will see how those who seek asylum are often subjected to cruel and inhumane processes even though they may already have suffered greatly:

> The ways in which we "see" the world, its story and destiny; the ways in which we "see" what human beings are, and what they are for, and how they are related to each other and the world around them; these things are shaped and structured by the stories that we tell ... What does the world look like? What do we look like? What does God look like?
>
> (Lash 2007: 130)

To love the stranger as oneself is to live as part of a community where human dignity is affirmed and where loving one's neighbour is exercised in mutual responsibility. In the light of this, sojourners are to be treated justly, protected from oppression, and, where they are poor and vulnerable, given comfort and support. The love of the stranger is to be fleshed out daily in homes, church congregations, communities, and at national level.

Communities nourished by the world in front of the text "can speak to impoverished debates in ways that enlarge and extend our political vision" (Messer & Paddison 2013: 207). This book offers no simple answers to the problems that force people to flee their homes and seek refuge in another country. But it does challenge readers to take the moral claims of refugees and asylum-seekers seriously and calls inhumanity and injustice into question. It shows how an engagement with the Bible can shape the way we see the world and make some Christian sense of things. This may in turn inform our attitudes and behaviours as citizens as we reckon with the political forces that constrain and shape what states can do with regard to refugees. But we must take heed: "unless we make that truth our own ... it will be chipped away, reshaped, eroded by the power of an imagining fed by other springs, tuned to quite different stories" (Lash 2007: 131).

By means of a cycle of reading and responding to the Bible, Christian identity and moral character become the narrative of our lives. As we see the sovereign rule of God breaking into the world, we are able to see the possibility of good in and beyond the current situation, however inhumane and unjust that might seem to be. We will stand committed to the reality of a world that is governed by justice and compassion, where the stranger is treated with dignity and respect.

BIBLIOGRAPHY

Abebe & Mengistu 2005. *Almaz Sayoum Albebe and Sisay Mengistu v. Alberto R. Gonzales, Attorney General*, 432 F. 3d1037 (9th Circuit 2005).

Achenbach, Reinhard 2011. "Ger-Nokhri-Toshav-Zar: Legal and Sacral Distinctions Regarding Foreigners in the Pentateuch". In *The Foreigner and the Law: Perspectives from the Hebrew Bible and the Ancient Near East*, Reinhard Achenbach, Rainer Albertz, & Jakob Wöhrle (eds). Wiesbaden: Harrassowitz Verlag: 29–51.

Adan 1999. *Adan v Secretary of State for the Home Department* [1999] 1 AC 293.

Adesina, Zach 2012. "Children with 'no stake' in the UK" (5 November). BBC *Inside Out*. http://www.bbc.co.uk/news/uk-england-london-20186588 (accessed June 2014).

Adler, D. & K. Rubinstein 2000. "International Citizenship: The Future of Nationality in a Globalised World". *Indiana Journal of Global Legal Studies* 7 (2): 519–548.

Agamben, Giorgio 1998. *Homo Sacer: Sovereign Power and Bare Life*, Daniel Heller-Roazen (trans.). Stanford, CA: Stanford University Press.

Ager, Alastair & Joey 2011. "Faith and the Discourse of Secular Humanitarianism". *Journal of Refugee Studies* 24 (3): 456–472.

Ahmed 1997. *Ahmed v Austria* (1997) 24 EHRR 278.

Ahn, John J. 2011. *Exile as Forced Migrations: A Sociological, Literary, and Theological Approach on the Displacement and Resettlement of the Southern Kingdom of Judah*. Berlin & New York: De Gruyter.

Aidani, Mammad 2010. *Welcoming the Stranger: Narratives of Identity and Belonging in an Iranian Diaspora*. Melbourne: Melbourne University Press.

Albertz, Rainer 2003. *Israel in Exile: The History and Literature of the 6th Century* BCE, David Green (trans.). Atlanta: Society of Biblical Literature; Leiden: Brill.

——2012. "More and Less than a Myth". In *By the Irrigation Canals of Babylon: Approaches to the Study of the Exile*, John J. Ahn & Jill Middlemas (eds). New York & London: T&T Clark: 20–33.

Al-Rasheed, Madawi 1994. "The Myth of Return: Iraqi Arab and Assyrian Refugees in London". *Journal of Refugee Studies* 7 (2–3): 199–219.

Amnesty International 2009. "Eritrea: Sent Home to Detention and Torture".

Appellant S395/2002. *Appellant S395/2002 v Minister for Immigration and Multicultural Affairs* (2003) 216CLR473 (Austl).

Arendt, Hannah 1982. *Lectures on Kant's Political Philosophy*, Ronald Beiner (ed.). Chicago: University of Chicago Press.

AS 2011. *AS v Secretary of State for the Home Department* [2011] EWHC 564 (Admin).

Assmann, Jan 2011. *Cultural Memory and Early Civilization: Writing, Remembrance and Political Imagination*. Cambridge & New York: Cambridge University Press.

Asylum Aid 2012. "The Human Rights of Unaccompanied Migrant Children and Young People in the UK". Asylum Aid's Submission to the Joint Committee on Human Rights (23 October).

Asylum Matters 2008. "Asylum Matters: Restoring Trust in the UK Asylum System". A Report by the Asylum and Destitution Working Group. London: Centre for Social Justice (December). http://www.centreforsocialjustice.org.uk/UserStorage/pdf/Pdf%20Exec%20summaries/AsylumMatters.pdf (accessed May 2014).

Awabdy, Mark A. 2014. *Immigrants and Innovative Law: Deuteronomy's Theological and Social Vision for the ger*. Tübingen: Mohr Siebeck.

Aynsley-Green, Sir Al 2010. "The Arrest and Detention of Children Subject to Immigration Control". London: 11Million.

Bacon, Hannah, Wayne Morris, & Steve Knowles (eds) 2011. *Transforming Exclusion: Engaging with Faith Perspectives*. London: T&T Clark.

Balentine, Samuel E. 2011. "The Prose and Poetry of Exile". In *Interpreting Exile: Displacement and Deportation in Biblical and Modern Contexts,* Brad E. Kelle, Frank Ritchel Ames, & Jacob L. Wright (eds). Atlanta: Society of Biblical Literature: 345–363.

Barstad, Hans M. 1996. *The Myth of the Empty Land: A Study in the History and Archaeology of Judah during the "Exilic" Period*. Oslo: Scandinavian University Press.

——2003. "After the 'Myth of the Empty Land': Major Challenges in the Study of Neo-Babylonian Judah". In *Judah and the Judeans in the Neo-Babylonian Period,* O. Lipschits & J. Blenkinsopp (eds). Winona Lake, IN: Eisenbrauns: 3–20.

Barton, John 1988. *People of the Book? The Authority of the Bible in Christianity*. London: SPCK.

——1998. *Ethics and the Old Testament*. London: SCM Press.

——2003. *Understanding Old Testament Ethics*. Louisville, KY: Westminster John Knox Press.

Bascom, Jonathan 2005. "The Long, 'Last Step'? Reintegration of Repatriates in Eritrea". *Journal of Refugee Studies* 18 (2): 165–180.

Beattie, D.R.G. 1978a. "Redemption in Ruth, and Related Matters: A Response to Jack M. Sasson". *Journal for the Study of the Old Testament* 5: 65–68.

——1978b. "Ruth III". *Journal for the Study of the Old Testament* 5: 39–48.

Becking, Bob 2011. "A Fragmented History of the Exile". In *Interpreting Exile: Displacement and Deportation in Biblical and Modern Contexts,* Brad E. Kelle, Frank Ritchel Ames, & Jacob L. Wright (eds). Atlanta: Society of Biblical Literature: 151–169.

——2012. "Global Warming and the Babylonian Exile". In *By the Irrigation Canals of Babylon: Approaches to the Study of the Exile,* John J. Ahn & Jill Middlemas (eds). New York & London: T&T Clark: 49–62.

Becking, Bob & Anne-Mareike Wetter 2013. "Boaz in the Gate (Ruth 4.1–12): Legal Transaction or Religious Ritual?". *Zeitschrift für altorientalische und biblische Rechtgeschichte* 19: 254–264.

Behavior and Law 2012. "Psychiatrists identify 'asylum seeker syndrome' - Yahoo 7". http://forpn.blogspot.co.uk/2012/05/psychiatrists-identify-asylum-seeker.html (accessed 22 December 2012).

Benhabib, Seyla 2004. *The Rights of Others: Aliens, Residents and Citizens*. Cambridge: Cambridge University Press.

Bernadotte 1948. *Progress Report of the UN Mediator*, 3rd Sess., Suppl. No. 11(A/648) (16 September).

Betz, Hans Dieter 1995. *The Sermon on the Mount*. Minneapolis: Fortress Press.

Birnberg Peirce & Partners, Medical Justice & NCADC 2008. "Outsourcing Abuse: The Use and Misuse of State-Sanctioned Force during the Detention and Removal".

Blenkinsopp, Joseph 1988. *Ezra-Nehemiah*. London: SCM Press.

——2002. "The Bible, Archaeology and Politics; or The Empty Land Revisited". *Journal for the Study of the Old Testament* 27 (2): 169–187.

Bockmuehl, Markus 2000. *Jewish Law in Christian Churches*. Edinburgh: T&T Clark.

Bögner, Diana, Jane Herlihy, & Chris R. Brewin 2007. "The Impact of Sexual Violence on Disclosure during the Home Office Interview". *British Journal of Psychiatry* 191: 75–81.

Boucher, David 2009. *The Limits of Ethics in International Relations: Natural Law, Natural Rights, and Human Rights in Transition*. Oxford: Oxford University Press.

Bouman, Stephen & Ralston Deffenbaugh 2009. *They Are Us: Lutherans and Immigration*. Minneapolis: Fortress Press.

Bovon, François 1996. *Das Evangelium nach Lukas*. 2. Teilbd. Zürich: Neukirchener Verlag.

——2002. *A Commentary on the Gospel of Luke*. Vol. 1, Christine M. Thomas (trans.), Helmut Koester (ed.). Minneapolis: Fortress Press.

Bralo, Zrinko *et al.* 2012. "Operation Integration: The Making of New Citizens". The Forum: London (February).

Bretherton, Luke 2010. *Christianity and Contemporary Politics: The Conditions and Possibilities of Faithful Witness*. Oxford: Wiley-Blackwell.

Brown, Malcolm D. 2012. "Institutional Islamophobia in the Cases of Ahmed Zaoui and Mohamed Haneef". In *Cultures in Refuge: Seeking Sanctuary in Modern Australia*, Anna Hayes & Robert Mason (eds). Farnham, Surrey: Ashgate: 149–162.

Brown, Raymond E. 1993. *The Birth of the Messiah*. New York & London: Doubleday.

Bryen, Shoshana 2012. "Israel and the Boat People". *The Times of Israel* (6 June). http://blogs.timesofisrael.com/israel-and-the-boat-people/ (accessed May 2014).

Buehrig, Edward H. 1971. *The UN and the Palestinian Refugees: A Study in Nonterritorial Administration*. Bloomington, IN: Indiana University Press.

Buis, P. & J. Leclerq 1963. *Le Deutéronome*. Paris: Sources Bibliques.

Bultmann, Christophe 1992. *Der Fremde im antiken Juda*. FRLANT 153: Göttingen: Vandenhoeck & Ruprecht.

Burke, Aaron A. 2011. "An Anthropological Model for the Investigation of the Archaeology of Refugees in Iron Age Judah and its Environs". In *Interpreting Exile: Displacement and Deportation in Biblical and Modern Contexts*, Brad E. Kelle, Frank Ritchel Ames, & Jacob L. Wright (eds). Atlanta: Society of Biblical Literature: 41–56.

Burnett, Jon *et al.* 2010. *State Sponsored Cruelty: Children in Immigration Detention*. Medical Justice. http://www.medicaljustice.org.uk/images/stories/reports/sscfullreport.pdf (accessed May 2014).

Burnside, Jonathan 2001. *The Status and Welfare of Immigrants*. Jubilee Centre.

Burridge, Richard A. 2007. *Imitating Jesus: An Inclusive Approach to New Testament Ethics*. Grand Rapids, Michigan & Cambridge, UK: Eerdmans.

Butler, Judith 2006. *Precarious Life: The Powers of Mourning and Violence*. London & New York: Verso.

——2010. *Frames of War: When is Life Grievable?* London & New York: Verso.

Byrne, Rosemary & Gregor Noll 2013. *International Criminal Justice, the Gotovina Judgment and the Making of Refugees*. University of Lund. http://works.bepress.com/gregor_noll/12/ (accessed May 2014).

Cahill, Lisa Sowle 2013. *Global Justice, Christology, and Christian Ethics*. Cambridge: Cambridge University Press.

Caird, George 1963. *Saint Luke*. Harmondsworth, Middlesex: Penguin Books.

Campbell, E.F. 1974. "The Hebrew Short Story: A Study of Ruth". In *A Light Unto My Path, fs J.M. Myers*, H.N. Bream (ed.). Gettysburg Theological Studies 4. Gettysburg: Temple University Press: 83–101.

Carr, David M. 2011. "Reading into the Gap: Refractions of Trauma in Israelite Prophecy". In *Interpreting Exile: Displacement and Deportation in Biblical and Modern Contexts*, Brad E. Kelle, Frank Ritchel Ames, & Jacob L. Wright (eds). Atlanta: Society of Biblical Literature: 295–308.

Carroll R., Daniel 2013. *Christians at the Border: Immigration, the Church, and the Bible*. 2nd edn revised. Grand Rapids, Michigan: Baker Publishing Group.

Carroll, Robert P. 1986. *Jeremiah*. London: SCM Press.

Cattin, Yves 1999. "Human Beings Cross Frontiers", John Bowden (trans.). In *Frontier Violations: The Beginnings of New Identities*, Felix Wilfred & Oscar Beozzo (eds). London: SCM Press & Maryknoll, NY: Orbis Books: 3–17.

Chahal 1997. *Chahal v the United Kingdom* (1997) 23 EHRR 413.

Chaichian, Mohammad A. 1997. "First-Generation Iranian Immigrants and the Question of Cultural Identity: The Case of Iowa". *International Migration Review* 31 (3): 612–627.

Charter 2008. Charter of the Rights of Women Seeking Asylum. London: Asylum Aid. http://www.asylumaid.org.uk/wp-content/uploads/2013/02/Charter.pdf (accessed June 2014).

Chen 2006. *Chen v US Att'y Gen.*, 463 F.3d 1228, 1233 (11th Circuit 2006).

Childs, Brevard S. 2001. *Isaiah*. Louisville, KY: Westminster John Knox Press.

Chimni, B.S. 2004. "From Resettlement to Involuntary Repatriation: Towards a Critical History of Durable Solutions to Refugee Problems". *Refugee Survey Quarterly* 23 (3): 55–73.

City of Sanctuary 2008. Core Principles. http://www.cityofsanctuary.org/content/core-principles (accessed May 2014).

Clayton, Pamela 1998. "Religion, Ethnicity and Colonialism as Explanations of the Northern Ireland Conflict". In *Rethinking Northern Ireland: Culture, Ideology and Colonialism*, David Miller (ed.). London & New York: Longman: 40–54.

Cleveland, J. *et al.* 2012. "The Impact of Detention and Temporary Status on Asylum Seekers' Mental Health". http://bit.ly/MSWzGe (accessed May 2014).

Clines, D.J.A. 1984. *Ezra, Nehemiah*. Waco, TX: Word Books.

——1990. *What Does Eve Do to Help? and Other Readerly Questions to the Old Testament*. JSOT Supplement Series 94. Sheffield: JSOT Press.

Cohen, Rina & Gerald Gold 1997. "Constructing Ethnicity: Myth of Return and Modes of Exclusion among Israelis in Toronto". *International Migration* 35 (3): 373–394.

Connor, P. 2010. "Explaining the Refugee Gap: Economic Outcomes of Refugees versus Other Immigrants". *Journal of Refugee Studies* 23 (3): 377–397.

Conway, Mary 2012. "Metaphor and Dialogue in Lamentations". In *Daughter Zion: Her Portrait, Her Response*, Mark J. Boda, Carol Dempsey, & LeAnn Snow Flesher (eds). Atlanta: Society of Biblical Literature: 101–126.

Cosa 2007. *Cosa v Mukasey*, 543 F.3d 1066, 1069–70 (9th Circuit 2008).

Cotter, David W. 2003. *Genesis*. Collegeville, MN: The Liturgical Press.

Council Directive 2004/83/EC of 29 April 2004 *on minimum standards for the qualification and status of third party nationals or stateless persons as refugees or as persons who otherwise need internal protection and the context of the protection granted.*

Crawley, Heaven 2001. *Refugees and Gender: Law and Process*. Bristol: Jordan.

——2010. "Chance or Choice? Understanding Why Asylum Seekers Come to the UK". Swansea University & The Refugee Council. http://www.refugeecouncil.org.uk/assets/0001/5702/rcchance.pdf (accessed June 2014).

Crüsemann, Frank 2003. *Masstab: Tora: Israels Weisung für christliche Ethik*. Gütersloh: Gütersloher Verlagshaus.

Cuéllar, G. Lee 2008. *Voices of Marginality: Exile and Return in Second Isaiah 40–55 and the Mexican Immigrant Experience*. Oxford: Peter Lang.

Curthoys, Ann 1999. "Expulsion, Exodus and Exile in White Australian Historical Mythology". *Journal of Australian Studies* 23 (61): 1–19.

Dapice, David & Nguyen Xuan Thanh 2013. *Creating a Future: Using Natural Resources for New Federalism and Unity*. http://www.ash.harvard.edu/Home/Programs/Institute-for-Asia/Publications/Occasional-Papers (accessed June 2014).

Darling, Jonathan 2008. "Creating the Hospitable City: Exploring Sheffield as a 'City of Sanctuary'". In *Good Asylum Conference*. Leeds Metropolitan University.

Daube, David 2003. *Biblical Law and Literature: Collected Works of David Daube Vol. 3*, Calum Carmichael (ed.). Berkeley: Robbins Collection (University of California).

Davidson, Steed Vernyl 2013. *Empire and Exile: Postcolonial Readings of the Book of Jeremiah*. London & New York: Bloomsbury.

Davies, Philip R. 1998. "Exile? What Exile? Whose Exile?". In *Leading Captivity Captive – "The Exile" as History and Ideology*, Lester L. Grabbe (ed.); JSOT Supplement Series 278. Sheffield: Sheffield Academic Press: 128–138.

Davies, W.D. & D.C. Allison 1988–97. *Matthew*. 3 vols. Edinburgh: T&T Clark.

De Luce, Daniel 2004. "Stumbling in the Dark". *Guardian* (24 May).

Demshuk, Andrew 2012. *The Lost German East: Forced Migration and the Politics of Memory, 1945–1970*. Cambridge: Cambridge University Press.

Deng, F. 1998. "Guiding Principles on Internal Displacement: Report of the Representative of the Secretary General". Geneva: UN Doc E/CN4/1998/53/Add2 (11 February).

Dennis, Judith 2012. "Not a Minor Offence: Unaccompanied Children Locked Up as Part of the Asylum System". Refugee Council. http://www.refugeecouncil.org.uk/assets/0002/5945/Not_a_minor_offence_2012.pdf (accessed June 2014).

Derrida, Jacques 2000. *Of Hospitality*, R. Bowlby (trans.). Stanford, CA: Stanford University Press.

Detention Action 2014. *Detention Action v Secretary of State for the Home Department* (2014) EWHC 2245 (Admin).

Dijk, Teun A. van 1991. *Racism and the Press*. London: Routledge.

Directive 2008. Directive 2008/115/EC of the European Parliament and of the Council of 16 December 2008 on Common Standards and Procedures in Member States for Returning Illegally Staying Third-Country Nationals. http://eur-lex.europa.eu/LexUriServ/LexUriServ.do?uri=OJ:L:2008:348:0098:0107:EN:PDF (accessed 22 December 2014).

Dominguez, J.I. 1990. "Immigration as Foreign Policy in US-Latin American Relations". In *Immigration and US Foreign Policy*, R.W.Tucker, C.B. Keely, & L. Wrigley (eds). Boulder, CO: Westview Press.

Dorling, Kamena *et al.* 2012. *Refused: The Experiences of Women Denied Asylum in the UK*. London: Women for Refugee Women.

Doyle, Lisa 2014. *Twenty-Eight Days Later: The Experiences of New Refugees in the UK*. London: Refugee Council.

Driver, S.R. 1890. *Notes on the Hebrew Text of the Books of Samuel with an Introduction on Hebrew Palaeography and the Ancient Versions*. Oxford: Clarendon Press.

Dummett, Michael 2001. *On Immigration and Refugees*. London: Routledge.

Dunn, James D.G. 1988. *The Theology of Paul the Apostle*. Edinburgh: T&T Clark.

Edwards, Alice 2006. "The Right to Work for Refugees and Asylum Seekers: A Comparative View". UNHCR Discussion Paper: Reception Standards (1) 2006: 5–20.

——2010. "Transitioning Gender: Feminist Engagement with International Refugee Law and Policy 1950–2010". *Refugee Survey Quarterly* 29 (2): 21–45.

El Karem & El Kott 2012. *Abed El Karem El Kott and ors v Bevándorlási és Állampolgársági Hivatal*, Court of Justice of the European Union, Case C-364/11.

Elliott, John H. 1981. *A Home for the Homeless*. London: SCM Press.

——1990. *A Home for the Homeless: A Sociological Examination of 1 Peter, Its Situation and Strategy*. Minneapolis: Fortress Press.

——2000. *1 Peter*. New York: Doubleday.

Esler, Philip F. 1987. *Community and Gospel in Luke-Acts*. Cambridge & New York: Cambridge University Press.

——(ed.) 1998. *Christianity for the Twenty-First Century*. Edinburgh: T&T Clark.

——2003. "Jesus in Social Context". In *Jesus: The Complete Guide,* James Leslie Houlden (ed.). London & New York: Continuum: 450–463.

Evans, C.F. 1990. *Saint Luke*. London: SCM Press & Philadelphia: Trinity Press International.

Exum, J. Cheryl 1992. *Tragedy and Biblical Narrative*. Cambridge: Cambridge University Press.

Faust, Avraham 2007. "Settlement Dynamics and Demographic Fluctuations in Judah from the Late Iron Age to the Hellenistic Period and the Archaeology of Persian Period Yehud". In *A Time of Change: Judah and its Neighbours in the Persian and Early Hellenistic Periods*, Yigal Levin (ed.). Library of Second Temple Studies 65. London: T&T Clark: 23–51.

——2011. "Deportation and Demography in Sixth-Century B.C.E. Judah". In *Interpreting Exile: Displacement and Deportation in Biblical and Modern Contexts*, Brad E. Kelle, Frank Ritchel Ames, & Jacob L. Wright (eds). Atlanta: Society of Biblical Literature: 91–103.

——2012. *Judah in the Neo-Babylonian Period: The Archaeology of Desolation*. Atlanta: Society of Biblical Literature.

Felman, Shoshana & Dori Laub 1991. *Testimony: Crises of Witnessing in Literature, Psychoanalysis, and History*. New York: Routledge.

Fischer, Michael M.J. 1995. "Starting Over: How, What, and for Whom Does One Write about Refugees? The Poetics and Politics of Refugee Film as Ethnographic Access in a Media-Saturated World". In *Mistrusting Refugees*, E. Valentine Daniel & John Chr. Knudsen (eds). Berkeley & London: University of California Press: 126–146.

Fishbane, Michael 1985. *Biblical Interpretation in Ancient Israel*. Oxford & New York: Oxford University Press.

Fishman, J.A. 1977. "Language and Ethnicity". In *Language, Ethnicity and Intergroup Relations,* H. Giles (ed.). European Monographs in Social Psychology 13. London: Academic Press: 15–58.

Fitzmaurice, Andrew 2008. "Anticolonialism in Western Political Thought: The Colonial Origins of the Concept of Genocide". In *Empire, Colony, Genocide: Conquest, Occupation and Subaltern Resistance in World History,* A. Dirk Moses (ed.). New York & Oxford: Berghahn Books: 55–80.

Fitzpatrick, Peter 2005. "Bare Sovereignty: *Homo Sacer* and the Insistence of Law". In *Politics, Metaphysics and Death: Essays on Giorgio Agamben's Homo Sacer*, Andrew Norris (ed.). Durham & London: Duke University Press: 49–73.

Flynn, Don 2005. "New Borders, New Management: The Dilemmas of Modern Immigration Policies". *Ethnic and Racial Studies* 28 (3): 463–490.

Fozdar, Farida 2012. "Beyond the Rhetoric of Inclusion: Our Response to Refugees". In *Cultures in Refuge: Seeking Sanctuary in Modern Australia,* Anna Hayes & Robert Mason (eds). Farnham, Surrey: Ashgate: 49–64.

Freedman, David Noel (ed.) 1992. *Anchor Bible Dictionary.* Vol. 5. London & New York: Doubleday: 940–946.

Freedman, Rosa 2014. *Failing to Protect: The UN and the Politicisation of Human Rights.* London: C. Hurst & Co.

From Deprivation to Liberty 2011. "From Deprivation to Liberty: Alternatives to Detention in Belgium, Germany and the UK" (December). http://lastradainternational.org/doc-center/2858/from-deprivation-to-liberty-alternatives-to-detention-in-belgium-germany-and-united-kingdom (accessed May 2014).

FS Iran 2004. *FS Iran* CG [2004] UKIAT 00303 Iran.

Galloway, Donald 2003. "Criminality and State Protection: Structural Tensions in Canadian Refugee Law". In *The Refugees Convention 50 Years On: Globalisation and International Law,* Susan Kneebone (ed.). Aldershot, Hampshire: Ashgate: 109–132.

Garber, David G. Jr. 2011. "A Vocabulary of Trauma in the Exilic Writings". In *Interpreting Exile: Displacement and Deportation in Biblical and Modern Contexts,* Brad E. Kelle, Frank Ritchel Ames, & Jacob L. Wright (eds). Atlanta: Society of Biblical Literature: 309–322.

Gerleman, Gillis 1965. *Ruth: Das Hohelied.* Biblischer Kommentar Altes Testament Band XVIII. Neukirches-Vluyn: Neukirchener Verlag des Erziehungsvereins.

Gerwen, Jef van 1995. "Refugee, Migrant, Stranger". *Ethical Perspectives* 2 (1): 3–10.

Gibney, Matthew J. 2003. "The State of Asylum: Democratisation, Judicialisation and Evolution of Refugee Policy". In *The Refugees Convention 50 Years On: Globalisation and International Law,* Susan Kneebone (ed.). Aldershot, Hampshire: Ashgate: 19–45.

——2004. *The Ethics and Politics of Asylum.* Cambridge: Cambridge University Press.

——2014. "Asylum: Principled Hypocrisy". In *Migration: A COMPAS Anthology,* B. Anderson & M. Keith (eds). Oxford: COMPAS.

Gillihan, Yonder 2011. *Civic Ideology, Organization and Law in the Rule Scrolls: A Comparative Study of the Covenanters' Sect and Contemporary Voluntary Associations in Political Context.* Leiden: Brill.

Girma, Marchu *et al.* 2014. *Detained: Women Asylum Seekers Locked Up in UK.* London: Women for Refugee Women.

Gitay, Zefira 1993. "Ruth and the Women of Bethlehem". In *A Feminist Companion to Ruth,* Athalya Brenner (ed.). Sheffield: Sheffield Academic Press: 178–190.

Gladwell, Catherine & Hannah Elwyn 2012. "Broken Futures: Young Afghan Asylum-Seekers in the UK and on Return to their Country of Origin". Geneva: UNHCR.

Goldingay, John 2014. *Isaiah 56–66*. London & New York: Bloomsbury T&T Clark.

Gonzaga, Jose Alvin C. 2003. "The Role of the United Nations High Commissioner for Refugees and the Refugee Definition". In *The Refugees Convention 50 Years On: Globalisation and International Law*, Susan Kneebone (ed.). Aldershot, Hampshire: Ashgate: 233–250.

Goodwin-Gill, Guy 1999. "Refugee Identity and Protection's Fading Prospect". In *Refugee Rights and Realities: Evolving International Concepts and Regimes*, F. Nicholson & P. Twomey (eds). Cambridge: Cambridge University Press: 220–249.

——2011. "The Right to Seek Asylum: Interception at Sea and the Principle of Non-Refoulement". An Inaugural Lecture given at the Palais des Académies, Bruxelles (16 February).

Goodwin-Gill, Guy & Jane McAdam 2007. *The Refugee in International Law*. 3rd edn. Oxford: Clarendon Press.

Grabbe, Lester L. 1998a. "Triumph of the Pious or Failure of the Xenophobes? The Ezra-Nehemiah Reforms and their Nachgeschichte". In *Jewish Local Patriotism and Self-Identification in the Graeco-Roman Period*, S. Jones & S. Pearce (eds). *Journal for the Study of the Pseudepigrapha Supplement* 25. Sheffield: Sheffield Academic Press: 48–63.

——1998b. *Ezra-Nehemiah*. London & New York: Routledge.

——2004. *A History of the Jews and Judaism in the Second Temple Period, vol. 1. Yehud: A History of the Persian Province of Judah*. London & New York: T&T Clark.

Granville-Chapman, Charlotte *et al.* 2004. *Harm on Removal: Excessive Force against Failed Asylum Seekers*. Medical Foundation. http://www.statewatch.org/news/2004/oct/Harm-on-Removal.pdf (accessed May 2014).

Gray, John 1964. *I and II Kings*. London: SCM Press.

Griffiths, Melanie 2012. "'Vile Liars and Truth Distorters': Truth, Trust and the Asylum System". *Anthropology Today* 28 (5): 8–12.

Guardian 2010. See the *Guardian*, quoting the Home Secretary (7 July). http://www.guardian.co.uk/uk/2010/jul/07/gay-asylum-seekers-rights-deportation?INTCMP=SRCH (accessed May 2014).

Guardiola-Saenz, Leticia 1997. "Borderless Women and Borderless Texts: A Cultural Reading of Matthew 15.21–28". *Semeia* 78: 69–81.

Gutiérrez, Gustavo 1984. *We Drink from Our Own Wells: The Spiritual Journey of a People*. London: SCM Press.

Hagedorn, Anselm 2011. "The Absent Presence: Cultural Responses to Persian Presence in the Eastern Mediterranean". In *Judah and the Judeans in the Achaemenid Period: Negotiating Identity in an International Context*, O. Lipschits, Gary N. Knoppers, & Manfred Oeming (eds). Winona Lake, IN: Eisenbrauns: 39–66.

——2014. "The Biblical Laws of Asylum between Mediterraneanism and Postcolonial Critique". Paper delivered at the 2014 SBL International Meeting in Vienna, Austria.

Hägglund, Fredrik 2008. *Isaiah 53 in the Light of Homecoming after Exile*. Tübingen: Mohr Siebeck.

Halperin, David J. 1993. *Seeking Ezekiel: Text and Psychology*. University Park: Pennsylvania State University Press.

Haneef 2007. *Minister for Immigration and Citizenship v Mohammed Haneef* (Haneef) [2007] FCAC 203.

Harding, Jeremy 2012. "Europe at Bay". *London Review of Books* 34 (3) (February).

Hargreaves, Russell 2014. "Dividing Lines: Asylum, the Media and Some Reasons for (Cautious) Optimism". London: Asylum Aid. http://www.asylumaid.org.uk/wp-content/uploads/2014/01/DividingLines_V3_highres.pdf (accessed June 2014).

Harrell-Bond, Barbara 1999. "The Experience of Refugees as Recipients of Aid". In *Refugees: Perspectives on the Experience of Forced Migration,* Alastair Ager (ed.). London & New York: Continuum: 136–168.

——2002. "Can Humanitarian Work with Refugees be Humane?" *Human Rights Quarterly* 24 (1): 51–85.

Harvey, Anthony 2009. *Asylum in Britain: A Question of Conscience.* Trowbridge, Wiltshire: Humanitas.

Harvey, Graham & Charles D. Thompson Jr. (eds) 2005. *Indigenous Diasporas and Dislocations.* Farnham, Surrey and Burlington, VT: Ashgate.

Hathaway, James C. 1991. *The Law of Refugee Status.* Toronto: Butterworths.

——1993. "Harmonizing for Whom? The Devaluation of Refugee Protection in the Era of European Economic Integration". *Cornell International Law Journal* 26 (3): 719–735.

——2005. *The Rights of Refugees under International Law.* Cambridge: Cambridge University Press.

Hayes, Anna & Robert Mason (eds) 2012. *Cultures in Refuge: Seeking Sanctuary in Modern Australia.* Farnham, Surrey: Ashgate.

Herlihy, Jane & Stuart Turner 2007. "Asylum Claims and Memory of Trauma: Sharing our Knowledge". *British Journal of Psychiatry* 191 (3–4).

——2009. "The Psychology of Seeking Protection". *International Journal of Refugee Law* 21 (2): 171–192.

——2013. "What Do We Know so far about Emotion and Refugee Law?" In *Northern Ireland Legal Quarterly* 64 (1): 47–62.

Herlihy, Jane *et al.* 2002. "Discrepancies in Autobiographical Memories–Implications for the Assessment of Asylum Seekers: Repeated Interviews Study". *British Medical Journal* 324: 324–327.

Herlihy, Jane *et al.* 2010. "What Assumptions about Human Behaviour Underlie Asylum Judgments?" *International Journal of Refugee Law* 22 (3): 351–366.

Herlihy, Jane *et al.* 2012. "Just Tell Us What Happened to You: Autobiographical Memory and Seeking Asylum". *Applied Cognitive Psychology* 26 (5): 661–676.

High Court 2011. *Plaintiff M70/2011 v Minister for Immigration and Citizenship, and Plaintiff M106 of 2011 v Minister for Immigration and Citizenship,* [2011] HCA 32, Australia: High Court, 31 August 2011. http://www.refworld.org/docid/4e5f51642html (accessed January 2015).

Hinton, Alex 2008. "Savages, Subjects, and Sovereigns: Conjunctions of Modernity, Genocide and Colonialism". In *Empire, Colony, Genocide: Conquest, Occupation and Subaltern Resistance in World History,* A. Dirk Moses (ed.). New York & Oxford: Berghahn Books: 440–459.

Hirsi Jamaa 2012. *Hirsi Jamaa and ors v. Italy* (2012) 55 EHRR 21.

HJ & HT 2011. *HJ (Iran) v Secretary of State for the Home Department and Another Case* [2011] 1 AC 596.

HMIP 2012. "Report on an Announced Inspection of Cedars Pre-Departure Accommodation, 30 April – 25 May 2012". HM Inspector of Prisons. (July). https://www.justice.gov.uk/downloads/publications/inspectorate-reports/hmipris/immigration-removal-centre-inspections/cedars/cedars-2012.pdf (accessed May 2014).

Hobbins, John F. 2012. "Zion's Plea that God See Her as She Sees Herself: Unanswered Prayer in Lamentations 1–2". In *Daughter Zion: Her Portrait, Her Response,* Mark J. Boda, Carol Dempsey, & LeAnn Snow Flesher (eds). Atlanta: Society of Biblical Literature: 149–176.

Home Office 2010. "Considering the Protection (Asylum) Claim and Assessing Credibility: Guidelines for Decision-Makers" (19 July).

——2011. "Call to End Violence against Women and Girls". Home Office Action Plan (March).

——2012. "Detained Fast Track Processes – Timetable Flexibility".

——2013. "Immigration Statistics, April to June 2013".

Hoop, R. de 2001. "The Use of the Past to Address the Present: The Wife–Sister Incidents (Gen. 12,10-20; 20,1-18; 26,1-16)". In *Studies in the Book of Genesis: Literature, Redaction and History*, A. Wénin (ed.). Leuven: Leuven University Press: 359–369.

Horrell, David G. 2008. *1 Peter*. London & New York: T&T Clark.

Horvath 2000. *Horvath v Secretary of State for the Home Department* [2000] 3 WLR 379.

Hossfeld, Frank Lothar & Erich Zenger 2011. *Psalms 3: A Commentary on Psalms 101–150,* Linda M. Maloney (trans.). Minneapolis: Fortress Press.

House of Commons 2004. "Foreign Affairs Committee, Iran: Third Report of Session 2003–4, Report, together with Appendix, Formal Minutes, Oral and Written Evidence, Ordered by the House of Commons to Be Printed 9 March 2004". http://www.publications.parliament.uk/pa/cm200304/cmselect/cmfaff/80/80.pdf (accessed May 2014).

Houston, Walter J. 1987. "'Today, in Your Very Hearing': Some Comments on the Christological Use of the Old Testament". In *The Glory of Christ in the New Testament: Studies in Christology in Memory of George Bradford Caird,* L.D. Hurst & N.T. Wright (eds). Oxford: Clarendon Press: 37–47.

——2004. "Was there a Social Crisis in the 8th Century?". In *In Search of Pre-Exilic Israel*, John Day (ed.). JSOT Supplement Series 406. London & New York: T&T Clark: 130–149.

——2008. *Contending for Justice: Ideologies and Theologies of Social Justice in the Old Testament*. 2nd edn revised. London & New York: T&T Clark.

——2013. *The Pentateuch*. London: SCM Press.

Houten, Christiana van 1991. *The Alien in Israelite Law*. Sheffield: Sheffield Academic Press.

Houtman, Cornelis 1993–2002. *Exodus*. 4 vols. Leuven: Peeters.

Hubbard, R.L. 1988. *The Book of Ruth*. New International Commentary 14. Grand Rapids, MI: Eerdmans.

Human Rights Watch 2001. "Refugees, Asylum Seekers, and Internally Displaced Persons". Human Rights Watch. http://www.hrw.org/wr2k1/special/refugees.html (accessed May 2014).

——2009. "Jailing Refugees". Human Rights Watch (29 December). Human Rights Watch. http://www.hrw.org/en/node/87369/section/2 (accessed May 2014).

——2010. "Deportation by Default: Mental Disability, Unfair Hearings, and Indefinite Detention in the US Immigration System (25 July)". Human Rights Watch. http://www.unhcr.org/refworld/docid/4c4d344c2.html (accessed May 2014).

Humphreys, W. Lee 1973. A *Life-Style for Diaspora: A Study of the Tales of Esther and Daniel*. *Journal of Biblical Literature* 92 (2): 211–223.

Hynes, Samuel 1992. *A War Imagined: The First World War and English Culture*. London: Pimlico.

IAC [Independent Asylum Commission] 2008a. *Safe Return*. London: IAC.

IAC [Independent Asylum Commission] 2008b. *Fit For Purpose Yet?* London: IAC.

IAC [Independent Asylum Commission] 2008c. *Deserving Dignity*. London: IAC.

IAC [Independent Asylum Commission] 2008d. *Saving Sanctuary*. London: IAC.

Ibrahim 2000. *Minister for Immigration and Multicultural Affairs (MIMA) v Haji Ibrahim (Ibrahim)* (2000) 204 CLR 1.

ICE Fact Sheet 2009. *US Immigration and Customs Enforcement Fact Sheet. 2009 Immigration Detention Reforms*. http://www.ice.gov/factsheets/2009detention-reform (accessed May 2014).

IDMC 2012. *Internal Displacement in Africa: A Development Challenge*. Geneva: Internal Displacement Monitoring Centre and Norwegian Refugee Council.

Iersel, Bas van & Anton Weiler (eds) 1987. *Exodus – A Lasting Paradigm*. Edinburgh: T&T Clark.

Independent Monitoring Board 2014. Report of the Independent Monitoring Board on the Non-Residential Short-Term Holding Facilities at London Heathrow Airport for the Year February 2013 to January 2014. http://www.justice.gov.uk/downloads/publications/corporate-reports/imb/annual-reports-2014/heathrow-2013-14.pdf (accessed December 2014)

Islam & Shah 1999. *Islam v Secretary of State for the Home Department* [1999] 2 AC 629.

Iyodu 2010. "Uganda: The Silent Practice of Deportations". *Pambazuka News* (6 May). http://pambazuka.org/en/category/features/64236 (accessed May 2014).

JCWI 2011. "A Study in Distortion – How *The Sun* Twists the Figures". The Joint Council for the Welfare of Immigrants (1 June). http://wp.me/pHWBa-Bu (accessed May 2014).

Jeremias, Joachim 1966. *Rediscovering the Parables*. London: SCM.

Jobes, Karen H. 2005. *1 Peter*. Grand Rapids, MI: Baker Academic Press.

Joosten, Jan 1996. *People and Land in the Holiness Code: An Exegetical Study of the Ideational Framework of the Law in Leviticus 17–26*. Leiden: Brill.

Joseph 2010. *Joseph v Holder*, 600 F. 3d 1235, 1240 (9th Circuit 2010).

Joyce, Paul M. 2007. *Ezekiel: A Commentary*. New York & London: T&T Clark.

JRS/USA 2012. World Detention Practices. Jesuit Refugee Service/USA. http://www.jrsusa.org/research?LID=172 (accessed May 2014).

Juss, Satvinder S. 2006. *International Migration and Global Justice*. Aldershot, Hampshire and Burlington, VT: Ashgate.

Kalin, W. 2001. "Non-State Agents of Persecution and the Inability of the State to Protect". *Georgetown Immigration Law Journal* 15: 427–482.

Kamya, Hugo 2011. "The Impact of War on Children: The Psychology of Displacement and Exile". In *Interpreting Exile: Displacement and Deportation in Biblical and Modern Contexts*, Brad E. Kelle, Frank Ritchel Ames, & Jacob L. Wright (eds). Atlanta: Society of Biblical Literature: 235–249.

Kee, Alistair 2004. "Blessed Are the Excluded". In *Public Theology for the 21st Century*, William F. Storrar & Andrew R. Morton (eds). London & New York: T&T Clark: 351–364.

Kelle, Brad E. 2011. "An Interdisciplinary Approach to the Exile". In *Interpreting Exile: Displacement and Deportation in Biblical and Modern Contexts*, Brad E. Kelle, Frank Ritchel Ames, & Jacob L. Wright (eds). Atlanta: Society of Biblical Literature: 5–38.

Kelle, Brad E., Frank Ritchel Ames, & Jacob L. Wright (eds) 2011. *Interpreting Exile: Interdisciplinary Studies of Displacement and Deportation in Biblical and Modern Contexts*. Leiden & Boston: Brill.

Kern, Paul Bentley 1999. *Ancient Siege Warfare*. Bloomington, IN: Indiana University Press.

Klocker, Natascha & Kevin M. Dunn 2003. "Who's Driving the Asylum Debate? Newspapers and Government Representations of Asylum Seekers". *Media International Australia Incorporating Culture and Policy* (November): 71–92. http://www.uws.edu.au/__data/assets/pdf_file/0010/26956/A17.pdf (accessed June 2014).

Kneebone, Susan 2003. "Moving Beyond the State: Refugees, Accountability and Protection". In *The Refugees Convention 50 Years On: Globalisation and International Law*, Susan Kneebone (ed.). Aldershot, Hampshire: Ashgate: 279–311.

Knierim, Rolf P. 1995. "The Interpretation of the Old Testament". In *The Task of Old Testament Theology*. Grand Rapids, MI: Eerdmans: 86–122.

Korac-Sanderson, Maja 2011. "Refugee-Centred versus State-Centred Approaches to Integration: Process, Practices and Narratives". Seminar paper presented under the Refugee Law Initiative, jointly with the British Red Cross, University of London (26 October).

Kristeva, Julia 1989. *Etrangers à nous-mêmes*. Paris: Gallimard.

Kuhrt, Amélie 1983. "The Cyrus Cylinder and Achaemenid Imperial Policy". *Journal for the Study of the Old Testament* 25: 83–97.

KV 2014. *KV (scarring-medical evidence) Sri Lanka* [2014] UKUT 230 (IAC).

Lacocque, A. 1990. *The Feminine Unconventional: Four Subversive Figures in Israel's Tradition*. Minneapolis: Fortress Press.

Lane, William L. 1991. *Hebrews*. 2 vols. Dallas: Word Books.

Langston, Scott M. 2006. *Exodus through the Centuries*. Oxford: Blackwell Publishing Ltd.

Larkin, Katrina J.A. 1996. *Ruth and Esther*. Sheffield: Sheffield Academic Press.

Lash, Nicholas 2007. "The Question of God Today". In *Transcending Boundaries in Philosophy and Theology: Reason, Meaning and Experience*, Kevin Vanhoozer & Martin Warner (eds). Aldershot, Hampshire and Burlington, VT: Ashgate: 129–143.

Law Society 2014. "Criminal Legal Aid". http://www.lawsociety.org.uk/policy-campaigns/campaigns/criminal-legal-aid/ (accessed December 2014).

Lee, Nancy C. & Carleen Mandolfo (eds) 2008. *Lamentations in Ancient and Contemporary Contexts*. Atlanta: Society of Biblical Literature.

Leveson 2012. The Right Honourable Lord Justice Leveson. "Representation of Women and Minorities". In *An Inquiry into the Culture, Practices and Ethics of the Press* (November), Section 8 vol II.

Levinson, Bernard M. 2004. "Is the Covenant Code an Exilic Composition? A Response to John van Seters". In *In Search of Pre-Exilic Israel*, John Day (ed.). London & New York: T&T Clark: 272–325.

Li 2011. *Li v Holder* 629 F.3d 1154 (9th Circuit 2011).

Liew, Jonathan 2012. "Fabrice Muamba: A True Battler Who Escaped Civil War". *The Daily Telegraph* (18 March). http://www.telegraph.co.uk/sport/football/teams/bolton-wanderers/9151126/Fabrice-Muamba-a-true-battler-who-escaped-civil-war.html (accessed May 2014).

Lifton, Robert Jay 1968. *Death in Life: Survivors of Hiroshima*. New York: Random House.

Lijnders, Laurie 2012. "Caught in the Borderlands: Torture Experienced, Expressed, and Remembered by Eritrean Asylum-Seekers in Israel". *Oxford Monitor of Forced Migration* 2 (1): 64–76.

Lipschits, Oded 2003. "Democratic Changes in Judah between the Seventh and the Fifth Centuries BCE". In *Judah and the Judeans in the Neo-Babylonian Period*, O. Lipschits & J. Blenkinsopp (eds). Winona Lake, IN: Eisenbrauns: 323–376.

——2011. "Shedding New Light on the Dark Years of the 'Exilic Period': New Studies, Further Elucidation, and Some Questions Regarding the Archaeology of Judah as an 'Empty Land'". In *Interpreting Exile: Displacement and Deportation in Biblical and Modern Contexts,* Brad E. Kelle, Frank Ritchel Ames, & Jacob L. Wright (eds). Atlanta: Society of Biblical Literature: 57–90.

Lipschits, Oded, Gary N. Knoppers, & Manfred Oeming (eds) 2011. *Judah and the Judeans in the Achaemenid Period: Negotiating Identity in an International Context.* Winona Lake, IN: Eisenbrauns.

Living Ghosts 2007. "Living Ghosts". Church Action on Poverty. http://www.church-poverty.org.uk/livingghosts (accessed December 2014).

Locking up Family Values 2007. *Locking up Family Values: The Detention of Immigrant Families.* Women's Refugee Commission and the Lutheran Immigration and Refugee Service (February).

Long, Lynellyn D. and Ellen Oxfeld (eds) 2004. *Coming Home? Refugees, Migrants, and Those Who Stayed Behind.* Philadelphia: University of Pennsylvania Press.

Lorek, Ann *et al.* 2009. "The Mental and Physical Health Difficulties of Children Held within a British Immigration Detention Center: A Pilot Study". *Child Abuse and Neglect: The International Journal* 33 (9): 573–585. http://www.ncbi.nlm.nih.gov/pubmed/19811830 (accessed May 2014).

Lundborg, Per 2013. "Refugees' Employment Integration in Sweden: Cultural Distance and Labor Market Performance". *Review of International Economics* 21 (2): 219–232.

Luz, Ulrich 1990. *Matthew 1–7: A Commentary,* Wilhelm C. Linss (trans.). Edinburgh: T&T Clark.

——2001. *Matthew 8–20: A Commentary,* James E. Crouch (trans.), Helmut Koester (ed.). Minneapolis: Fortress Press.

——2005a. *Matthew 21–28: A Commentary,* James E. Crouch (trans.), Helmut Koester (ed.). Minneapolis: Fortress Press.

——2005b. *Studies in Matthew,* Rosemary Selle (trans.). Grand Rapids, MI and Cambridge, UK: Eerdmans.

Lynch, P. & P. O'Brien 2001. "From Dehumanisation to Demonisation: The MV Tampa and the Denial of Humanity". *Alternative Law Journal* 26 (5): 215–218.

MacCulloch, Diarmaid 2009. *A History of Christianity: The First Three Thousand Years.* London: Allen Lane.

Mandolfo, Carleen 2007. *Daughter Zion Talks Back to the Prophets: A Dialogic Theology of the Book of Lamentations.* Atlanta: Society of Biblical Literature.

Maritime Incident Committee Report 2002. Government of Australia. http://www.aph.gov.au/binaries/senate/committee/maritime_incident_ctte/report/report.pdf (accessed December 2014).

Marfleet, Philip 2011. "Understanding 'Sanctuary': Faith and Traditions of Asylum". *Journal of Refugee Studies* 24 (3): 440–455.

Mason, Robert 2012. "Coalitions of Justice: Articulating Democratic Transition in Australia's Salvadoran Community". In *Cultures in Refuge: Seeking Sanctuary in Modern Australia,* Anna Hayes & Robert Mason (eds). Farnham, Surrey: Ashgate: 95–112.

Matter of Toboso-Alfonso 1990. *Matter of Toboso-Alfonso* (Case A23-220-664, Board of Immigration Appeals, 12 March 1990).

Mayes, A.D.H. 1979. *Deuteronomy,* R.E. Clements & M. Black (eds). Grand Rapids, MI: Eerdmans & London: Marshall, Morgan and Scott Publishers Ltd.

McConville, J.G. 2002. *Deuteronomy*. Leicester, Leicestershire and Downers Grove, IL: Intervarsity Press.

McGinley, Ali & Adeline Trude 2012. "Positive Duty of Care? The Mental Health Crisis in Immigration Detention". A briefing paper by the Mental Health in Immigration Detention Project (May).

McIntyre, Philippa 2011. *Refugee Council Submission to the Leveson Enquiry*. http://www.refugeecouncil.org.uk/latest/blogs/3555_refugee_council_submission_to_the_leveson_enquiry (accessed June 2014).

——2012. "Between a Rock and a Hard Place: The Dilemma Facing Refused Asylum Seekers". London: The Refugee Council. http://www.refugeecouncil.org.uk/assets/0000/1368/Refugee_Council_Between_a_Rock_and_a_Hard_Place_10.12.12.pdf (accessed June 2014).

Meier, J.P. 2009. *A Marginal Jew: Rethinking the Historical Jesus*. Vol. 4: *Law and Love*. New Haven & London: Yale University Press.

Mein, Andrew 2001. *Ezekiel and the Ethics of Exile*. Oxford & New York: Oxford University Press.

Merrill, Jamie & Emily Dugan 2014. "Local Councils Forced to Reject Syrian Refugees without more Government Funding". *The Independent* (24 May).

Messer, Neil & Angus Paddison 2013. "The Bible and Public Policy: What Kind of Authority?" In *The Bible, Culture, Community, Society*, Angus Paddison & Neil Messer (eds). London and New York: Bloomsbury T&T Clark: 189–207.

Meverden, Amy 2011. "Daughter Zion as *Homo Sacer*: The Relationship of Exile, Lamentations, and Giorgio Agamben's Bare Life Figure". In *Interpreting Exile: Displacement and Deportation in Biblical and Modern Contexts*, Brad E. Kelle, Frank Ritchel Ames, & Jacob L. Wright (eds). Atlanta: Society of Biblical Literature: 395–407.

Meynet, Roland 2009. *Called to Freedom*, Patricia Kelly (trans.). Miami: Convivium Press.

Middlemas, Jill 2012a. "The Future of the 'Exile'". In *By the Irrigation Canals of Babylon: Approaches to the Study of the Exile*, John J. Ahn & Jill Middlemas (eds). New York & London: T&T Clark: 63–82.

——2012b. "Speaking of Speaking: The Form of Zion's Suffering in Lamentations". In *Daughter Zion: Her Portrait, Her Response*. Mark J. Boda, Carol Dempsey, & LeAnn Snow Flesher (eds). Atlanta: Society of Biblical Literature: 39–54.

Migrant and Refugee Woman of the Year Awards 2013. http://awards.migrantforum.org.uk/2013-winners (accessed December 2014).

Migration Observatory 2014. *Briefing – Migration to the UK: Asylum*. http://migration observatory.ox.ac.uk/briefings/migration-uk-asylum (accessed December 2014)

Miles, Nathanael 2010. "No Going Back: Lesbian and Gay People and the Asylum System". Stonewall. http://www.stonewall.org.uk/documents/no_going_back_1.pdf (accessed June 2014).

Milgrom, Jacob 1991–2001. *Leviticus*. 3 vols. New York: Doubleday.

Millbank, Jenni 2012. "The Rights of Lesbians and Gay Men to Live Freely, Openly and on Equal Terms is Not Bad Law: A Reply to Hathaway and Pobjoy". *International Law and Politics* 44 (2): 497–527.

MK 2012. *MK and anor v Secretary of State for the Home Department and anor* [2012] EWCC 1896 (Admin).

Modrzejewski, Joseph Mélèze 1997. *The Jews of Egypt: From Rameses II to Emperor Hadrian*, Robert Cornman (trans.). Princeton: Princeton University Press.

Montefiore, H.W. 1964. *The Epistle to the Hebrews*. London: Adam & Charles Black.

Moore, Megan Bishop & Brad E. Kelle 2011. *Biblical History and Israel's Past: The Changing Study of the Bible and History*. Grand Rapids, MI and Cambridge, UK: Eerdmans.

Moorehead, Caroline 2005. *Human Cargo: A Journey among Refugees*. London: Chatto and Windus.

——2006. "Soft Target". *Guardian* G2 (9 June; 23 August).

Moreno-Lax, Violeta 2012. "*Hirsi Jamaa and Others v Italy* or the Strasbourg Court versus Extraterritorial Migration Control?" *Human Rights Law Review* 12 (3): 574–598.

Moreton-Robinson, Aileen 2004. "The Possessive Logic of Patriarchal White Sovereignty: The High Court and the Yorta Yorta Decision". *Borderlands e-journal* 3 (2). http://www.borderlands.net.au/vol3no2_2004/moreton_possessive.htm (accessed May 2014).

Moses, A. Dirk (ed.) 2008. *Empire, Colony, Genocide: Conquest, Occupation and Subaltern Resistance in World History*. New York & Oxford: Berghahn Books.

Moughtin-Mumby, Sharon 2008. *Sexual and Marital Metaphors in Hosea, Jeremiah, Isaiah, and Ezekiel*. Oxford & New York: Oxford University Press.

MSF 2012. "Dadaab Refugee Camps Back to Square One". Briefing paper, *Médecins sans Frontières* (February).

Mudge, Lewis S. 2001. *Rethinking the Beloved Community: Ecclesiology, Hermeneutics, Social Theory*. Geneva: World Council of Churches.

Muecke, Marjorie A. 1995. "Trust, Abuse of Trust, and Mistrust among Cambodian Refugee Women: A Cultural Interpretation". In *Mistrusting Refugees*, E. Valentine Daniel & John Chr. Knudsen (eds). Berkeley & London: University of California Press: 36–55.

Muggeridge, Helen & Chen Maman 2011. "Unsustainable: The Quality of Initial Decision-Making in Women's Asylum Claims". London: Asylum Aid. http://www.asylumaid.org.uk/wp-content/uploads/2013/02/unsustainableweb.pdf (accessed June 2014).

Myers, Ched & Matthew Colwell 2012. *Our God is Undocumented: Biblical Faith and Immigrant Justice*. Maryknoll, NY: Orbis Books.

Nafziger, James A.R. 1983. "The General Admission of Aliens under International Law". *American Journal of International Law* 77 (4): 804–847.

Napolitano 2012. US Citizenship and Immigration Services. http://uscis.gov (accessed June 2014).

Nasar, Sema 2013. *Violence against Women: A Bleeding Wound in the Syrian Conflict*. Copenhagen: Euro-Mediterranean Human Rights Network.

Nelson, R.D. 2002. *Deuteronomy*. Louisville, KY & London: Westminster John Knox Press.

Newey, Glen 2011. "Limits of Civility", Review of Wendy Brown *Walled States, Waning Sovereignty* (Zone 2010). London Review of Books 33 (6) (March).

Newman, Ines & Peter Ratcliffe (eds) 2011. *Promoting Social Cohesion: Implications for Policy and Evaluation*. Bristol: Policy Press.

Newton, John 1987. "Analysis of Programmatic Texts of Exodus Movements". In *Exodus – A Lasting Paradigm*, Bas van Iersel & Anton Weiler (eds). Edinburgh: T&T Clark: 56–62.

NICER 2012. "Report of the National Independent Commission on Enforced Removals with Additional Findings and Recommendations". London: Citizens UK. http://www.citizensuk.org (accessed June 2014).

Niditch, Susan 2008. *Judges*. Louisville, KY & London: Westminster John Knox Press.

NM 2009. *NM (Christian Converts) Afghanistan* CG [2009] UKAIT 00045.

Noll, Gregor 2006. "Asylum Claims and the Translation of Culture into Politics". *Texas International Law Journal* 41 (3): 491–502.

Nora, Pierre 1989. "Between Memory and History: *Les Lieux de Mémoire*". *Representations* 26: 7–24.

O'Connor, Kathleen 2008. "Voices Arguing about Meaning". In *Lamentations in Ancient and Contemporary Cultural Contexts,* Nancy C. Lee & Carleen Mandolfo (eds). Atlanta: Society of Biblical Literature: 27–32.

O'Sullivan, Maria 2009. "The Intersection between the International, the Regional and the Domestic: Seeking Asylum in the UK". In *Refugees, Asylum-Seekers and the Rule of Law: Comparative Perspectives*, Susan Kneebone (ed.), Cambridge: Cambridge University Press: 228–280.

Ogletree, Thomas W. 1985. *Hospitality to the Stranger: Dimensions of Moral Understanding*. Philadelphia: Fortress Press.

Olick, Jeffrey K. 2007. *The Politics of Regret: On Collective Memory and Historical Responsibility*. New York & London: Routledge.

OSC. *Refugees and Asylees Have the Right to Work*. Office of Special Counsel for Immigration-Related Unfair Employment Practices. U.S. Department of Justice, Civil Rights Division. http://www.justice.gov/crt/about/osc/htm/employer.php (accessed December 2014)

Oswald, Wolfgang 2012. "Foreign Marriages and Citizenship in Persian Period Judah". *Journal of Hebrew Scriptures* 12 (6). https://drive.google.com/file/d/0B6smVijz2aFdanB4Q2tnOW10ajg/edit?usp=sharing (accessed June 2014).

Othman 2012. *Othman v UK* (2012) 55 EHRR 1.

Ott, E. 2013. "The Labour Market Integration of Resettled Refugees". Policy Development and Evaluation Service. Geneva: UNHCR.

Otto, Eckart 1994. *Theologische Ethik des Alten Testaments*. Theologische Wissenschaft 3, 2. Stuttgart: Kohlhammer.

Ozick, Cynthia 1993. *"Ruth": A Feminist Companion to Ruth,* Athalya Brenner (ed.). Sheffield: Sheffield Academic Press.

Pearce, Laurie E. 2011. "'Judean': A Special Status in Neo-Babylonian and Achemenid Babylonia?" In *Judah and the Judeans in the Achaemenid Period: Negotiating Identity in an International Context,* O. Lipschits, Gary N. Knoppers, & Manfred Oeming (eds). Winona Lake, IN: Eisenbrauns: 267–275.

Pinter, Ilona 2012. *"I Don't Feel Human": Experiences of Destitution among Young Refugees and Migrants*. London: The Children's Society.

Pizor, Andrew G. 1993. "Sale v Haitian Centers Council: The Return of Haitian Refugees". *Fordham International Law Journal* 17 (4): 1061–1115.

PJCHR 2007. "The Treatment of Asylum Seekers". The Parliamentary Joint Committee on Human Rights (HL paper 81, HC 60).

Podeszfa, Leana & Charlotte Manicom 2012. "Avoiding Refoulement: The Need to Monitor Deported Failed Asylum Seekers". *Oxford Monitor of Forced Migration* 2 (2): 10–15.

Pohl, Christine D. 1999. *Making Room: Recovering Hospitality as a Christian Tradition*. Grand Rapids, MI and Cambridge, UK: Eerdmans.

——2006. "Responding to Strangers: Insights from the Christian Tradition". *Studies in Christian Ethics* 19 (1): 81–101.

Poynder, Nick 2003. "'Mind the Gap': Seeking Alternative Protection under the Convention against Torture and the International Covenant on Civil and Political Rights". In *The Refugees Convention 50 Years On: Globalisation and International Law,* Susan Kneebone (ed.). Aldershot, Hampshire: Ashgate: 173–192.

Prior, Michael 1997. *The Bible and Colonialism: A Moral Critique*. Sheffield: Sheffield Academic Press.

Pritchard, James B. 1969. *Ancient Near Eastern Texts Relating to the Old Testament*. 3rd edn. Princeton: Princeton University Press.

Propp, William H.C. 1998, 2006. *Exodus* 2 vols. New York: Doubleday.

Querton, Christel 2012. "'I Feel Like as a Woman I'm Not Welcome': A Gender Analysis of UK Asylum Law, Policy and Practice". London: Asylum Aid. http://www.asylumaid.org.uk/wp-content/uploads/2013/02/Ifeelasawoman_EXEC_SUM_WEB.pdf. (accessed June 2014).

R 1803. *R v Inhabitants of Eastbourne* [1803] 4 East 103.

——1984. *R v Governor of Durham Prison Ex p. Singh* [1984] 1 WLR. 704.

——1997. *R v Secretary of State for Social Security Ex p. Joint Council for the Welfare of Immigrants and Another Case* [1997] 1 WLR 275, CA.

——2003. *R (Q and others) v Secretary of State for the Home Department* [2003] EWCA Civ 364.

——2005. *R (on the application of Hoxha) v Special Adjudicator and Another Case* [2005] 1 WLR 1063.

——2010. *R v M, MV, M and N* [2010] EWCA Crim 2400.

——2011. *R (on the application of Kambadzi) v Secretary of State for the Home Department* [2011] 1 WLR 1299.

——2012a. *R (on the application of SA (Iran)) v Secretary of State for the Home Department* [2012] EWHC 2575 (Admin).

——2012b. *R (on the application of AM (Angola)) v Secretary of State for the Home Department* [2012] EWCA Civ 521.

——2014a. *R (on the application of MD) v Secretary of State for the Home Department* [2014] EWHC 2249 (Admin).

——2014b. *R (on the application of Refugee Action) v Secretary of State for the Home Department* [2014] EWHC 1033 (Admin).

Rad, Gerhard von 1961. *Genesis: A Commentary*, John H. Marks (trans.). London: SCM Press.

——1964. *Deuteronomy: A Commentary*. London: SCM Press.

Ramirez Kidd, José E. 1999. *Alterity and Identity in Israel: The Ger in the Old Testament*. Berlin & New York: De Gruyter.

Ramos, C. 2011. "Unsafe Return: Refoulement of Congolese Asylum Seekers". Justice First. http://justicefirst.org.uk/wp-content/uploads/UNSAFE-RETURN-DECEMBER-5TH-2011.pdf (accessed May 2014).

Reagan, Ronald 1982. Executive Order No. 12,324, 3 C.F.R. 180, 180–181.

Red Cross 2010. "Not Gone but Forgotten: The Urgent Need for a More Humane Asylum System". London: The British Red Cross.

Refugee Act 1980. Pub. L. no. 96–212, 94 Stat. 102.

Refugee Council 2007. "The New Asylum Model". Refugee Council. http://www.refugeecouncil.org.uk/policy_research/policy_work/p.14 (accessed June 2014).

Richardson, M.E.J. 2000. *Hammurabi's Laws: Text, Translation and Glossary*. Sheffield: Sheffield Academic Press.

Ricoeur, Paul 1981. "The Model of the Text: Meaningful Action Considered as a Text". In *Hermeneutics and the Human Sciences: Essays on Language, Action, and Interpretation*, John B. Thompson (ed.). Cambridge: Cambridge University Press: 131–144.

——1982. "Mimesis and Representation". *Annals of Scholarship* 2 (2): 15–32.

——1984. *Time and Narrative*. Vol. 1. Kathleen McLaughlin & David Pellauer (trans.). Chicago: University of Chicago Press.

——1986. *Du texte à l'action: Essais d'herméneutique II*. Paris: Editions du Seuil.

Robertson, Edward 1950. "The Plot of the Book of Ruth". *Bulletin of the John Rylands Library* 32: 207–228.

Robins, Jon (ed.) 2011. "Unequal before the Law? The Future of Legal Aid". *Solicitors' Journal* (June).

Robinson, V. 1993. "Marching into the Middle Classes? The Long-Term Resettlement of East African Asians in the UK". *Journal of Refugee Studies* 6 (3): 230–247.

Rogerson, John W. 2007. *According to the Scriptures? The Challenge of Using the Bible in Social, Moral and Political Questions*. London & Oakville, CT: Equinox.

Rom-Shiloni, Dalit 2011. "From Ezekiel to Ezra-Nehemiah: Shifts of Group Identities within Babylonian Exilic Ideology". In *Judah and the Judeans in the Achaemenid Period: Negotiating Identity in an International Context,* Oded Lipschits, Gary N. Knoppers, & Manfred Oeming (eds). Winona Lake, IN: Eisenbrauns: 127–151.

Ross, Ellie 2013. "Afghan Refugee Wins Scholarship to Eton College". *The Sun* (20 February). http://www.thesun.co.uk/sol/homepage/news/4804386/Afghan-refugee-wins-scholarship-to-David-Camerons-school-Eton-College.html (accessed May 2014).

Ruiz, Jean-Pierre 2011. *Readings from the Edges: The Bible and People on the Move*. Maryknoll, NY: Orbis Books.

Saadi 2009. *Saadi v Italy* (2009) 49 EHRR 30.

Sagovsky, Nicholas 2003. "Natural Law and Social Theology". In *God in Society: Doing Social Theology in Scotland Today*, William Storrar & Peter Donald (eds). Edinburgh: Saint Andrew Press: 54–81.

Said, Edward W. 1986. "Michael Walzer's 'Exodus and Revolution': A Canaanite Reading". *Grand Street* 5 (2): 86–106.

Sale 1993. *Sale v Haitian Centers Council, Inc.*, 113 S.Ct. 2549 (1993).

Salters, R.B. 2010. *A Critical and Exegetical Commentary on Lamentations*. London & New York: T&T Clark.

Sanders, Edward P. 1985. *Jesus and Judaism*. London: SCM Press.

Sasson, Jack M. 1978. "The Issue of Ge'Ullah in Ruth". *Journal for the Study of the Old Testament* 3 (5): 52–64.

——1979. *Ruth: A New Translation with a Philological Commentary and a Formalist-Folklorist Interpretation*. Baltimore & London: Johns Hopkins University Press.

Schaper, Joachim 2011. "Torah and Identity in the Persian Period". In *Judah and the Judeans in the Achaemenid Period: Negotiating Identity in an International Context*, Oded Lipschits, Gary N. Knoppers, & Manfred Oeming (eds). Winona Lake, IN: Eisenbrauns: 27–38.

Schüssler Fiorenza, Elisabeth 1983. *In Memory of Her: A Feminist Theological Reconstruction of Christian Origins*. London: SCM Press.

Schwartz, Regina 1997. *The Curse of Cain*. Chicago & London: University of Chicago Press.

Scott, James C. 1990. *Domination and the Arts of Resistance: Hidden Transcripts*. New Haven & London: Yale University Press.

Seabrook, Jeremy 2009. *The Refuge and the Fortress: Britain and the Flight from Tyranny*. Basingstoke, Hampshire & New York: Palgrave Macmillan.

Shacknove, Andrew E. 1985. "Who is a Refugee?" *Ethics* 95 (2): 274–284.

Significant Harm 2009. "Intercollegiate Briefing Paper: Significant Harm – The Effects of Administrative Detention on the Health of Children, Young People and their

Families". Royal College of Psychiatrists. http://www.rcpsych.ac.uk/pdf/Significant%20Harm%20intercollegiate%20statement%20Dec09.pdf (accessed May 2014).

Smith, Adrian 2008. Submitted in Evidence to: Asylum Matters: Restoring Trust in the UK Asylum System. London: Centre for Social Justice. (December). http://www.centreforsocialjustice.org.uk/UserStorage/pdf/Pdf%20Exec%20summaries/AsylumMatters.pdf (accessed May 2014).

Smith, Daniel L. 1989. *The Religion of the Landless: The Social Context of the Babylonian Exile*. Bloomington, IN: Meyer-Stone Books.

Smith, James F. 1995. "A Nation that Welcomes Immigrants? An Historical Examination of US Immigration Policy". *UC Davis Journal of International Law and Policy* 1 (2): 228–247.

Smith, William Robertson 1927. *Lectures on the Religion of the Semites: The Fundamental Institutions*. New York: Macmillan.

Smith-Christopher, Daniel L. 1994. "The Mixed Marriage Crisis in Ezra 9–10 and Nehemiah 13: A Study of the Sociology of the Post-Exilic Judean Community". In *Second Temple Studies 2: Temple and Community in the Persian Period,* Tamara C. Eskenazi & Kent H. Richards (eds). JSOT Supplement Series 175. Sheffield: Sheffield Academic Press: 243–265.

——1996. "Between Ezra and Isaiah: Exclusion, Transformation and Inclusion of the 'Foreigner' in Post-exilic Biblical Theology". In *Ethnicity and the Bible*, M.G.Brett (ed.). Leiden: Brill: 117–44.

——2002. *A Biblical Theology of Exile*. Minneapolis: Fortress Press.

——2011. "Reading War and Trauma: Suggestions Toward a Social-Psychological Exegesis of Exile and War in Biblical Texts". In *Interpreting Exile: Displacement and Deportation in Biblical and Modern Contexts*, Brad E.Kelle, Frank Ritchel Ames, & Jacob L. Wright (eds). Atlanta: Society of Biblical Literature: 253–274.

——2012. "Reading Exile Then: Reconsidering the Methodological Debates for Biblical Analysis with Sociological and Literary Analysis". In *By the Irrigation Canals of Babylon: Approaches to the Study of the Exile,* John J. Ahn & Jill Middlemas (eds). New York & London: T&T Clark: 141–159.

Snyder, Susanna 2007. "The Dangers of 'Doing our Duty': Reflections on Churches' Engagement with People Seeking Asylum in the UK". *Theology* 110 (857): 351–360.

——2011. "Un/settling Angels: Faith-Based Organizations and Asylum-Seeking in the UK". *Journal of Refugee Studies* 24 (3): 565–585.

——2012. *Asylum-Seeking, Migration and Church*. Farnham, Surrey & Burlington, VT: Ashgate.

Soggin, J. Alberto 1987. *Judges: A Commentary*, John Bowden (trans.). London: SCM Press.

Southwood, Katherine E. 2011a. "The Holy Seed: The Significance of Endogamous Boundaries and their Transgression in Ezra 9–10". In *Judah and the Judeans in the Achaemenid Period: Negotiating Identity in an International Context*, Oded Lipschits, Gary N. Knoppers, & Manfred Oeming (eds). Winona Lake, IN: Eisenbrauns: 189–224.

——2011b. "'And They Could Not Understand Jewish Speech': Language, Ethnicity, and Nehemiah's Intermarriage Crisis". *Journal of Theological Studies* 62 (1): 1–19.

——2012. *Ethnicity and the Mixed Marriage Crisis in Ezra 9–10: An Anthropological Approach*. Oxford: Oxford University Press.

Spencer, Jon *et al.* 2014. "Law, Order and Irregularity: Undocumented Migrants and UK Immigration Policy". Migrants' Rights Network. http://www.law.manchester.ac.

uk/medialibrary/Main%20site/CCCJ/Migrants/Undocumented-migrants-policy-briefing.pdf (accessed December 2014).

Spencer, Nick 2004. *Asylum and Immigration: A Christian Perspective on a Polarised Debate*. Milton Keynes, Buckinghamshire: Paternoster Press.

Spina, Frank Anthony 1983. "Israelites as Gerim, 'Sojourners' in Social and Historical Context". In *The Word of the Lord Shall Go Forth*, C.L. Myers & M.P. O'Connor (eds). *fs* D.N. Freedman. Winona Lake, IN: Eisenbrauns: 321–335.

——2005. *The Faith of the Outsider*. Grand Rapids, MI & Cambridge, UK: Eerdmans.

SPIU 2010. "Refugees' Experiences and Views of Poverty in Scotland". Glasgow: Scottish Poverty Information Unit (October).

Statelessness Convention 1954. Geneva: UNHCR. http://www.unhcr.org/pages/4a2535c3d.html (accessed June 2014).

Stefansson, Anders H. 2004. "Refugee Returns to Sarajevo and their Challenge to Contemporary Narratives of Mobility". In *Coming Home? Refugees, Migrants and Those Who Stayed Behind*, Lynellyn D. Long & Ellen Oxfeld (eds). Philadelphia: University of Pennsylvania Press: 170–186.

Still Human Still Here 2009. http://stillhumanstillhere.wordpress.com/ (accessed December 2014).

Stiver, Dan R. 2001. *Theology after Ricoeur: New Directions in Hermeneutical Theology*. Louisville, KY & London: Westminster John Knox Press.

——2007. "Felicity and Fusion: Speech Act Theory and Hermeneutical Philosophy". In *Transcending Boundaries in Philosophy and Theology: Reason, Meaning, and Experience*, Kevin Vanhoozer & Martin Warner (eds). Aldershot, Hampshire & Burlington, VT: Ashgate: 145–158.

Storrar, William F. & Andrew R. Morton (eds) 2004. *Public Theology for the 21st Century*. London & New York: T&T Clark.

Strik, Tineke 2012. "Lives Lost in the Mediterranean Sea: Who is Responsible?" Report for the Parliamentary Assembly Committee on Migration, Refugees and Displaced Persons. Council of Europe (29 March).

Sufi 2012. *Sufi and Elmi v the United Kingdom* [2012] ECHR 1045.

SZ & JM 2008. *SZ & JM (Christians-FS confirmed) Iran* CG [2008] UKAIT 00082.

Taylor, Vincent 1959. *The Gospel according to St Mark: The Greek Text*. London: Macmillan & New York: St Martin's Press.

Tazreiter, Claudia 2012. "The Politics of Asylum and Identities in Exile: Negotiating Place and Meaning". In *Cultures in Refuge: Seeking Sanctuary in Modern Australia*, Anna Hayes & Robert Mason (eds). Farnham, Surrey: Ashgate: 31–47.

Templeton, Elizabeth 1990. "'Person' and Risk". In *The Divine Risk*, Richard Holloway (ed.). London: Darton, Longman and Todd: 67–78.

Terrien, Samuel 2003. *The Psalms*. 2 vols. Grand Rapids, MI & Cambridge, UK: Eerdmans.

The Forum 2013. Available at: http://migrantforum.org.uk/joint-2013-winner-woman-of-the-year-remzije-sherifi/ (accessed December 2014).

Thomasset, Alain 2005. "L'imagination dans la pensée de Paul Ricoeur: Fonction poétique du langage et transformation du sujet". *Études Théologiques et Religieuses* 80 (4): 525–541.

Todorov, Tzvetan 1982. *La conquête de l'Amérique: La question de l'autre*. Paris: Editions du Seuil.

Torrey, Charles 1910. "The Exile and the Restoration". In *Ezra Studies*. New York: KTAV 1970 [1910]: 285–340.

Tracy, David 1987. "Exodus: Theological Reflection". In *Exodus – A Lasting Paradigm*, Bas Van Iersel & Anton Weiler (eds). Edinburgh: T&T Clark: 118–124.

Trible, Phyllis 1976. "Two Women in a Man's World: A Reading of the Book of Ruth". *Soundings* 59 (3): 251–279.

——1978. *God and the Rhetoric of Sexuality*. Philadelphia: Fortress Press.

——1982. "Of Human Comedy: The Book of Ruth". In *Literary Interpretations of Biblical Narratives,* Vol. 2, K.R.R. Gros Louis and J.S. Ackerman (eds). Nashville: Abingdon Press: 161–190.

——1984. *Texts of Terror: Literary-Feminist Readings of Biblical Narratives*. Philadelphia: Fortress Press.

Truman, Harry S. 1963. *Public Papers of the Presidents of the United States: Harry S. Truman, January 1 to December 31, 1947*. Washington, DC: US Government Printing Office, 421.

Tsangarides, Natasha 2012. "'The Second Torture': The Immigration Detention of Torture Survivors". London: Medical Justice.

Tulloch, Jonathan 2009. "For Whom the Drums Beat". *The Tablet* (14 November).

Türk, Volker 2012a. "Introductory Statement: Standing Committee of the Executive Committee of the High Commissioner's Programme". Geneva: UNHCR. (June).

——2012b. "Responding to the Changing Dynamics of Displacement". Keynote address delivered at the Canadian Association for Refugee and Forced Migration Studies (CARFMS) conference at York University, Toronto (16 May).

Turner, Stuart 1995. "Torture, Refuge and Trust". In *Mistrusting Refugees*, E. Valentine Daniel & John Chr Knudsen (eds). Berkeley & London: University of California Press: 56–72.

UKBA 2010. "Asylum Instruction on Gender Issues in the Asylum Claim". London: United Kingdom Border Agency.

——2011. "Revised Guidance: Sexual Orientation in the Asylum Claim". London: United Kingdom Border Agency.

UKLGIG 2010. "Failing the Grade: Home Office Initial Decisions on Lesbian and Gay Claims for Asylum". UK Lesbian and Gay Immigration Group.

——2013. "Missing the Mark: Decision-Making on Lesbian, Gay (Bisexual, Trans and Intersex) Asylum Claims". UK Lesbian and Gay Immigration Group.

UN DOC A/CONF.2/SR.19. *Conference of Plenipotentiaries on the Status of Refugees and Stateless Persons: Summary Record of the Nineteenth Meeting.*

UNHCR 1996. "Protecting Refugees: Questions and Answers". Geneva: UNHCR. http://www.unhcr.org/3b779dfe2.html (accessed May 2014).

——2010. "Convention and Protocol Relating to the Status of Refugees". Geneva: UNHCR. http://www.unhcr.org/3b66c2aa10.html (accessed June 2014).

——2012a. "Internally Displaced People". Geneva: UNHCR. http://www.unhcr.org/pages/49c3646c146.html (accessed May 2014).

——2012b. "Asylum Levels and Trends in Industrialised Countries". Geneva: UNHCR. http://www.unhcr.org/5149b81e9.html (accessed June 2014).

——2013. "A New Beginning: Refugee Integration in Europe, September 2013". Geneva: UNHCR. http://www.refworld.org/docid/522980604.html (accessed June 2014).

——2014. "Resettlement". Geneva: UNHCR. http://www.unhcr.org/pages/4a16b1676.html (accessed June 2014).

United Nations 1945. "Charter of the United Nations and Statute of International Court of Justice". http://www.un.org/en/documents/charter/index.shtml (accessed June 2014).

——1948. "Universal Declaration of Human Rights". GA Res.217 A(III), UN Doc. A/810. Paris.

——1951. United Nations Convention and Protocol Relating to the Status of Refugees. http://www.unhcr.org/3b66c2aa10.html (accessed May 2014).

US Code: Title 8. 8 USC §1101 (a) (42) (A). http://www.law.cornell.edu/uscode/text/8 (accessed December 2014).

Vahali, Honey Oberoi 2009. *Lives in Exile: Exploring the Inner World of Tibetan Refugees*. London: Routledge.

Vallely, Paul 2010. "No Place for the Innocent". *The Independent* (12 January).

Van Hear, Nicholas 1998. *New Diasporas: The Mass Exodus, Dispersal and Regrouping of Migrant Communities*. London: University College London Press.

Van Seters, John 1975. *Abraham in History and Tradition*. Yale: Yale University Press.

Vickroy, L. 2005. "The Traumas of Unbelonging: Reinaldo Arena's Recuperations of Cuba". *MELUS* 30 (4): 109–128.

Vikman, Elisabeth 2005a. "Ancient Origins: Sexual violence in warfare", Part I. *Anthropology and Medicine* 12 (1): 21–31.

——2005b. "Ancient Origins: Sexual violence in warfare", Part II. *Anthropology and Medicine*,12(1): 33–46.

Vine, John 2010. *Family Removals: A Thematic Inspection, January–April*. London: United Kingdom Border Agency.

——2011a. "A Thematic Inspection of how the UKBA Manages Foreign National Prisoners". London: United Kingdom Border Agency.

——2011b. "Asylum: A Thematic Inspection of the Detained Fast Track. July–September". London: United Kingdom Border Agency.

——2012. "An Inspection of the United Kingdom Border Agency's Handling of Legacy Asylum and Migration Cases". London: United Kingdom Border Agency.

——2013. "An Inspection into the Handling of Asylum Applications Made by Unaccompanied Children. February to June 2013". London: Home Office.

Walker, Kristen 2003. "New Uses of the Refugees Convention: Sexuality and Refugee Status". In *The Refugees Convention 50 Years On: Globalisation and International Law*, Susan Kneebone (ed.). Aldershot, Hampshire: Ashgate: 251–277.

Walzer, Michael 1985. *Exodus and Revolution*. New York: Basic Books.

Ward 1993. *Ward v Attorney-General (Canada)* [1993] 2 SCR 689.

Webber, Frances 2012. *Borderline Justice: The Fight for Refugee and Migrant Rights*. London: Pluto Press.

Weinfeld, Moshe 1972. *Deuteronomy and the Deuteronomic School*. Oxford: Clarendon Press.

Wenham, Gordon J. 1991. *Genesis 1–15*. Waco, TX: Word Books.

——1994. *Genesis 16–50*. Dallas: Word Books.

——2000. *Story as Torah: Reading the Old Testament Ethically*. Edinburgh: T&T Clark.

Westermann, Claus 1981. *Praise and Lament in the Psalms*. Edinburgh: T&T Clark.

——1985–87. *Genesis*. 3 vols. John J. Scullion (trans.). London: SPCK & Minneapolis: Fortress Press.

——1994. *Lamentations: Issues and Interpretations*. Edinburgh: T&T Clark.

Westin, Charles 1999. "Regional Analysis of Refugee Movements: Origins and Response". In *Refugees: Perspectives on the Experience of Forced Migration*, Alastair Ager (ed.). London & New York: Continuum: 24–45.

Williamson Jr., Robert 2008. "Lament and the Arts of Resistance: Public and Hidden Transcripts in Lamentations 5". In *Lamentations in Ancient and Contemporary Cultural Contexts*, Nancy C. Lee & Carleen Mandolfo (eds). Atlanta: Society of Biblical Literature: 67–80.

Williamson, Hugh G.M. 1985. *Ezra, Nehemiah*. Waco, TX: Word Books.

Wilsher, Daniel 2003. "Non-State Actors and the Definition of a Refugee in the UK". *International Journal of Refugee Law* 15 (1): 68–112.

Wilson, Erin 2011. "Much to be Proud of, Much to be Done: Faith-Based Organizations and the Politics of Asylum in Australia". *Journal of Refugee Studies* 24 (3): 548–564.

Wilson, Robert R. 2012. "Forced Migration and the Formation of the Prophetic Literature". In *By the Irrigation Canals of Babylon: Approaches to the Study of the Exile*, John J. Ahn & Jill Middlemas (eds). New York & London: T&T Clark: 125–140.

Wilson-Shaw, Lucy *et al.* 2012. "Non-Clinicians' Judgments about Asylum Seekers' Mental Health: How Do Legal Representatives of Asylum Seekers Decide When to Request Medico-Legal Reports?" *European Journal of Psychotraumatology* 3: 18406. http://www.ncbi.nlm.nih.gov/pubmed/23082238 (accessed May 2014).

Winter, Jay 2006. *Remembering War: The Great War between Memory and History in the Twentieth Century*. New Haven & London: Yale University Press.

Women's Refugee Commission 2009. "US Immigration Policy Harms Women, Families. Briefing to Congress" (June 24). http://www.womensrefugeecommission.org/about/staff/press-room/811-us-immigration-policy-harms-women-families (accessed May 2014).

Wood, Alexis L. 2011. "How Long is Indefinite?". Glocal Films (September). http://www.glocalfilms.net/how-long-is-indefinite/ (accessed May 2014).

Wright, Jacob L. 2011. "The Deportation of Jerusalem's Wealth and the Demise of Native Sovereignty in the Book of Kings". In *Interpreting Exile: Displacement and Deportation in Biblical and Modern Contexts*, Brad E. Kelle, Frank Ritchel Ames, & Jacob L. Wright (eds). Atlanta: Society of Biblical Literature: 105–133.

Yorta Yorta 2002. *Members of the Yorta Yorta Aboriginal Community v Victoria* (2002) HCA 58; 214 CLR 422; 194 ALR 538; 77 ALJR 356.

Zaoui 2006. *Z v Attorney General* [2005] NZSC 38; [2006] 1 NZLR 289.

Zetter, Roger 1999. "International Perspectives on Refugee Assistance". In *Refugees: Perspectives on the Experience of Forced Migration*, Alastair Ager (ed.). London & New York: Continuum: 46–82.

Zi Lin Chen 2004. *Zi Lin Chen v Ashcroft*, 362 F. 3d 611,617 (9th Circuit 2004).

Zimmerli, Walther 1979, 1983. *Ezekiel*. 2 Vols. Philadelphia: Fortress Press.

ZNS 2012. *ZNS v. Turkey* (2012) 55 EHRR 11.

INDEX OF BIBLICAL REFERENCES

SUBJECT AND AUTHOR INDEX